IMAGES
of America

MacArthur Park

On the Cover: A young person finds a moment of respite and contemplation while sitting in MacArthur Park, one of Los Angeles' oldest, imminently attractive, and most democratic parks. MacArthur Park evolved alongside its home city as Los Angeles was becoming the modern metropolis it is today. The park has experienced multiple physical transformations and a name change, but it has never lost its intent and purpose to serve the millions of souls that call Los Angeles home. (Courtesy of the Los Angeles Public Library Photo Collection.)

IMAGES
of America

MacArthur Park

Jose A. Gardea

ARCADIA
PUBLISHING

ISBN 978-1-4671-3345-6

Published by Arcadia Publishing
Charleston, South Carolina

Printed in the United States of America

Library of Congress Control Number: 2015939110

For all general information, please contact Arcadia Publishing:
Telephone 843-853-2070
Fax 843-853-0044
E-mail sales@arcadiapublishing.com
For customer service and orders:
Toll-Free 1-888-313-2665

Visit us on the Internet at www.arcadiapublishing.com

For my wife, Susana—one more book for our bookcase; and my sons, Zacharias and Sebastian—view the world with wide eyes one book at a time, it is a beautiful responsibility.

Contents

ACKNOWLEDGMENTS

MacArthur Park is a unique place in Los Angeles. This accolade is only possible because unique people have always appreciated the park's role in nurturing community and building our city. It is well documented since the inception of Westlake Park that this public space has had many champions fighting for causes and resources that are critical to the preservation and restoration of this great park. It would be a mistake on my part to try to name these champions across the generations of time who have accepted the challenge of advocating for MacArthur Park. It is indeed a long list. But, believe me, they have all left their marks in the park. Perhaps this subject can be articulated at a different time and under a different format. For now, however, thank you all.

A thank-you goes to those individuals and organizations that allowed me the use of the archival photographs: the Los Angeles City Archives (Michael Holland and Todd Gaydowski), the Los Angeles Public Library, the Natural History Museum of Los Angeles County (John Cahoon), the USC Digital Collection, the *Los Angeles Times* photograph collection, the Watson Family Photography Archives (thank you, Dan Watson), Karen Mack from LA Commons, Joe Colleti from IURD, and the good folks from CicLAvia.

I want to thank Liz Hirsch and her fellow board members from the Levitt Pavilion for their support and encouragement. Keep the music playing at the park!

Many of the modern-day photographs in this book were taken by the incredible Meeno Peluce (Meeno), a Los Angeles–based photographer who always amazes me with his skills and talent. Thank you for your poetic perspective of the park.

A thank-you goes to the editors at Arcadia Publishing for their direction and patience. I truly appreciated the journey.

One final thank-you goes to the millions of immigrants from across the world who have called the Westlake neighborhood home and MacArthur Park their public space to recreate and gather. In particular, I want to thank Eva Gardea, my mother, for the courage to come to a new country and arriving to this neighborhood. Her story is shared by so many, a story of sacrifice and hope. May the millions who will come in the future continue to see Westlake and MacArthur Park as portals for opportunity and growth.

INTRODUCTION

Los Angeles is a big city, but MacArthur Park makes it a democratic place. I am reminded of this every time I sit in the park. I remind myself that I am sitting in the middle of one of the most crowded neighborhoods in the country, where hundreds of thousands of immigrant souls, primarily from Mexico and Central America, live in high-rise buildings that once reached elegantly for the clear, blue sky, but today strain under years of deafening hardship and trembling turmoil.

I remind myself that beyond the transparent borders of this neighborhood expands a metropolis of 13 million dreamers, searchers, and workers. This is a city that, since its founding along the Rio de Nuestra Señora la Reina de Los Ángeles de Porciúncula, has been hungry to grow its territorial boundaries and search for precious water to accommodate its collective thirst.

Westlake Park, as MacArthur Park was originally called, fulfilled both realities. The creation of the park in 1886 solidified the western edge of a dusty town already searching for its manifest destiny to the Pacific Ocean. The early city surveyors established the city's western boundary a few hundred yards west of the lands that would become Westlake Park, an area unclaimed by the local ranchos and not known for its physical attractiveness. But the sea was still many miles away, and local property owners were eager to prosper.

Los Angeles was indeed dusty, both because of its desertlike geography and the constant threat of drought in this part of California during the late 19th century. As a result, the capture and storage of water became a matter of survival for the emerging city, an assignment that the new public park and reservoir was given.

Westlake Park and the expanse between the new park and the original city border to the east quickly became points of pride for local stakeholders and ambitious elected officials. The new park was photogenic, and the new city needed a relief valve for its residents to gather, breath, and recreate. Thus, the people's park was born.

For much of the 20th century, Westlake/MacArthur Park served as a mirror for the entire city of Los Angeles. The park and the neighborhood around it were a microcosm of the infrastructure, social, transportation, and economic forces that created the second-largest city in the country. As the city's watershed and requisite engineering challenges needed to better manage its water increased, so did the importance of the park as a catchment area. With the sea many miles to the west of the original pueblo, the city grew in that fateful direction. The neighborhood around Westlake Park experienced the first critical levels of population density as the decades passed. Many observers will argue that the city was unprepared, or perhaps unwilling, to adequately manage the population explosion that occurred in this neighborhood as the postwar decades progressed. Clearly, the lack of strategic thought and action on this issue heavily impacted the park itself. Although the park always patiently endured periods of municipal neglect, the strain on its resources created an environment of fear and lawlessness—a phase the park is still trying to recover from.

When cars and people needed to move to the west side of the city to shop or work, the park sacrificed its green space for this objective to be achieved. On the economic front, as the city's workforce went from a "base of makers to a base of servers," the Westlake neighborhood became home to the largest group of immigrants that served our food and cleaned our homes and offices.

During this period, the park experienced two distinct and significant traumas. Two major construction projects (the Wilshire Viaduct and the Los Angeles County Metropolitan Transportation Authority's Red Line subway) permanently scarred the design and biological ecosystem of the park, and the second injury was the renaming of the park after Gen. Douglas MacArthur, an act that on its own was not fatal to the park. However, the injury was inflicted on the local community, which was unhappy with the name change.

At MacArthur Park, memory, culture, and imagination share the same stage across time. A child at play with his miniature boat on the natural bottom lake during the early 20th century shares the same youthful enthusiasm of a youngster enjoying a soccer game on a synthetic turf field in the park during the early 21st century. A visitor partaking of a musical performance in the park's band shell in 1900, 1960, or 2010 experienced the same sensory pleasures. A writer's mind captures the mystery, magic, and majesty of an arcadian park populated by characters traversing generations and eras.

MacArthur Park welcomes people, regardless of intent, purpose, and desire. It is a park that has never had a fence encircling its edges. People sit in the park to contemplate. Students draw in the park to document its beauty. Children run in the park to remind us of optimism. Visitors protest in the park to exercise our collective values. It is the knowledge and appreciation of this beauty, optimism, and values that has always driven local stakeholders to protect and serve the park, especially as it enters a new century.

Over the last 25 years, MacArthur Park, like the city it serves, has attempted to understand its role for the next 100 years. Local residents are rediscovering the city's original neighborhoods, as well as remaking the city's urban parks. This dynamic is framed as either revitalization or gentrification, the two great urban forces transforming and, some might say, confusing cities across the country.

At stake in this conversation is the future of MacArthur Park. Will this conversation preserve the original intent of the park as a green oasis in the middle of our great concrete city? Does this conversation take into account the importance of maintaining an open and free park for the pleasure of all? And will we allow for all voices—local, immigrant, newcomer, visitor—to participate in this same conversation to dream about MacArthur Park, the people's park?

I remind myself that MacArthur Park, like Los Angeles, is still a work in progress.

One

The Most Beautiful Park in the City

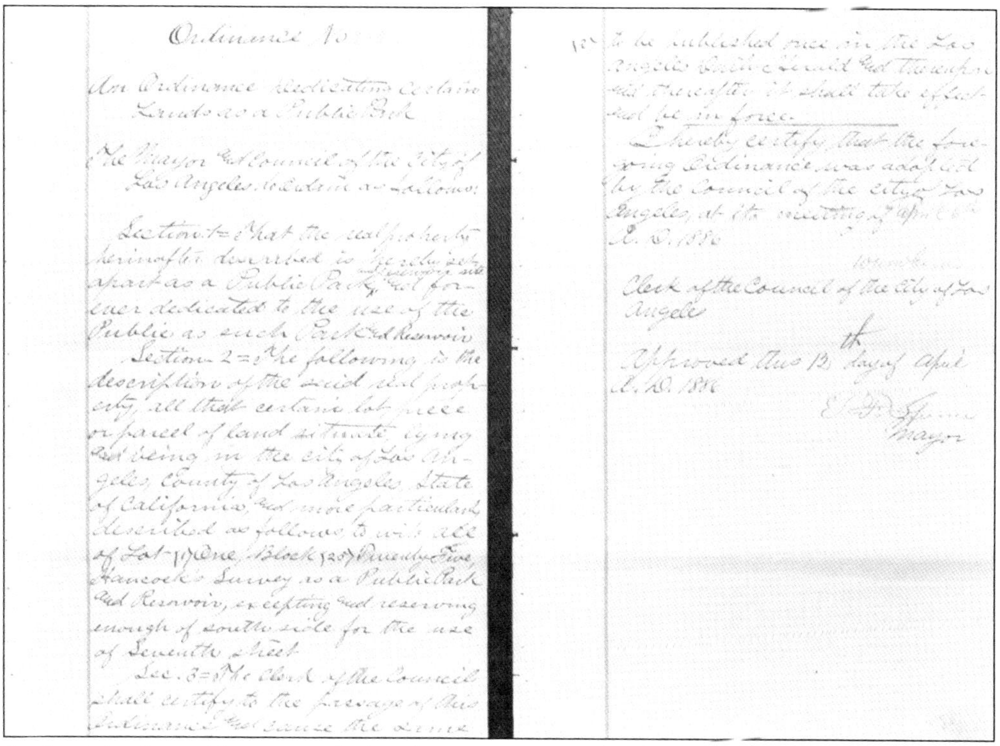

Ordinance No [illegible]

An Ordinance Dedicating Certain Lands as a Public Park

The Mayor and Council of the City of Los Angeles do ordain as follows:

Section 1 = That the real property hereinafter described is hereby set apart as a Public Park and reservoir and forever dedicated to the use of the Public as such Park and Reservoir

Section 2 = The following is the description of the said real property, all that certain lot piece or parcel of land situate, lying and being in the city of Los Angeles, County of Los Angeles, State of California, and more particularly described as follows to wit: All of Lot (1) One, Block (25) Twenty-Five, Hancock's Survey as a Public Park and Reservoir, excepting and reserving enough of south side for the use of Seventh street

Sec. 3 = The Clerk of the Council shall certify to the passage of this Ordinance and cause the same to be published once in the Los Angeles Daily Herald and thereupon and thereafter it shall take effect and be in force.

I hereby certify that the foregoing Ordinance was adopted by the Council of the City of Los Angeles, at its meeting of April 6th A. D. 1886

[illegible]

Clerk of the Council of the City of Los Angeles

Approved this 13th day of April A. D. 1886

E. F. Spence
Mayor

And so it begins, with paper and a handwritten municipal ordinance. The park that came to be known as Westlake Park was born on an early spring day in 1886 as a public park and reservoir, "forever dedicated to the use of the public as such park and reservoir." A little over a century after the founding of city, Los Angeles had its westernmost public park, with the city's early boundary located only a few blocks to the west, where Hoover Street and Commonwealth Avenue today cascade down towards Wilshire Boulevard. (Courtesy of the City of Los Angeles Archives.)

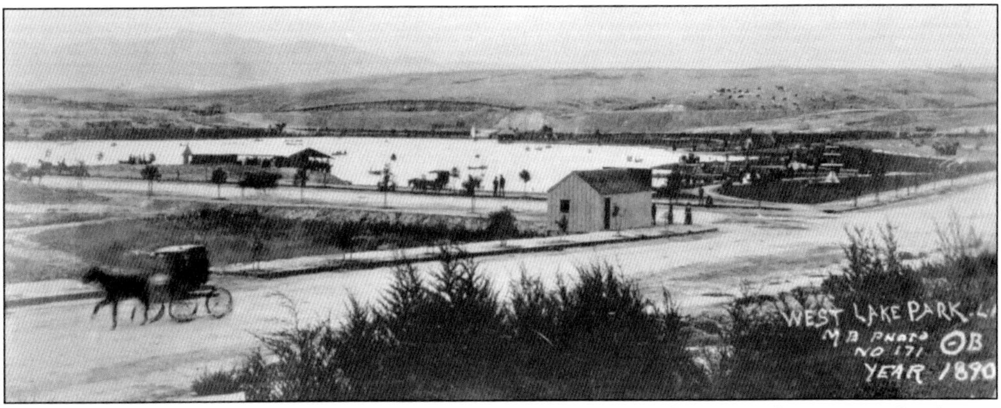

Although the park was still a distance from the original center of town at the time, it clearly was already exerting a gravitational pull for residents in 1890. From its earliest days, boating was the most popular recreational activity for visitors to the park. As a testament to the semiarid climate of Southern California, note the barren hills surrounding the new lake, a contrast that visitors took notice of at the time. (Courtesy of the City of Los Angeles Archives.)

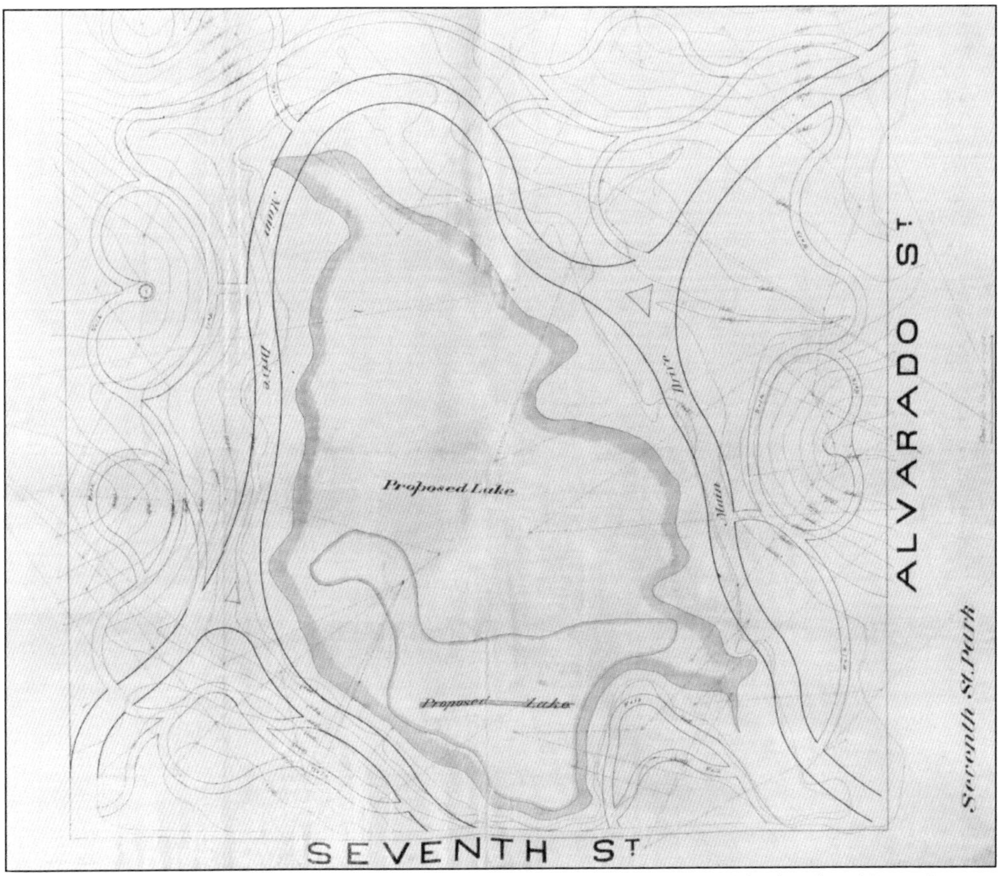

Researchers of the park have debated the accurate original ownership of the land and how the city came to negotiate its possession. This early map for "Seventh Street Park" showcases a thoughtful design for the emerging park. The design illustrates multiple grand entrances, various walking paths, and of course the lake itself. (Courtesy of the City of Los Angeles Archives.)

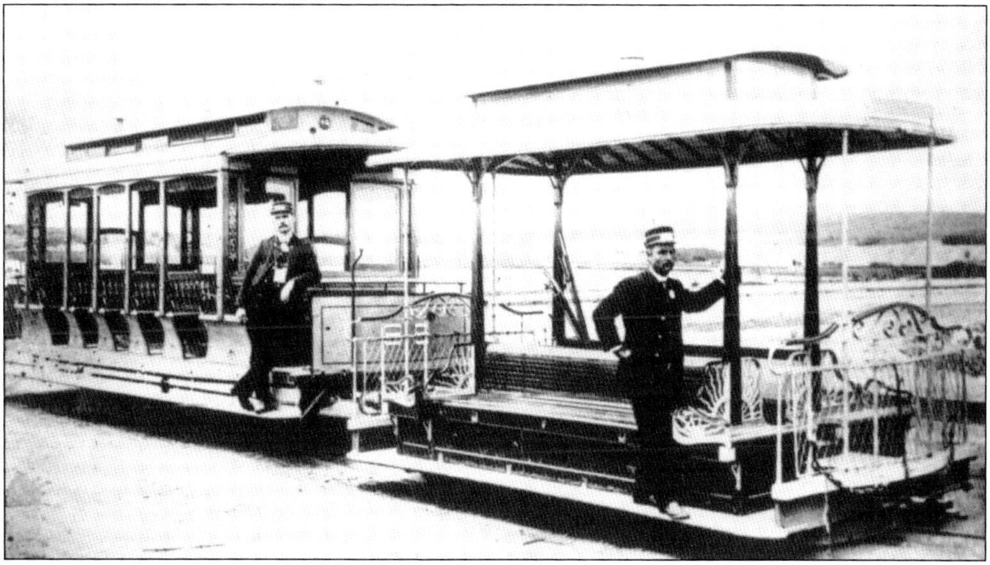

As further evidence of the growing importance of the nascent neighborhoods to the west of the old pueblo, public transportation carried visitors to the park. With Westlake Park in the background, one can appreciate the rudimentary public transport of the region's early railway system. (Courtesy of the Natural History Museum of Los Angeles County.)

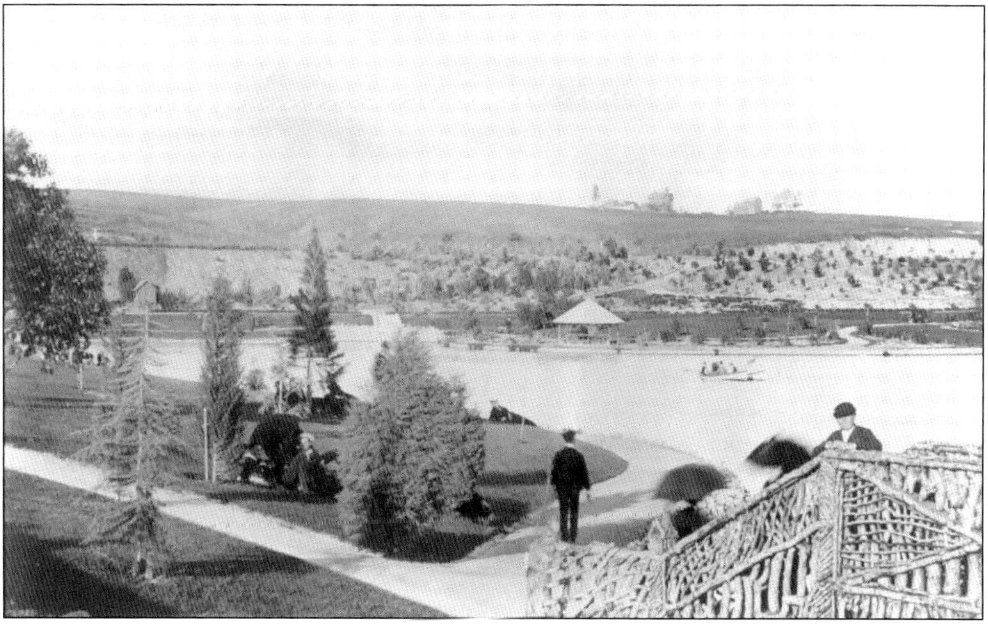

Only a few years after the park's formal grand opening, this photograph from 1892 clearly illustrates the basin topography that defined the purpose of the new public space. One can observe on the northern edge of the new park the heavy engineering of the hillside, which included the addition of a bulkhead and dam on the rim of the reservoir. These improvements were envisioned to facilitate the capture and retention of water throughout the year. (Courtesy of the Natural History Museum Los Angeles County.)

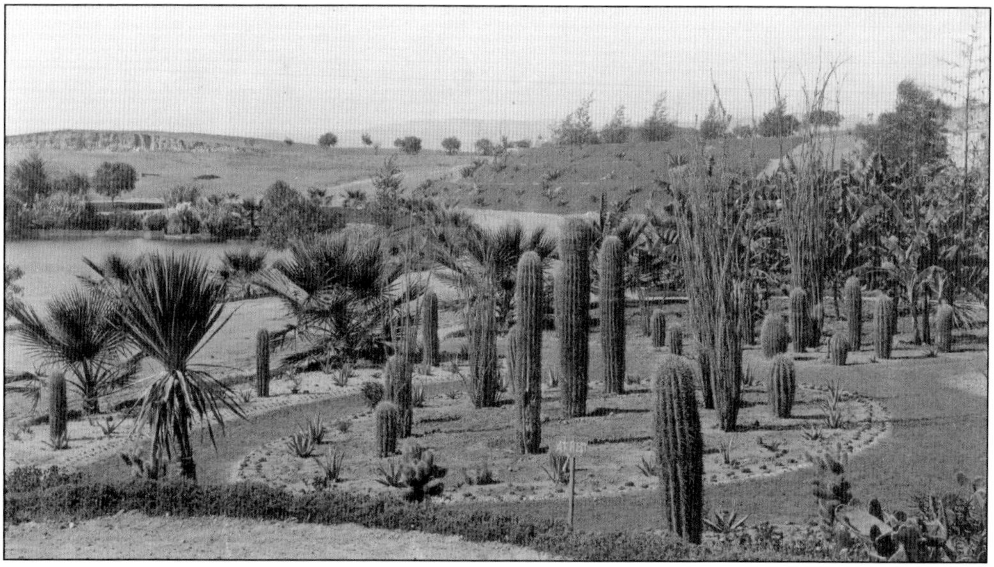

In a city that had yet to rediscover its native flora palette and long removed from the alkali mounds that were prevalent in the pre-reservoir basin, the trees and shrubs that were used to landscape the new park were a mixture of styles and heights. Clearly, the landscape architect in charge was aggressive in importing plants to overcome the barrenness of the site and to expedite the creation of a true green space. (Courtesy of Los Angeles Public Library Photo Collection.)

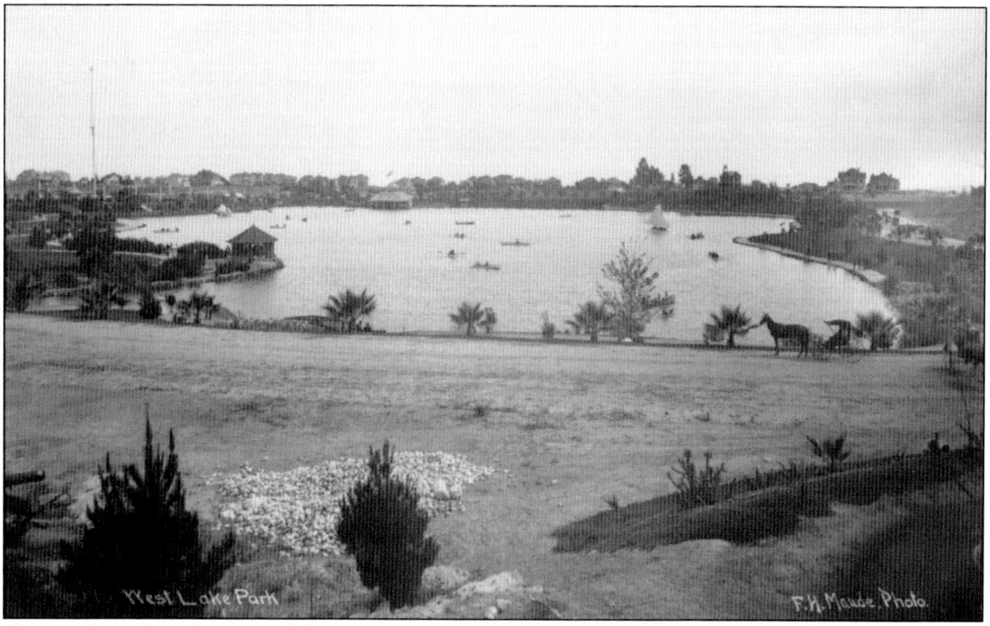

This early 1900s photograph bears witness to the 32-acre park and lake's natural beauty while depicting the emergence of the adjacent neighborhood to the east of the park. As a new century dawned on the rapidly expanding city, the park became known as a resort that could motivate local investors to build grand homes and institutions. It worked. The quality of the architecture in this neighborhood rivaled anything that had been built in the young city. Many examples of the architecture of this era still stand today. Although not abandoned, they are underutilized as housing. (Courtesy of the Natural History Museum of Los Angeles County.)

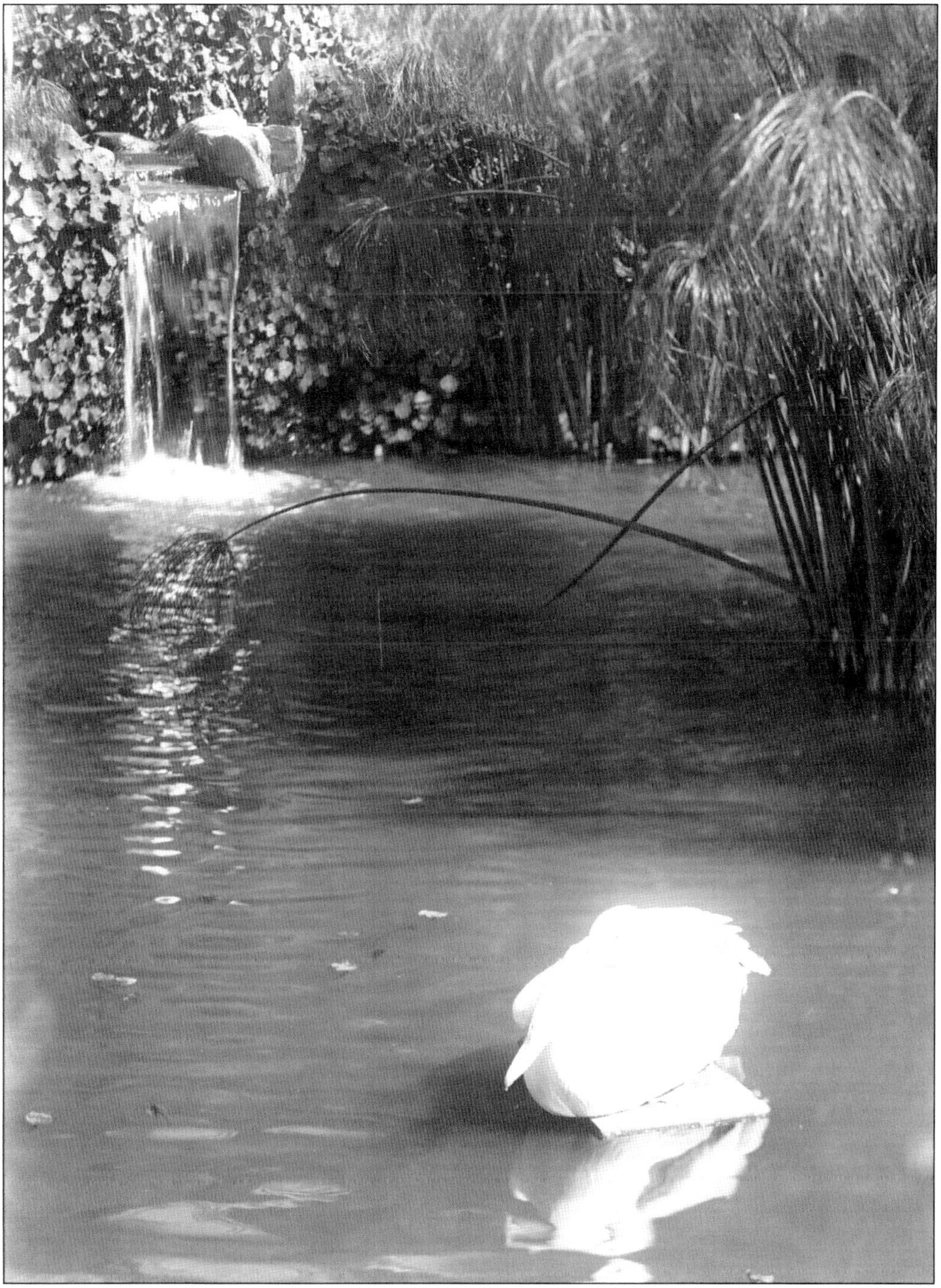

One of the unique landscape features of the park was a series of rocky cascades that fed the reservoir. Known as the Rockery, the waterfall was a welcome relief for the local fauna. The population of ducks increased so much that it forced the recreation department to proactively sell off the duck population, stating in a letter to a potential suitor, "This department has a surplus number of young ducks at Westlake Park which we desire to dispose of. We can sell you 12 ducks which we value at 35 cents each." (Courtesy of the Natural History Museum of Los Angeles County.)

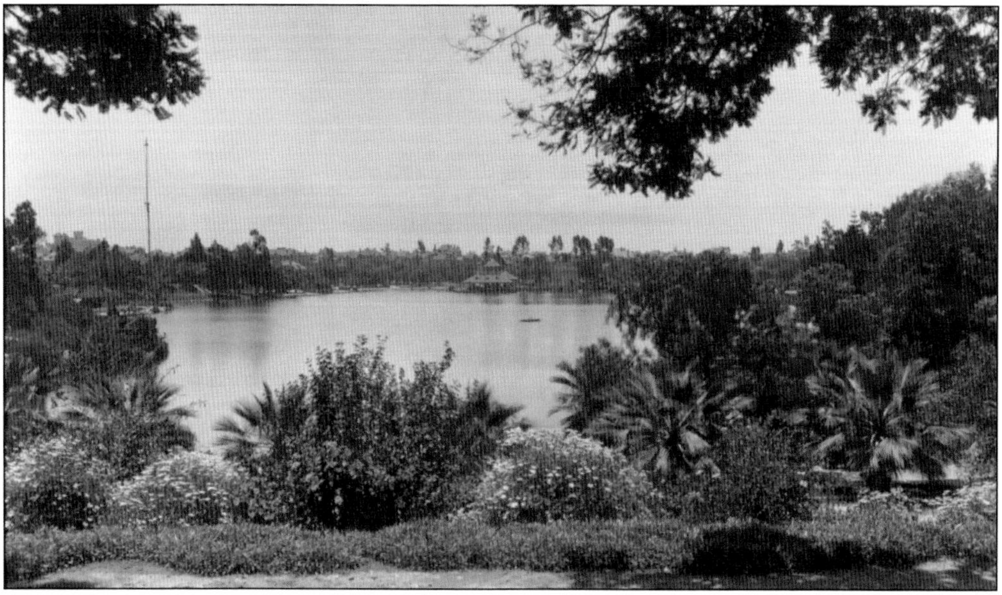

A decade into the new century, Westlake Park was an established natural area. Like the trees and shrubs themselves, the park had matured into an urban oasis for a city that was growing in all directions. The pride of local leaders was clear. An editorial from the *Westlake Weekly* asserts, "Westlake Park is the most beautiful and popular of the city's playgrounds . . . approximately 10,000 people visit the park each week, or about a half million every year." (Courtesy of the Natural History Museum of Los Angeles County.)

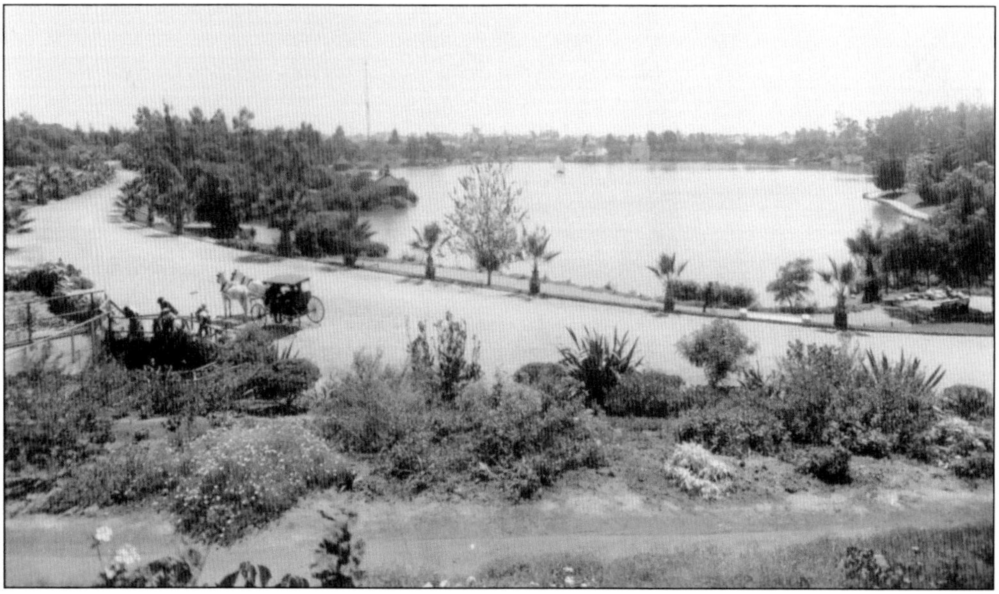

One of the reasons so many visitors enjoyed the park was the buggy trail that encircled a portion of the lake. The trail was later renamed Palm Drive to create a more elegant atmosphere for not only visitors but also the elite who were quickly populating the surrounding neighborhood. In this photograph, one can observe the newly planted palms along the edge of the roadway. A number of these palms survived many decades in the park. (Courtesy of the Natural History Museum of Los Angeles County.)

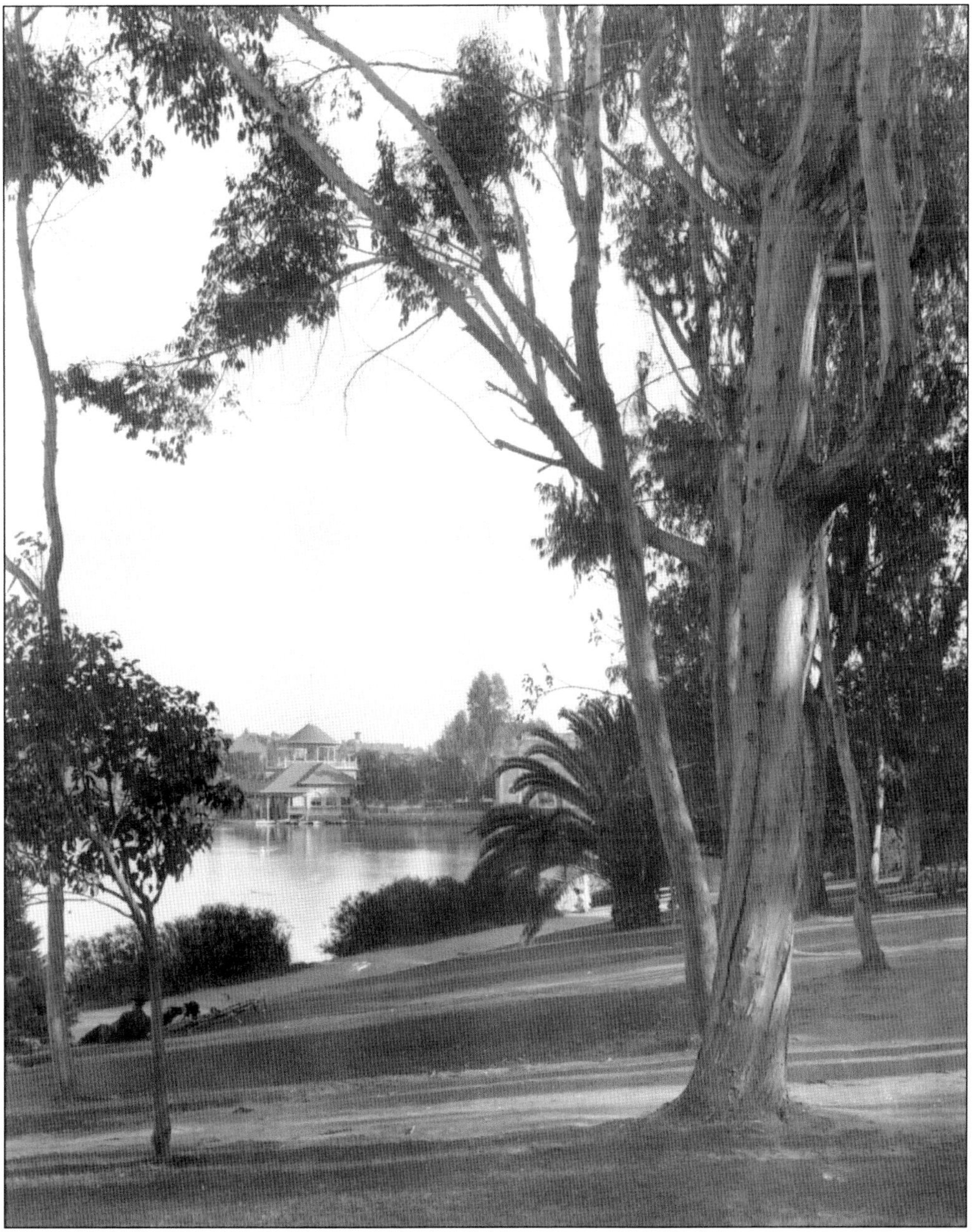

With popularity came challenges for the young park. Although the parks department employed up to 15 men in 1910 to provide upkeep for the park (at a total salary cost of $806 for all), local users were expressing their concerns with the condition of the property. The park may appear pristine in this photograph, but a local resident, in a letter to the city, stated that "it may be the park department is spending too much money on Griffith Park, and neglecting some of the city parks." (Courtesy of the Natural History Museum of Los Angeles County.)

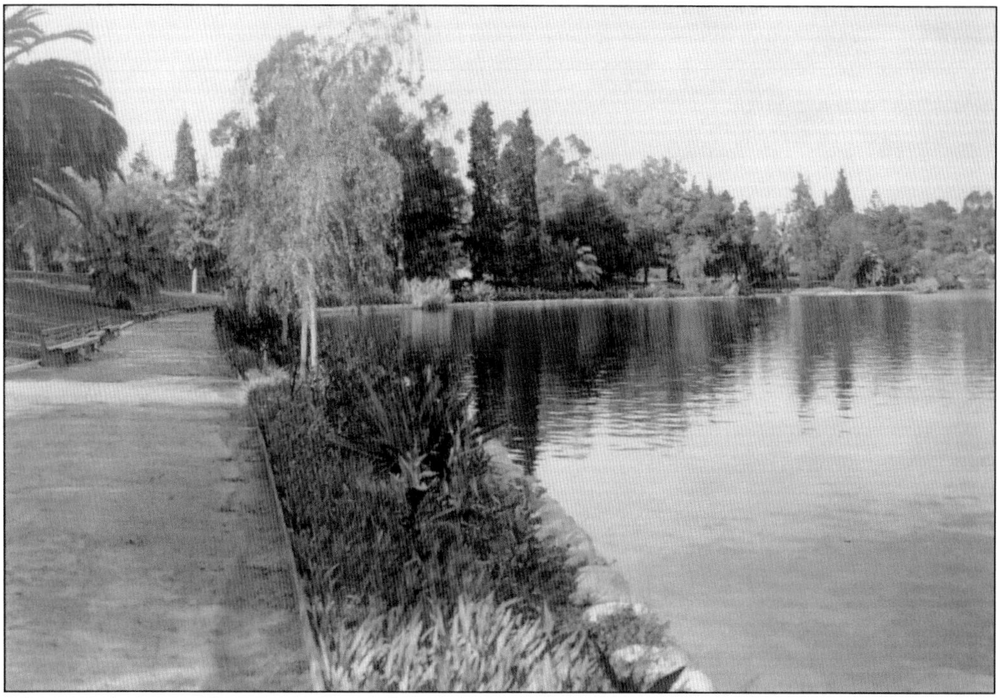

Through design and programming, the park became a place of leisure for all Angelenos. This pathway offered a relaxing atmosphere for pedestrians in 1929. But pedestrians beware! Perhaps as a precursor of the Wilshire Viaduct controversy that would emerge a few years later, a representative from the Auto Club of America approached the board of park commissioners and "requested that Westlake Park be opened to automobile traffic." Fortunately, the board was opposed to the opening of the park to traffic. (Courtesy of the Los Angeles Public Library Photo Collection.)

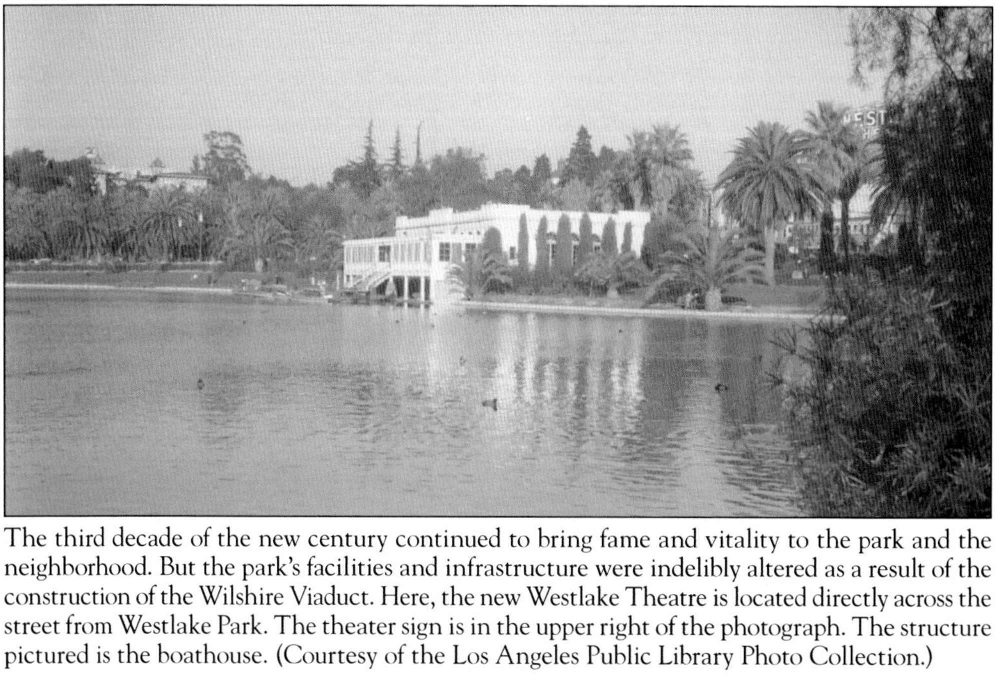

The third decade of the new century continued to bring fame and vitality to the park and the neighborhood. But the park's facilities and infrastructure were indelibly altered as a result of the construction of the Wilshire Viaduct. Here, the new Westlake Theatre is located directly across the street from Westlake Park. The theater sign is in the upper right of the photograph. The structure pictured is the boathouse. (Courtesy of the Los Angeles Public Library Photo Collection.)

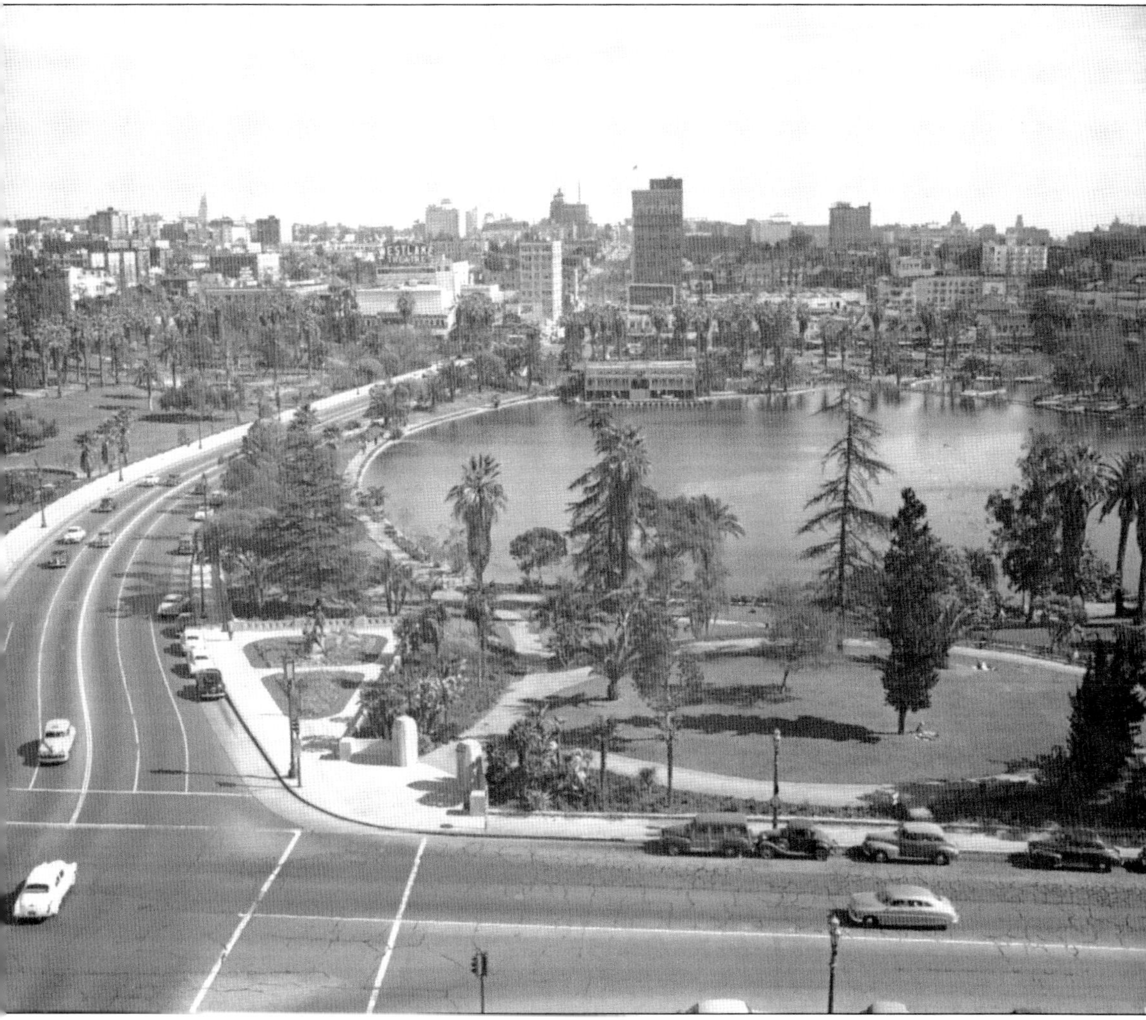

Westlake Park, pictured here in the postwar years, is now in two sections. This view is looking east towards downtown Los Angeles, with Wilshire Boulevard, the major thoroughfare, running up the center of the photograph. In the distance to the left is city hall, the tallest building in the downtown area at the time. With the hurtful memory of the construction of Wilshire Boulevard still fresh for many local residents, the city again brought traumatic change to the park when in May 1942 the board of park commissioners approved the change of name with Resolution No. 57: "Be it resolved that the name Westlake Park be, and it is hereby changed to General Douglas MacArthur Park, effective this date." Local stakeholders were stunned. (Courtesy of the Natural History Museum of Los Angeles County.)

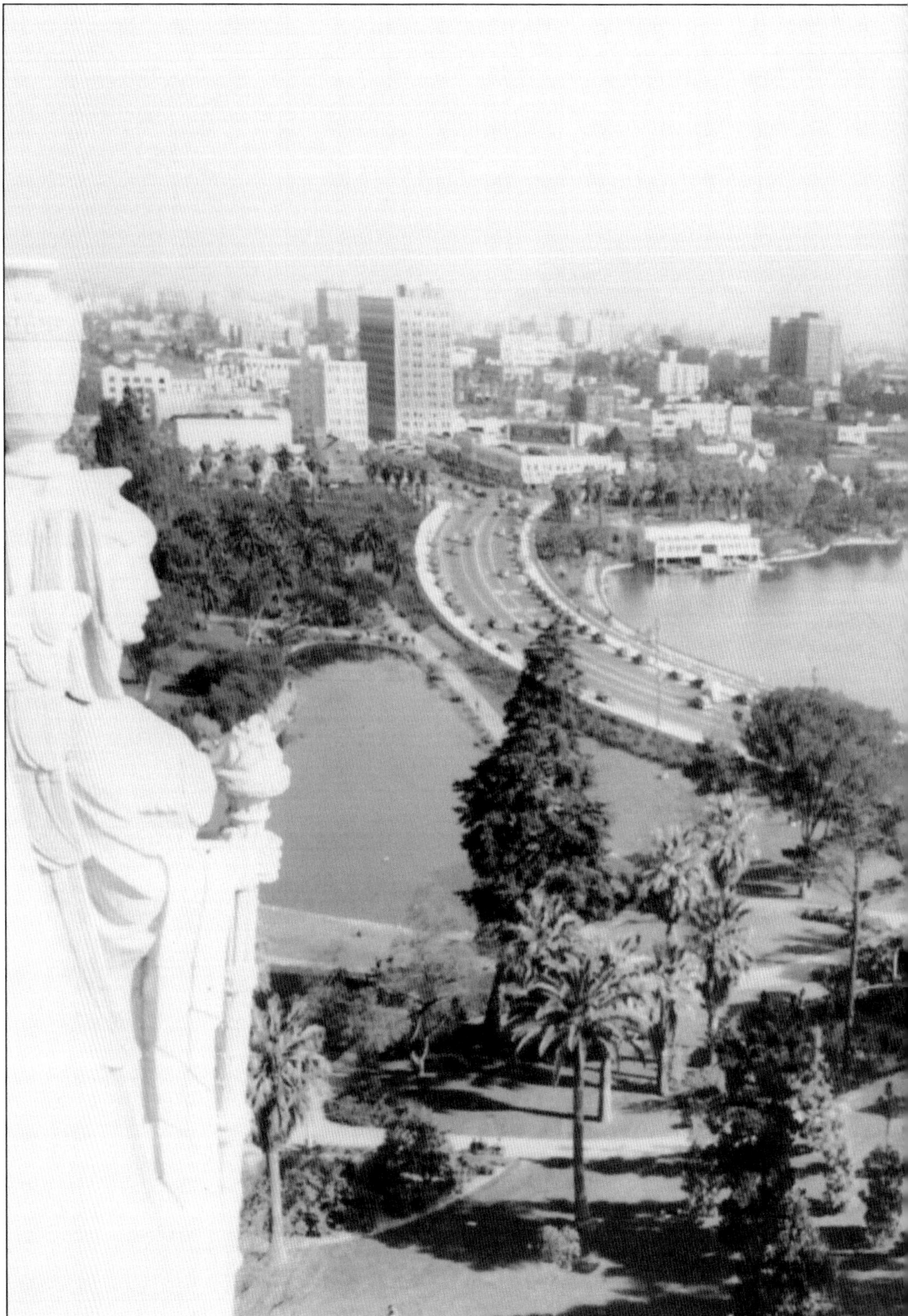

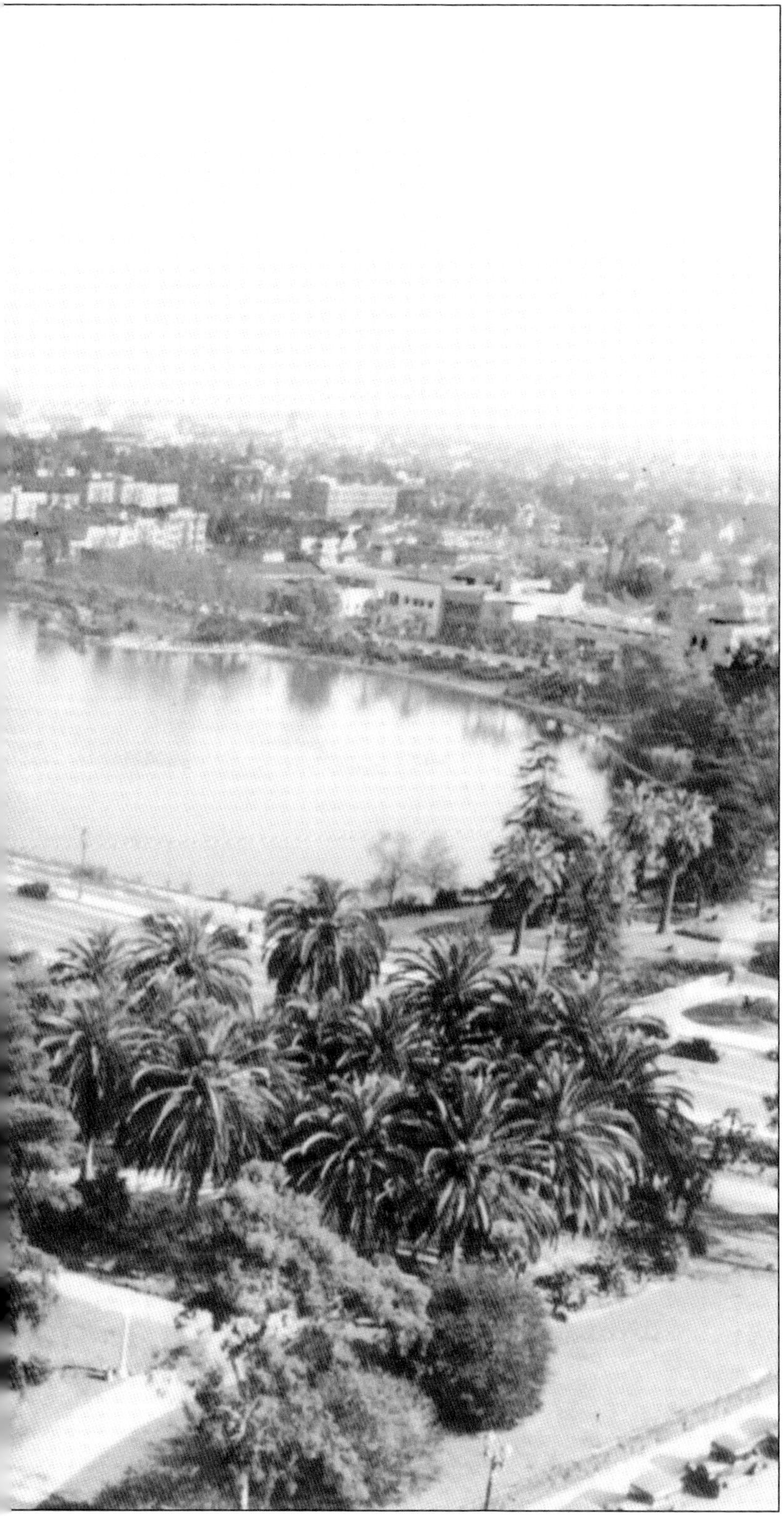

The expansiveness of the park is evident in this photograph taken from the Park Plaza (Elks Lodge) building across from the western edge of the park. What is special, however, is the proximity of the exterior figurine that adorns the now historic building, standing guard over the changing green space directly to the east. But it was the economic and demographic forces occurring to the west of the park that would leave a permanent imprint in the neighborhood. (Courtesy of the Los Angeles Public Library Photo Collection.)

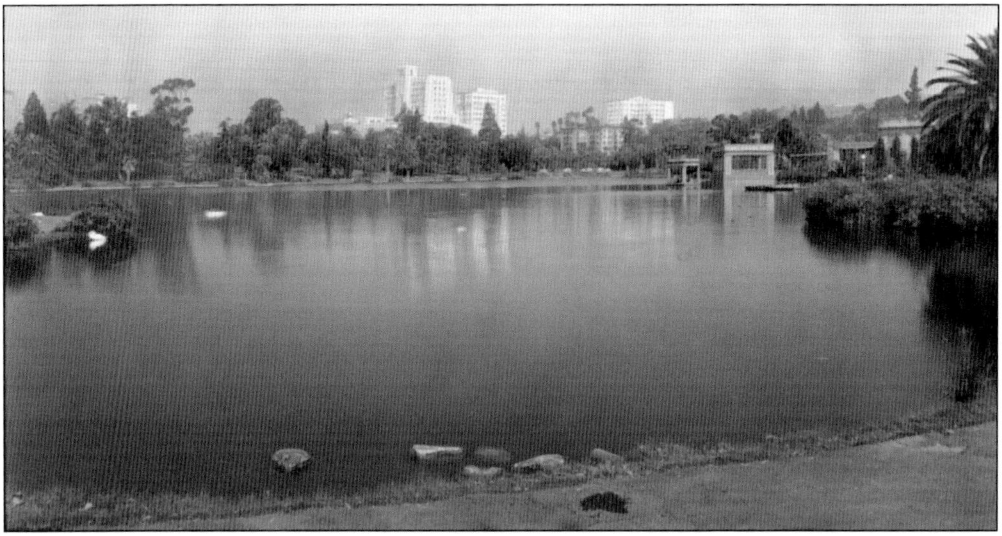

The construction of the Wilshire Viaduct altered the design and biological health of the lake. The natural features of the lake were still visible, including the soft edges of the banks. Westlake Park was a survivor, but it could not survive the political machinations behind the name change. N.I. Scott, a local booster, in attempting to influence the reversal of the name change, wrote, "Westlake Park is an appropriate name which is known the country over by millions of persons who at one time or another have visited it. The name has a sentimental value." (Courtesy of the Natural History Museum of Los Angeles County.)

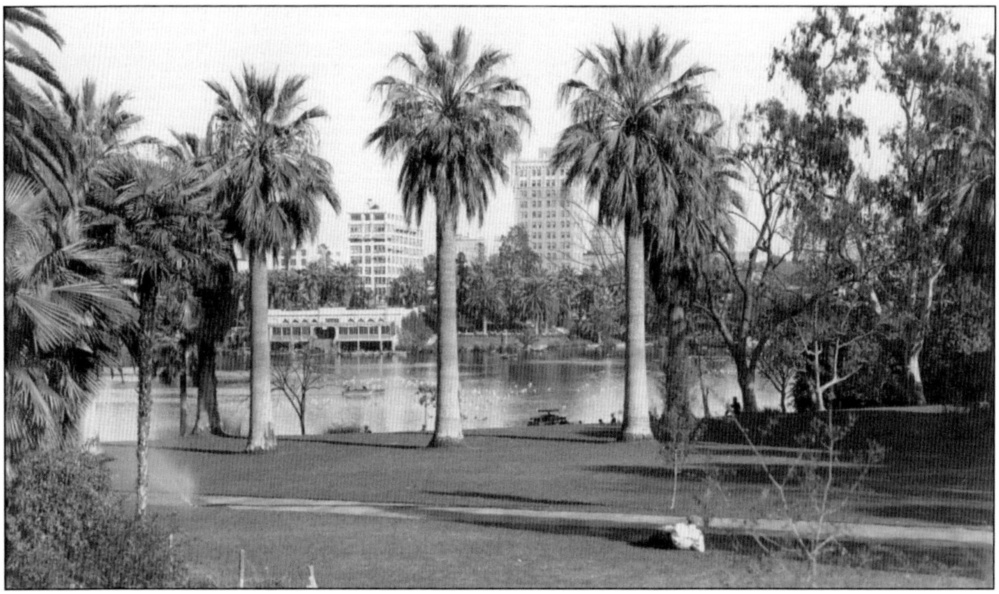

The name change was not embraced by all residents, business owners, and visitors. The City of Los Angeles Archives contains dozens of letters from concerned parties relative to the action, an action that most stakeholders believed was rushed without any community discussion. Local resident W.O. Gilkey wrote to the board: "Again, political aspirations along with hasty judgment and hero worship, you have sanctioned the change of the name of one of the city's recreational areas, without the consent of the property owners or the general public." (Courtesy of the Natural History Museum of Los Angeles County.)

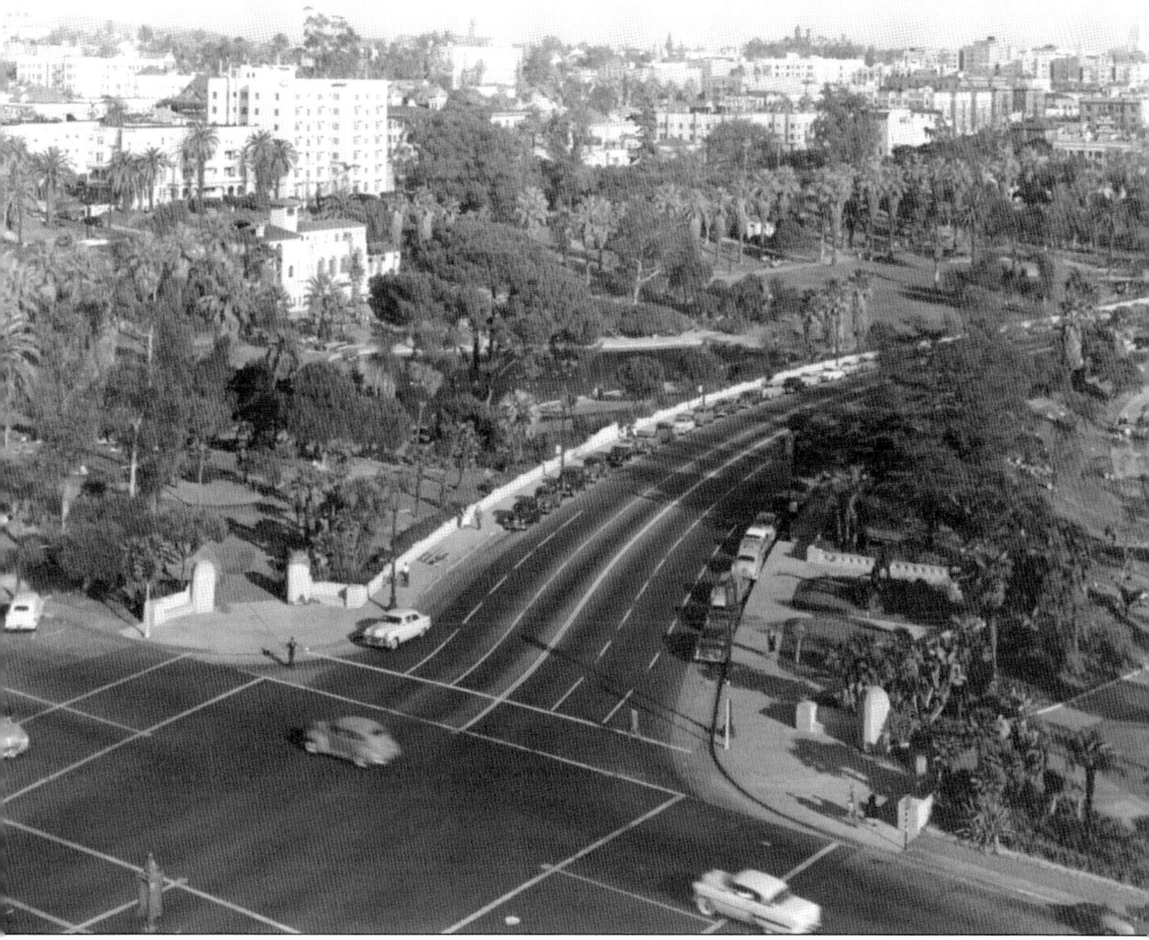

Hero worship was indeed a defining motivator for the name change. It was William Randolph Hearst, in his quest to promote General MacArthur as a viable presidential candidate, who first proposed renaming the park. Arthur Day, a local business owner, pleaded against the change, stating, "I feel that we should at least wait until after the war." The board, after recognizing the level of opposition, including from the local council member, deferred on a final decision "pending receipt of an expression from the people in the district of their wishes." (Courtesy of the Natural History Museum of Los Angeles County.)

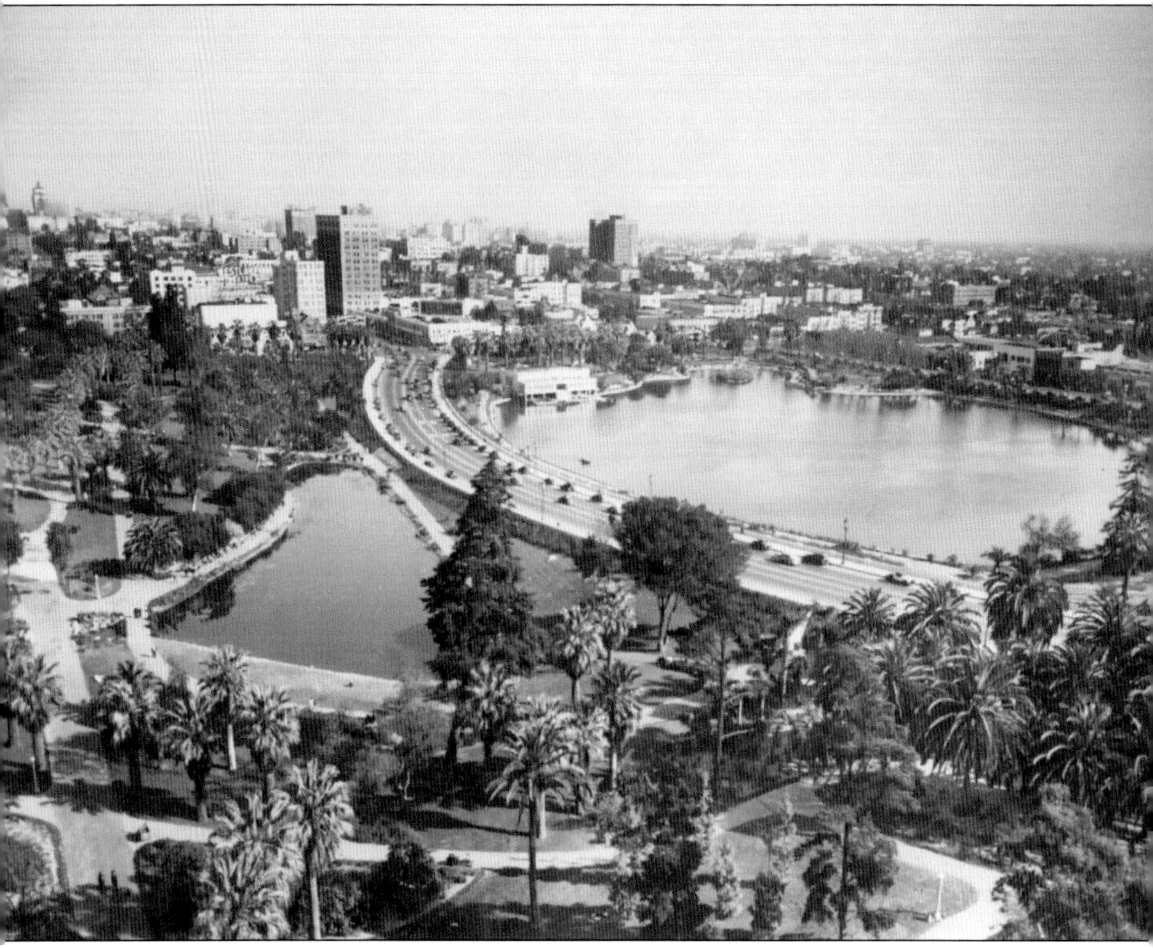

The hope that the board would reverse the decision was short-lived. Three weeks later, the board, with Los Angeles mayor Fletcher Bowron present, approved the action. The meeting minutes read as follows: "Mayor Bowron was also present at the meeting and stated that on May 19 he notified General MacArthur that Los Angeles had named a park in his honor and the mayor read a cablegram from the general extending his thanks for the honor thus conferred. It was therefore the opinion of most of those present that as General MacArthur had already been notified that the city had named the park after him, nothing further could be done in regard to restoring the name. The Mayor extended an invitation to the representatives of the Westlake district to participate in the dedication ceremonies at the park on June 13." Political machinations indeed: the ceremony had already been scheduled. The public sentiment may have been defeated, but the park, now with two lakes, would continue on its journey as an urban oasis into the next decades. (Courtesy of the Natural History Museum of Los Angeles County.)

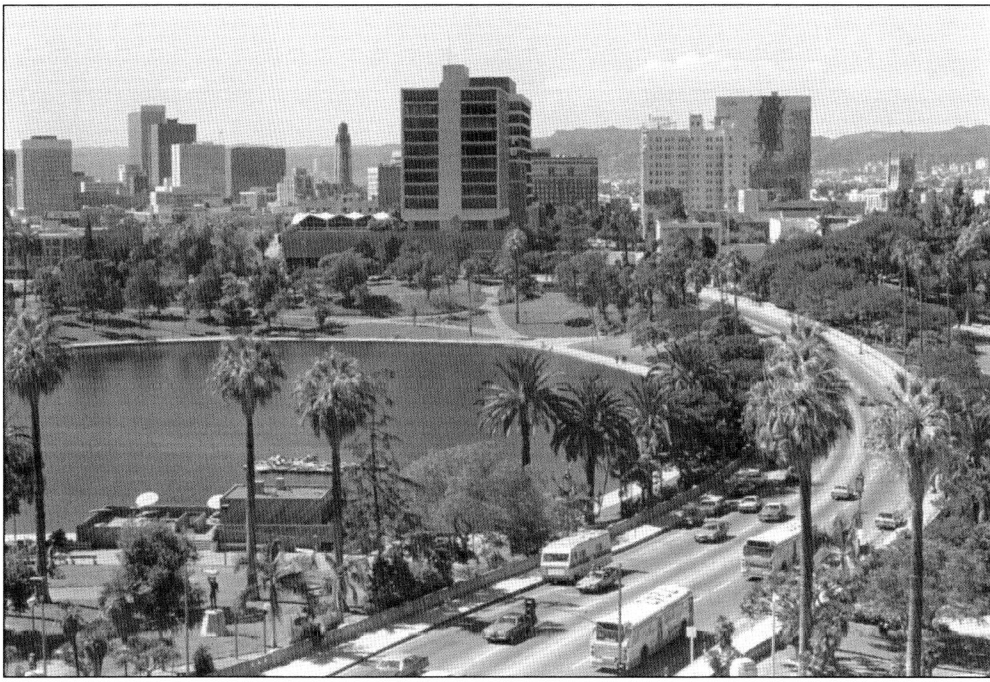

By the 1970s, with the passage of time, the failing infrastructure, and perhaps the grind of millions of feet walking, running, and marching atop it, MacArthur Park was to see a significant physical upgrade. This change would not be as environmentally damaging as the Wilshire Boulevard extension construction, or as emotionally draining on the local residents and visitors. The city's hardscape improvements included a concrete edge to the lake as well as other beautification efforts that were intended to make the entire park safer and more attractive for local families. Despite these improvements, the park's passive status was maintained by the city. (Courtesy of the Los Angeles Public Library Photo Collection.)

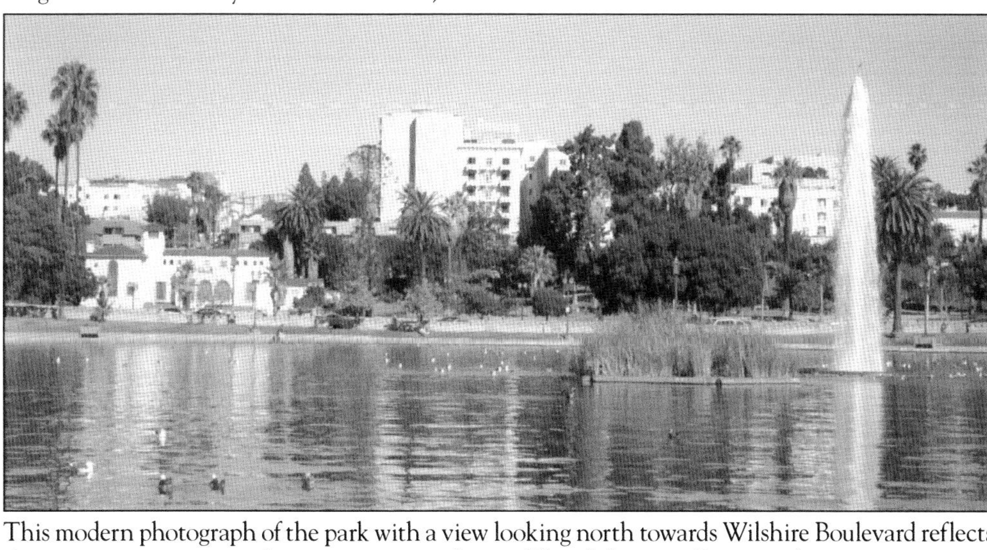

This modern photograph of the park with a view looking north towards Wilshire Boulevard reflects the continuing nature of a green oasis in the middle of the city. Due to subway construction, the bottom of the lake is no longer natural, but concrete. Wilshire Boulevard continues to move commuters from the western end of the city to downtown. (Author's collection.)

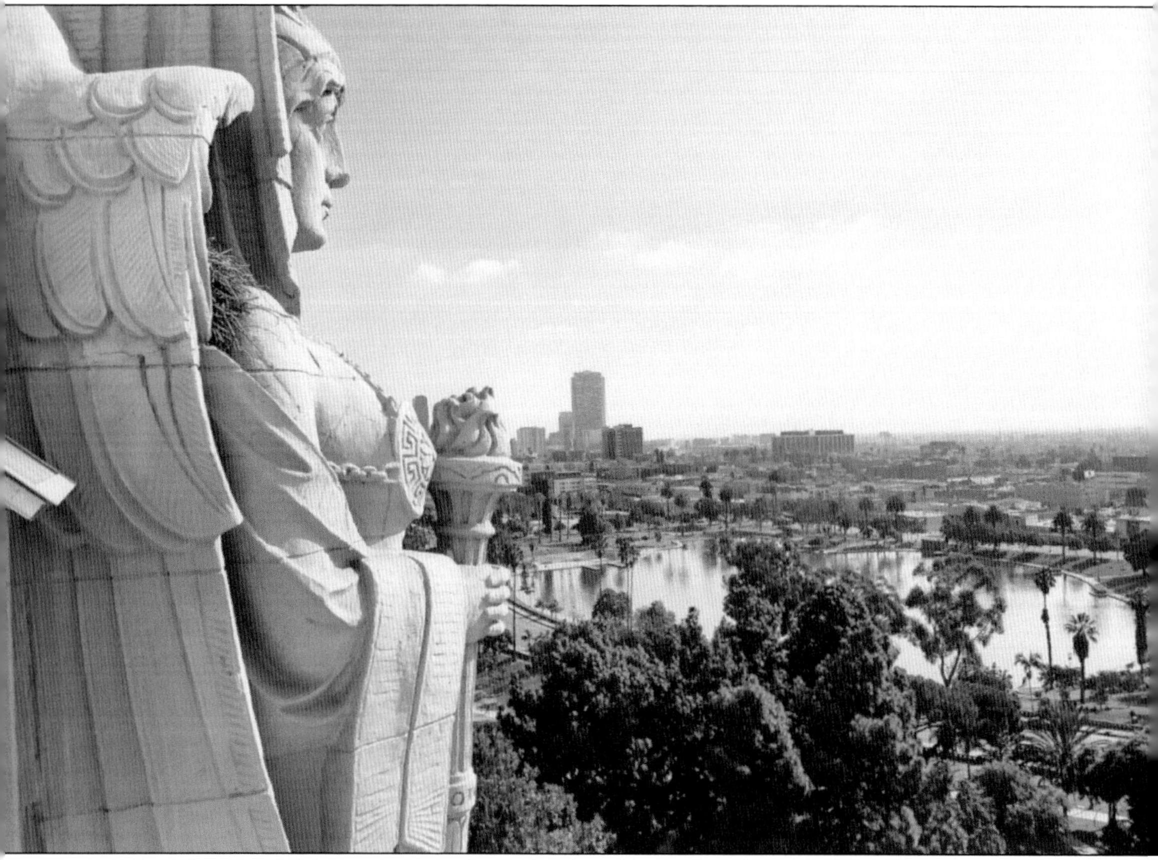

Today, the view of the park from the Park Plaza (formerly Elks Lodge) looks similar to images from earlier decades. A key difference is the disappearance of the second lake north of Wilshire Boulevard, replaced by the latest version of the band shell and the newly installed synthetic turf field. But history does not hide, and the high water table continues to wreak havoc with park engineering. (Courtesy of Meeno.)

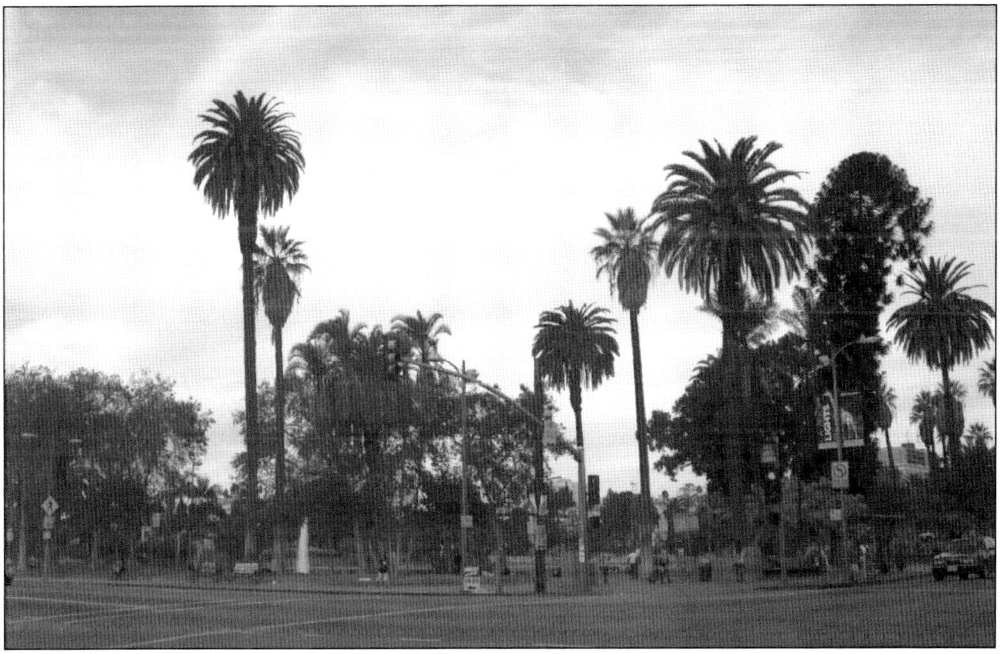

The southeastern entrance to the park continues to be the most popular entry point for local residents seeking a green refuge from the heavily urbanized neighborhood. This section of the park, along with the intersection, frequently floods during heavy winter rains. The drainage system is unable to carry away the rainwater fast enough. Perhaps it is a reminder of the park's reservoir history. (Author's collection.)

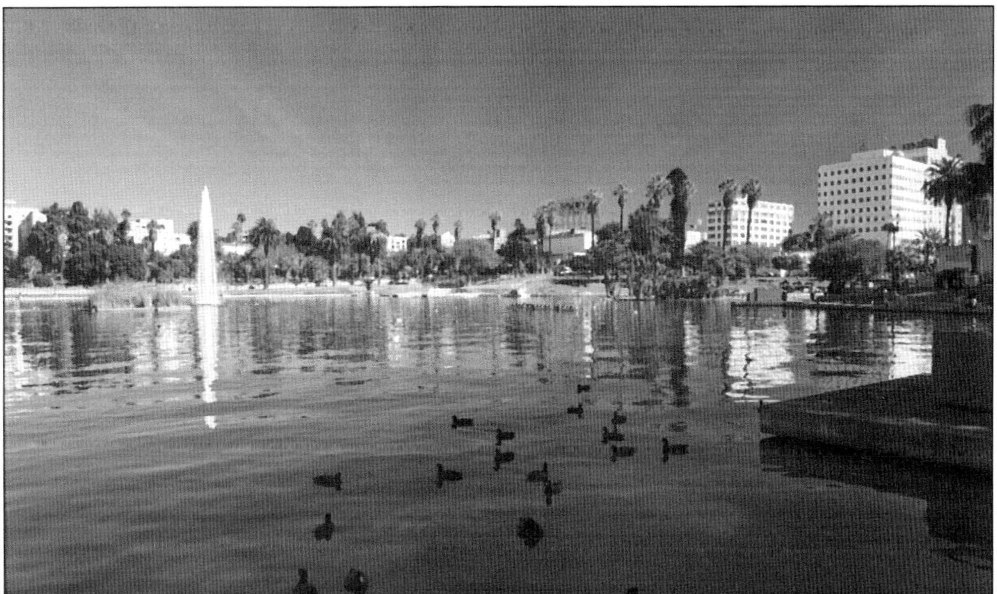

Looking west across the lake, one can still appreciate the serenity of the lake within its natural catchment basin. The condition of the water has improved over the last decade as the city has increased the circulation capacity of the aeration system, which was installed after the subway project was completed. Fishing, however, is still discouraged. (Courtesy of Meeno.)

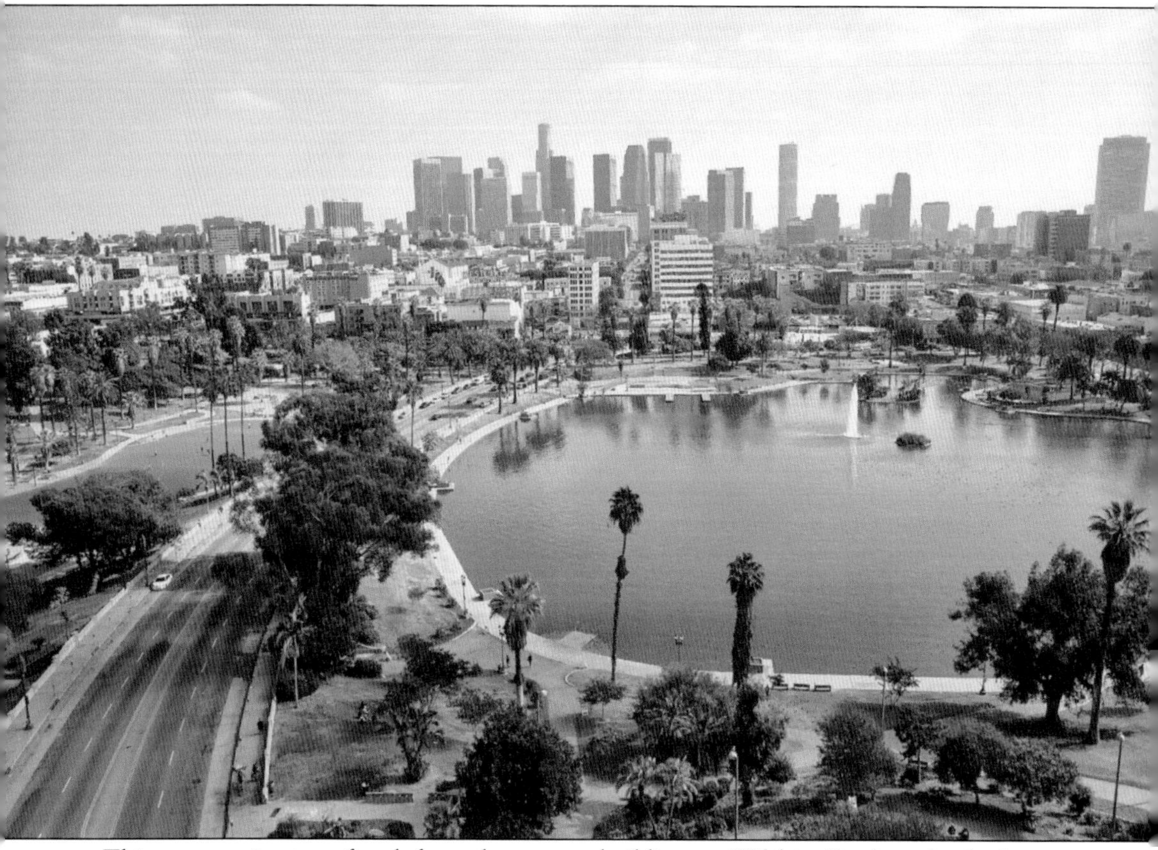

This panoramic view of park from the cement building on Wilshire Boulevard is looking east toward the modern and dramatic downtown skyline. On any given day of the week, thousands of families continue to visit the park seeking relief from what troubles them. Although public safety within the park has exponentially improved over the last 10 years, visitors from outside the neighborhood are relatively rare today. (Courtesy of Meeno.)

Two

THE CENTER OF THE CITY

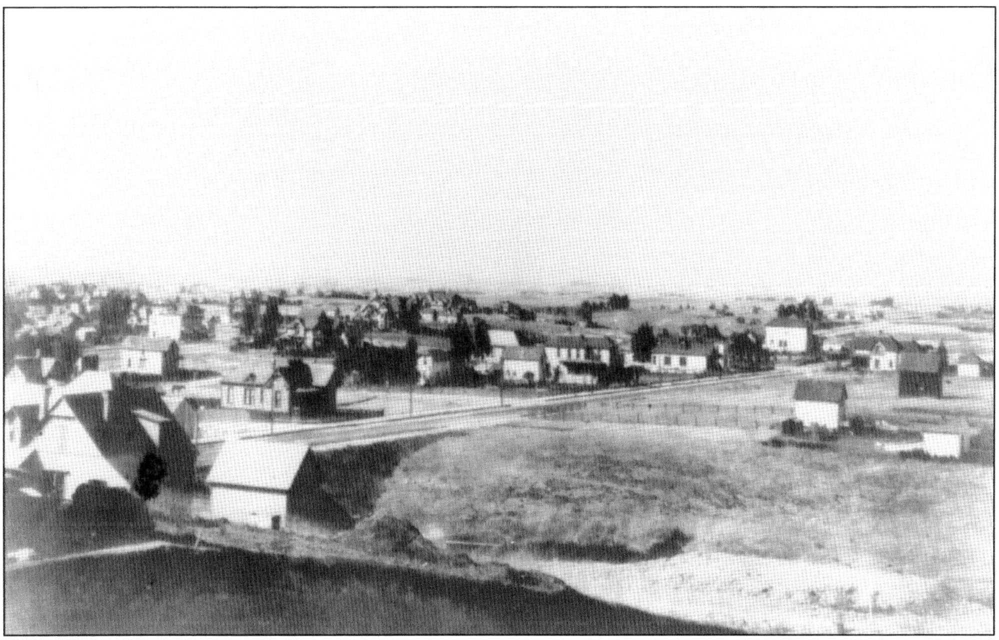

The 19th century was coming to a close, and Los Angeles' population was growing and looking optimistically towards the new century. The neighborhoods to the west of historic Bunker Hill and the Old Plaza were the harbingers of change for the city, and Westlake Park the new jewel for a town that had worldly aspirations. Here is a view from 1890 looking southwest near the corner of Seventh and Witmer Streets, a few blocks east of the recently inaugurated Westlake Park. (Courtesy of the Natural History Museum of Los Angeles County.)

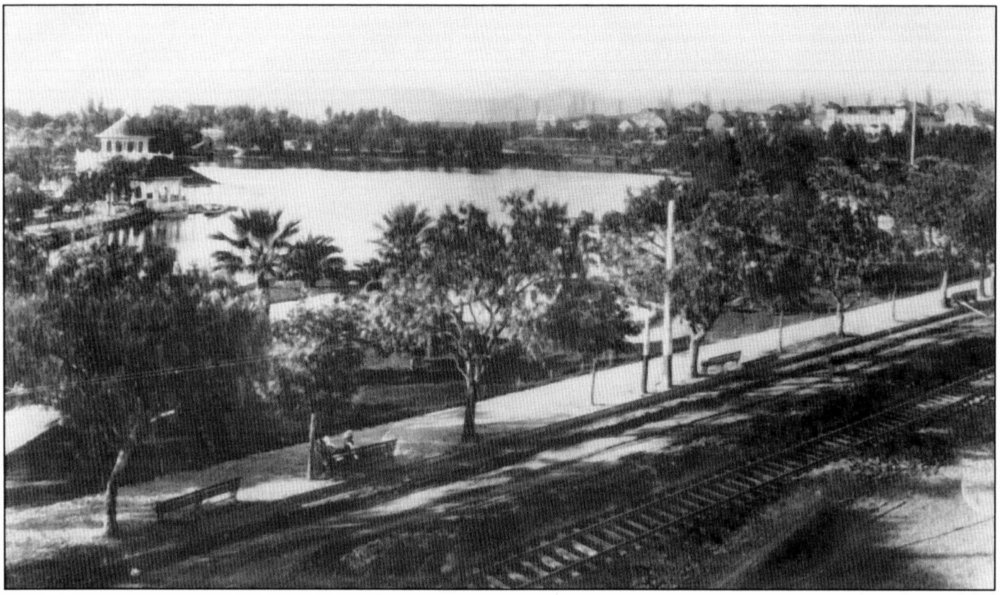

The rail line seen in this photograph from the early 1900s provided service between the neighborhoods around Westlake Park and extended east to the growing neighborhood of Boyle Heights. This railway served the city until the mid-20th century, when a newer and more modern light-rail line replaced it. Over its century of existence, Westlake Park (and later MacArthur Park) has been positioned as a transportation hub for the entire region, beginning with streetcars and now with subway service. (Courtesy of the Los Angeles Public Library Photo Collection.)

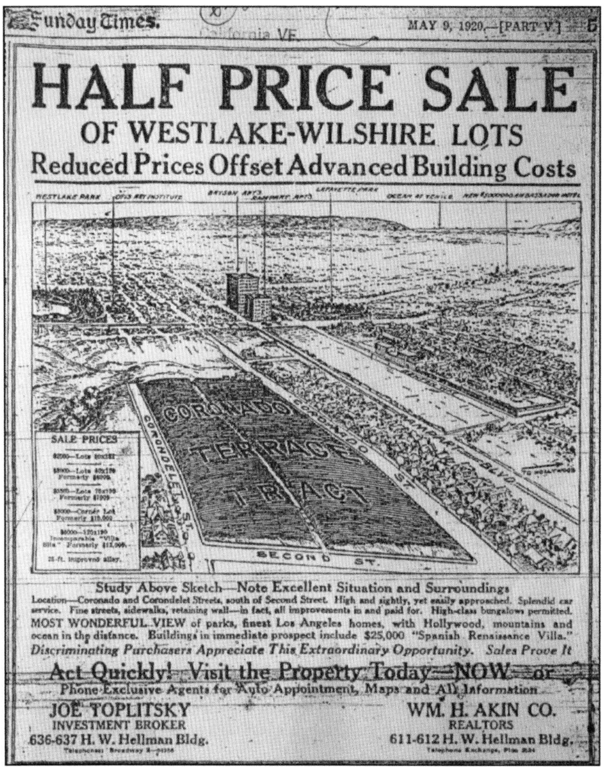

After the park opened, the city's population doubled again over the next decade. The real estate industry speculators—as commonplace in Los Angeles as the aromatic sagebrush—rushed in to fill the need for housing. This advertisement from the *Los Angeles Times* in 1920 showcases the hilly Coronado Terrace Tract just north of Westlake Park. The area is described as "high and sightly, yet easily approached." The street at the top of this tract is still called Ocean View Avenue due to its elevation and view of the Pacific Ocean. (Courtesy of the *Los Angeles Times*.)

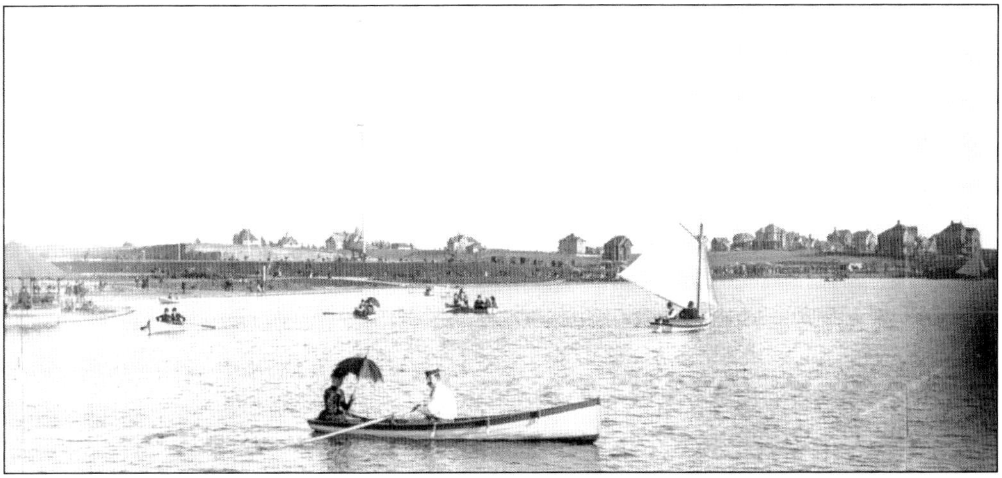

This early photograph of the neighborhood to the east of the park features the emerging grandiosity of the houses. As the park itself continued to be beautified, local boosters engendered a resort-like environment to attract the city's elite. When a local property owner proposed to bring in an undesirable commercial establishment, a local resident circulated a petition that in part stated its opposition because of the "exclusive, high-class residence district long famed as Westlake." (Courtesy of the Natural History Museum of Los Angeles County.)

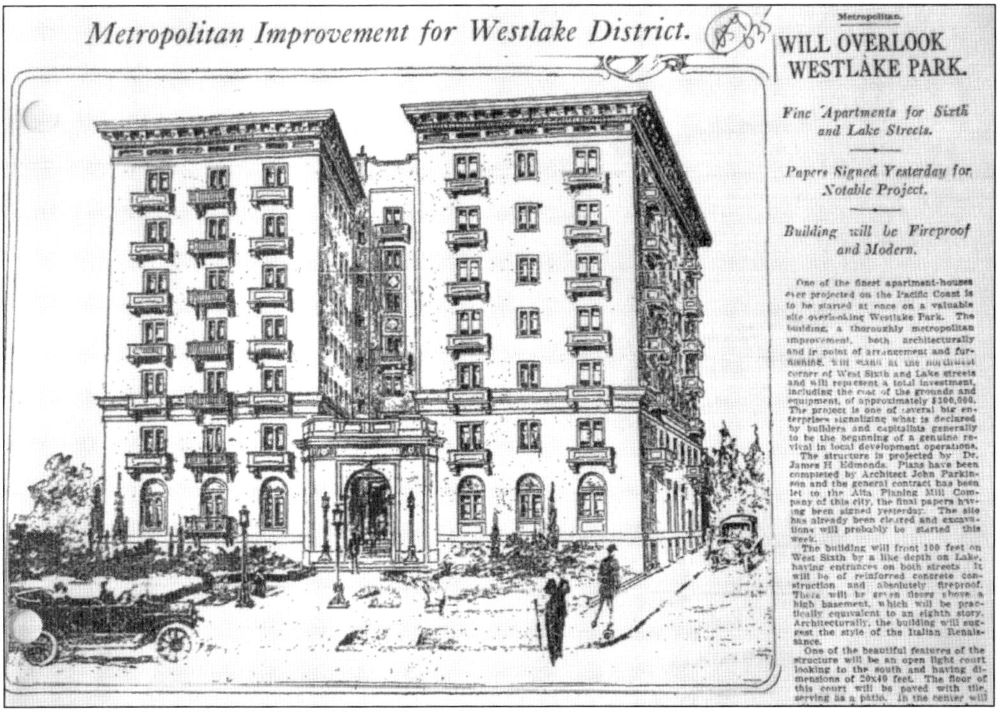

Metropolitan Improvement for Westlake District.

Metropolitan.

WILL OVERLOOK WESTLAKE PARK.

Fine Apartments for Sixth and Lake Streets.

Papers Signed Yesterday for Notable Project.

Building will be Fireproof and Modern.

One of the finest apartment-houses ever projected on the Pacific Coast is to be started at once on a valuable site overlooking Westlake Park. The building, a thoroughly metropolitan improvement, both architecturally and in point of arrangement and furnishing, will stand at the northwest corner of West Sixth and Lake streets and will represent a total investment, including the cost of the grounds and equipment, of approximately $100,000. The project is one of several big enterprises signalizing what is declared by builders and capitalists generally to be the beginning of a genuine revival in local development operations.

The structure is projected by Dr. James H. Edmonds. Plans have been completed by Architect John Parkinson and the general contract has been let to the Alta Planing Mill Company of this city, the final papers having been signed yesterday. The site has already been cleared and excavations will probably be started this week.

The building will front 100 feet on West Sixth by a like depth on Lake, having entrances on both streets. It will be of reinforced concrete construction and absolutely fireproof. There will be seven floors above a high basement, which will be practically equivalent to an eighth story. Architecturally, the building will suggest the style of the Italian Renaissance.

One of the beautiful features of the structure will be an open light court looking to the south and having dimensions of 20x40 feet. The floor of this court will be paved with tile, serving as a patio. In the center will

Of the many streets fronting Westlake Park, Sixth Street was the street that received the most beautiful architecture, primarily because of its elevated frontage adjacent to the park. This apartment house, designed by John Parkinson (the architect of such notable local landmarks as Los Angeles City Hall, Union Station, and the Bullock's Wilshire, which is just a few blocks west of Westlake Park), is described as "the finest apartment-houses ever projected on the Pacific Coast." (Courtesy of the *Los Angeles Times*.)

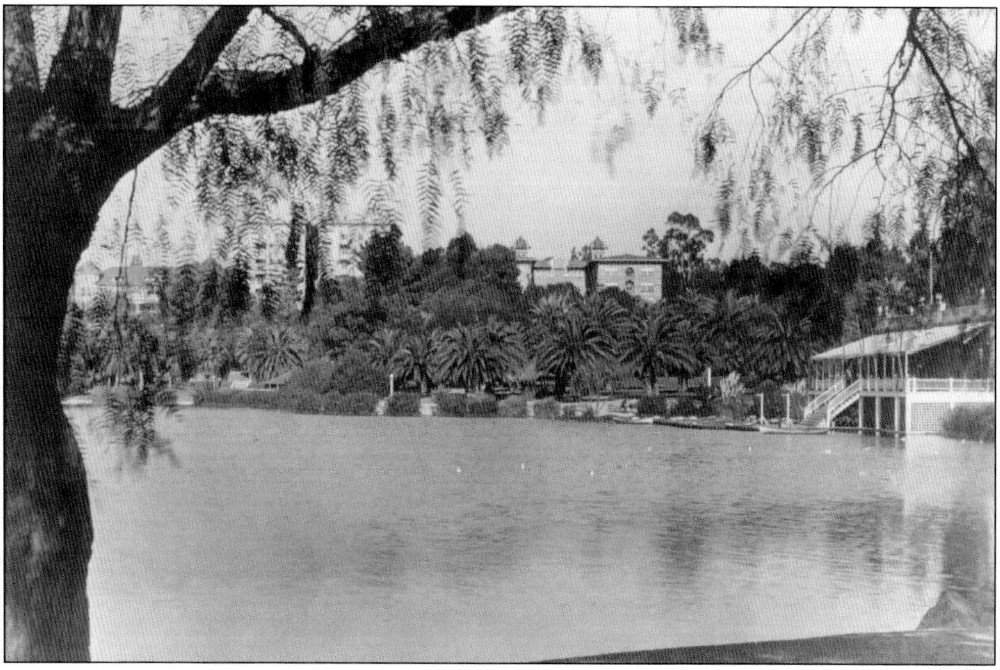

This photograph shows a glimpse of the architecture fronting the pseudo-tropical foliage of the park. Buildings with haughty names like the Bryson, Leighton, Arcady, and the classiest of them all, the Asbury, symbolized the brick-and-mortar fashionableness of the new neighborhood. An advertisement for the new Hotel Californian, located a block from the park, describes its interior: "All rooms with bath or shower, radio in every room, European plan, and rates moderate." (Courtesy of the Natural History Museum of Los Angeles County.)

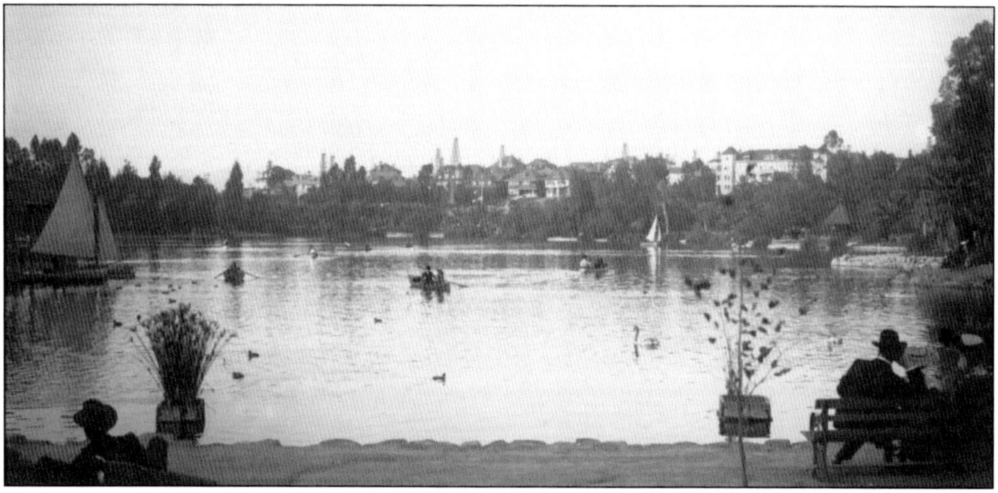

Real estate speculation created wealth in this neighborhood, and so did oil. One of the original oil fields discovered underneath the Los Angeles basin had its westernmost boundary directly below the surface of the Westlake neighborhood. The oil derricks are clearly visible in the hills north of the park, and, yes, the oil industry attempted to drill near the park. Fortunately, local stakeholders blocked all efforts. Oil was ingloriously exhumed for many decades around the neighborhood. Starting in the 1960s, many oil wells were capped due to their lack of production. (Courtesy of the Natural History Museum of Los Angeles County.)

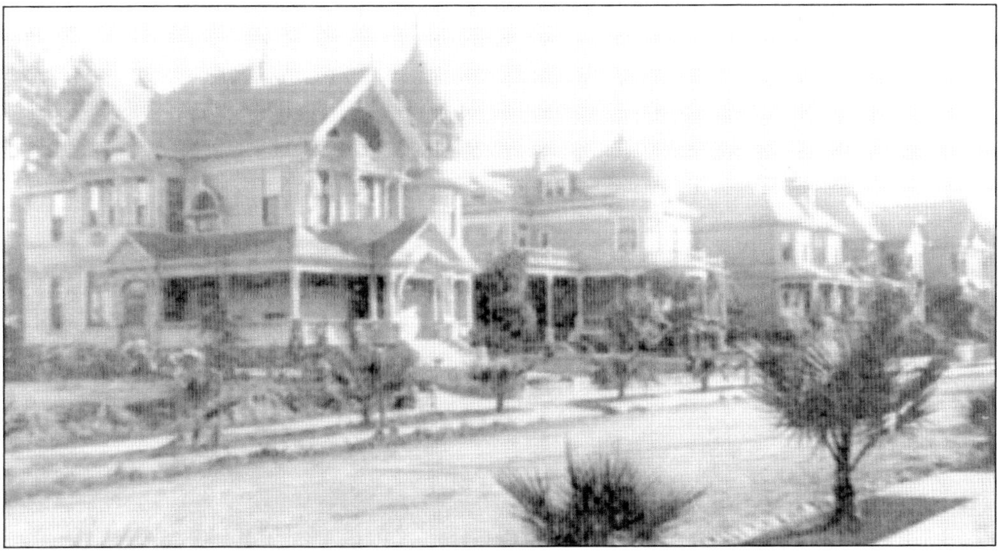

Elegant apartment houses were not the only architectural improvements that took root in the Westlake neighborhood in the early part of the 20th century. Along thoroughfares like Bonnie Brae Street (pictured), Lake Street, Miramar Street (Spanish for "ocean view"), and Westlake Avenue, monumental Queen Anne and Eastlake homes were constructed to house the city's wealthy, weekend vacationers, and newly arrived celebrities. A house built by and for Charlie Chaplin still stands today a couple of blocks south of the park. (Courtesy of the Los Angeles Public Library Photo Collection.)

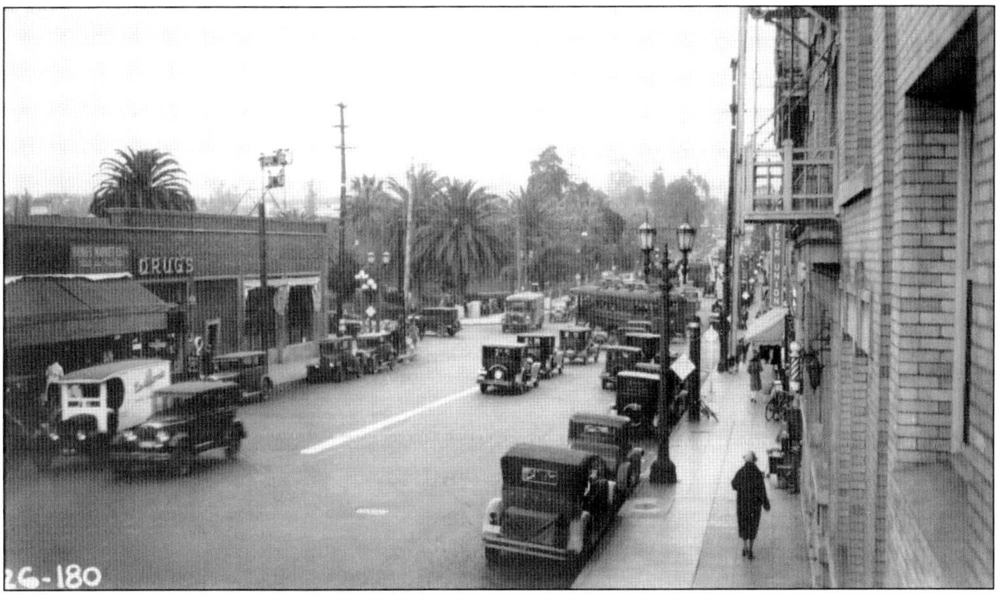

The Westlake neighborhood was a mixed-use and vibrant place, an early model of the type of density that would define the land-use patterns for the entire city during the first few decades of the new century. In this view looking north on Alvarado Street from the south side of Seventh Street in 1926, the southeast entrance to Westlake Park is in the distance. The streetcar is rolling by on its way to eastern neighborhoods. (Courtesy of the University of Southern California Libraries.)

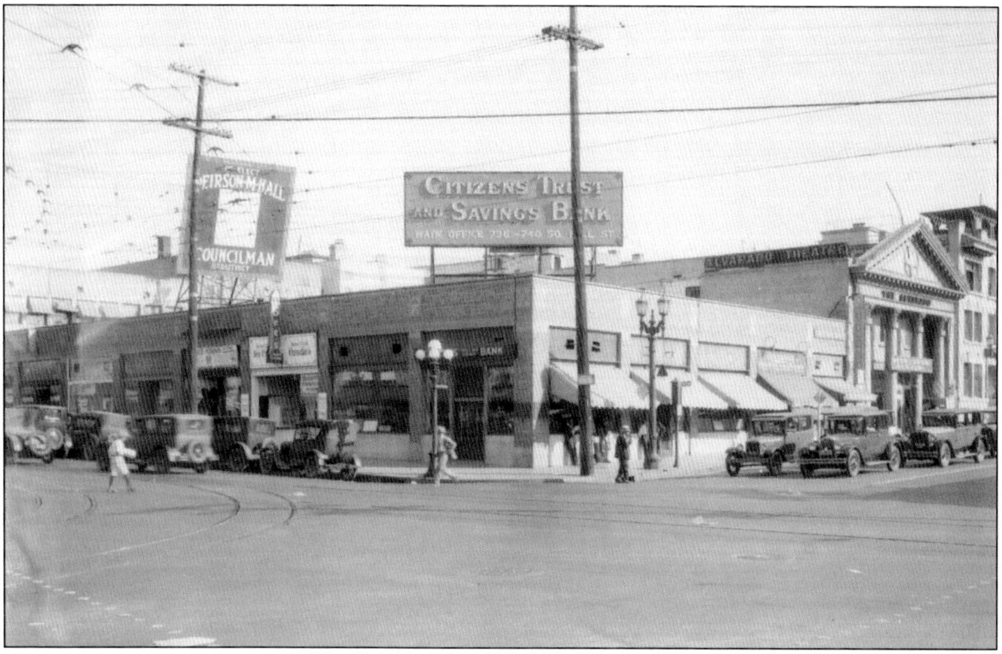

If a person survived crossing the street as the streetcar was turning, then he would be standing at the northwest corner of Seventh and Alvarado Streets (at the entrance of Westlake Park), the location from which this photograph was taken in 1927. The signs of a healthy neighborhood are clear—a bank, retail shops, the proverbial Los Angeles traffic, and, of course, a billboard with political propaganda. (Courtesy of the University of Southern California Libraries.)

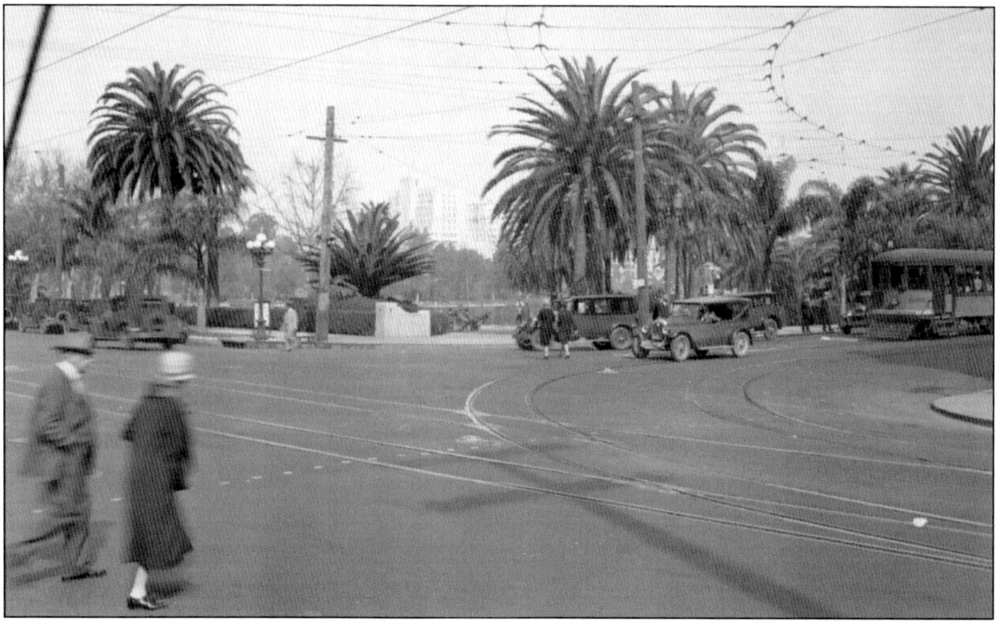

The green oasis that is the park serves as a retreat for local residents and visitors from the traffic and general urban commotion. This view is what a person would have seen standing in front of the bank (southeast corner of Seventh and Alvarado Streets) and looking towards Westlake Park (Courtesy of the Los Angeles Public Library Photo Collection.)

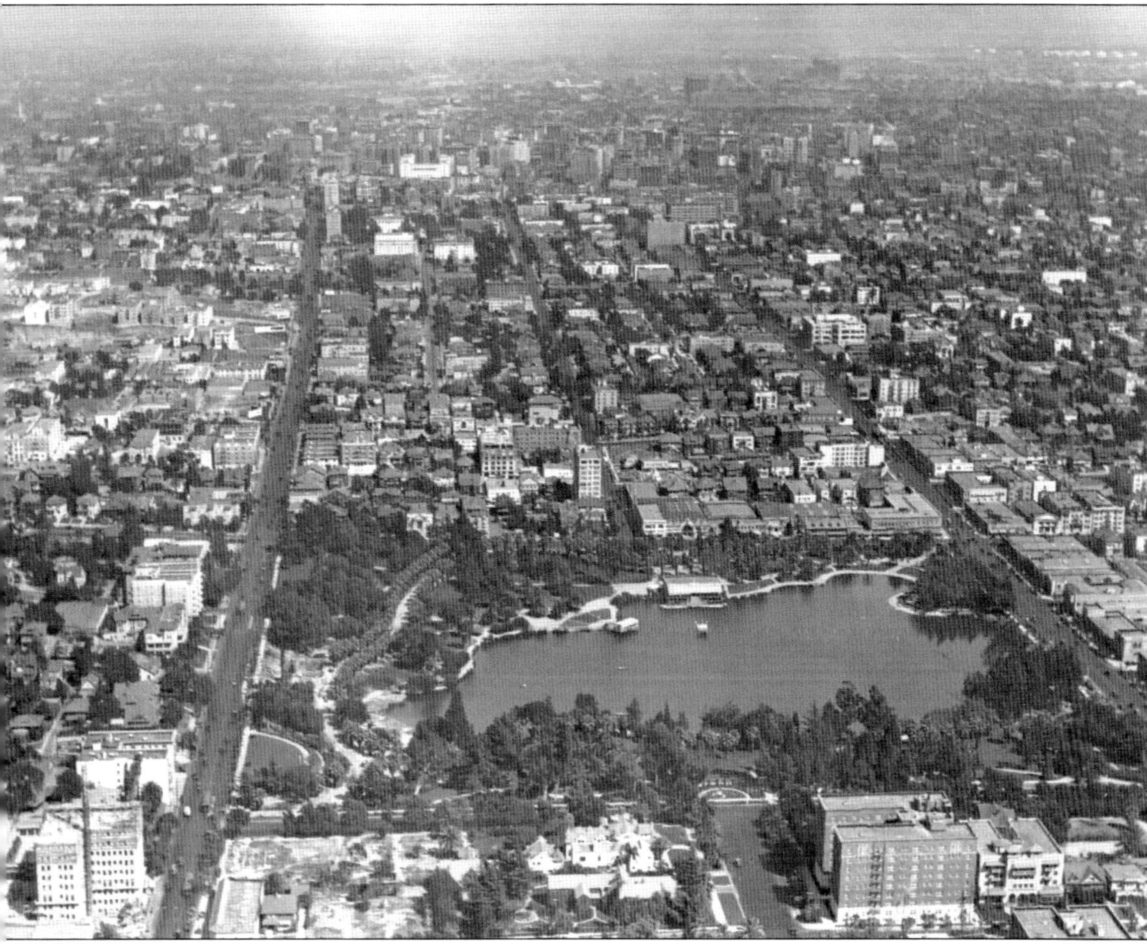

This aerial from the 1920s of the park and neighborhood demonstrates the growing density of the area. In the upper part of the photograph is downtown Los Angeles and the center right captures the corner of Seventh and Alvarado Streets. The newly built Asbury Apartments are visible in the lower right. Some of the original design features of the park such as the Palm Drive can be seen along the left side of the park. (Courtesy of the Los Angeles Public Library Photo Collection.)

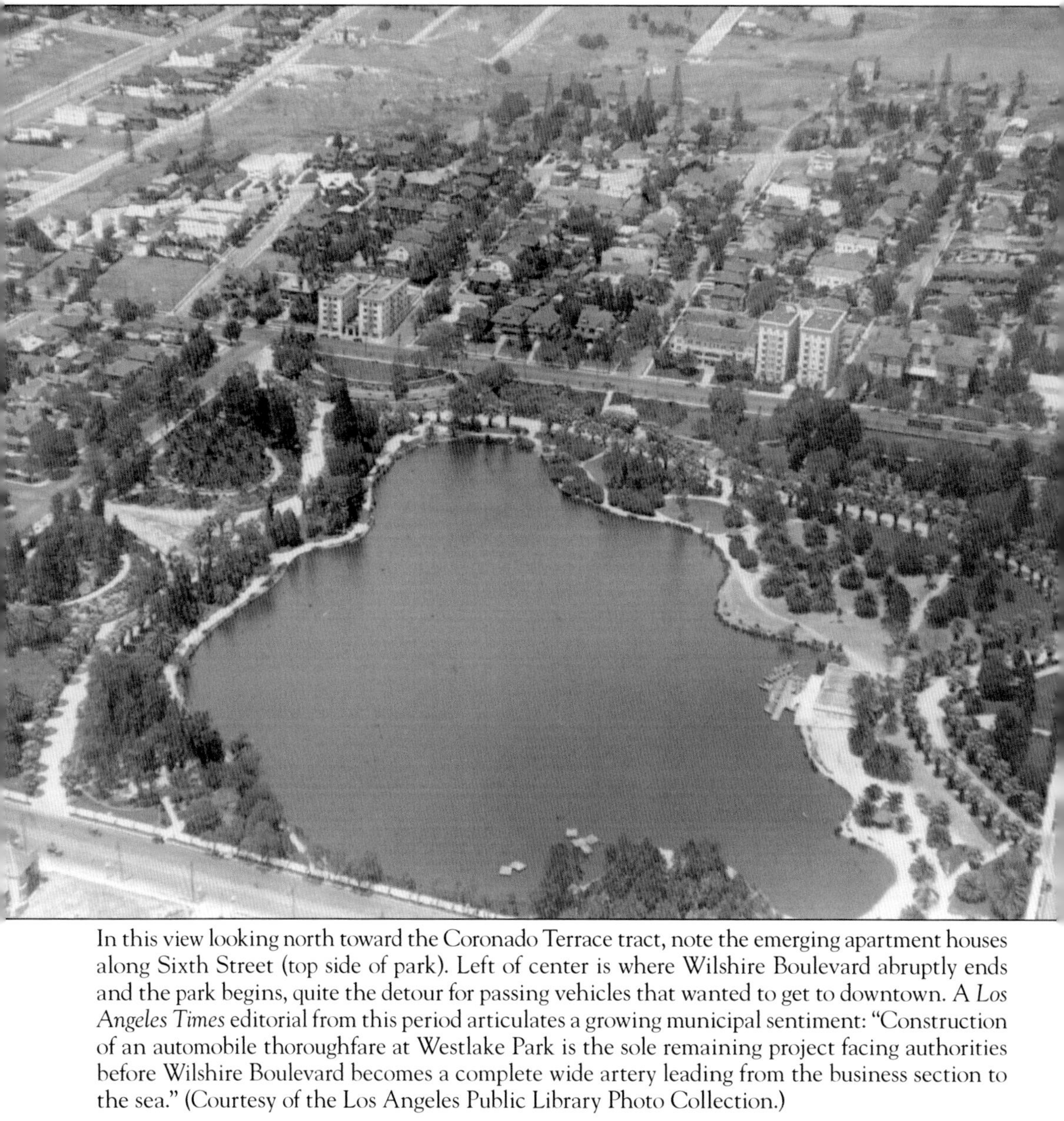

In this view looking north toward the Coronado Terrace tract, note the emerging apartment houses along Sixth Street (top side of park). Left of center is where Wilshire Boulevard abruptly ends and the park begins, quite the detour for passing vehicles that wanted to get to downtown. A *Los Angeles Times* editorial from this period articulates a growing municipal sentiment: "Construction of an automobile thoroughfare at Westlake Park is the sole remaining project facing authorities before Wilshire Boulevard becomes a complete wide artery leading from the business section to the sea." (Courtesy of the Los Angeles Public Library Photo Collection.)

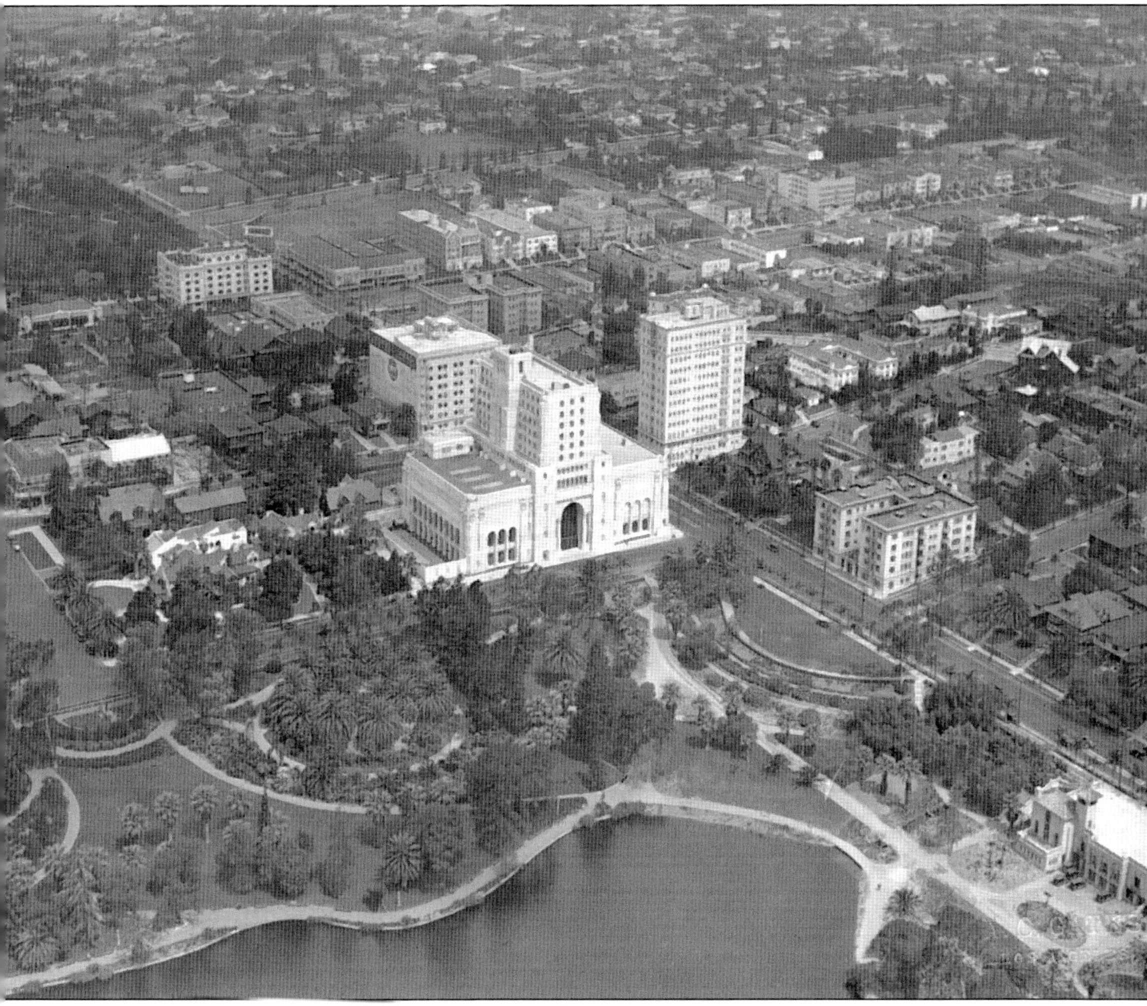

While city leaders were preparing for the fight that was certain to come with the bisecting of the park for the Wilshire Viaduct, construction of what would become architectural landmarks continued. The Elks Lodge building was an instant classic for the neighborhood. The building included retail space, a residential tower, an Olympic-size pool in the basement, and large banquet centers. The members who visited the club gravitated to the park. The park itself became an extension of the lodge, hosting a variety of community events for the Elks. (Courtesy of the Los Angeles Public Library Photo Collection.)

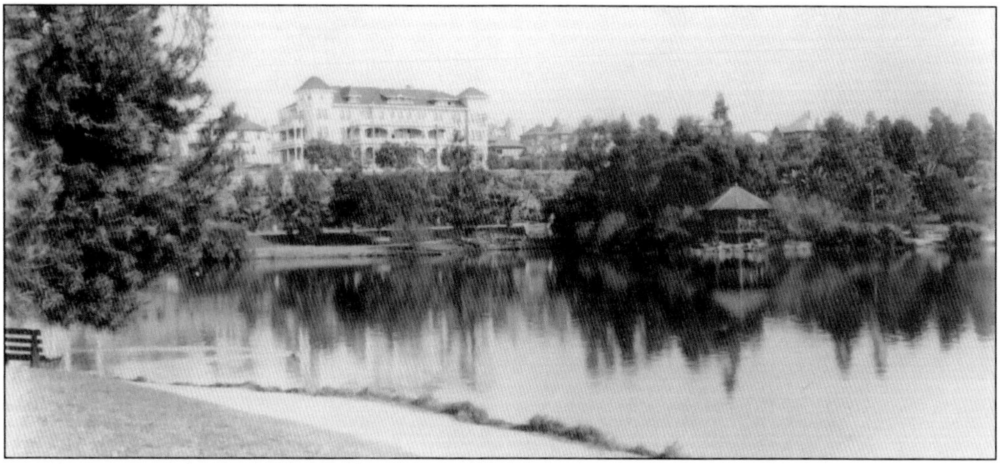

Another instant design icon was the Park View Hotel on Sixth Street, Although photographs of the hotel are somewhat rare, this one shows the size of the building and its strategic location across from the park. As would be expected with its view, the hotel became a popular destination for visitors to the neighborhood. (Courtesy of the Los Angeles Public Library Photo Collection.)

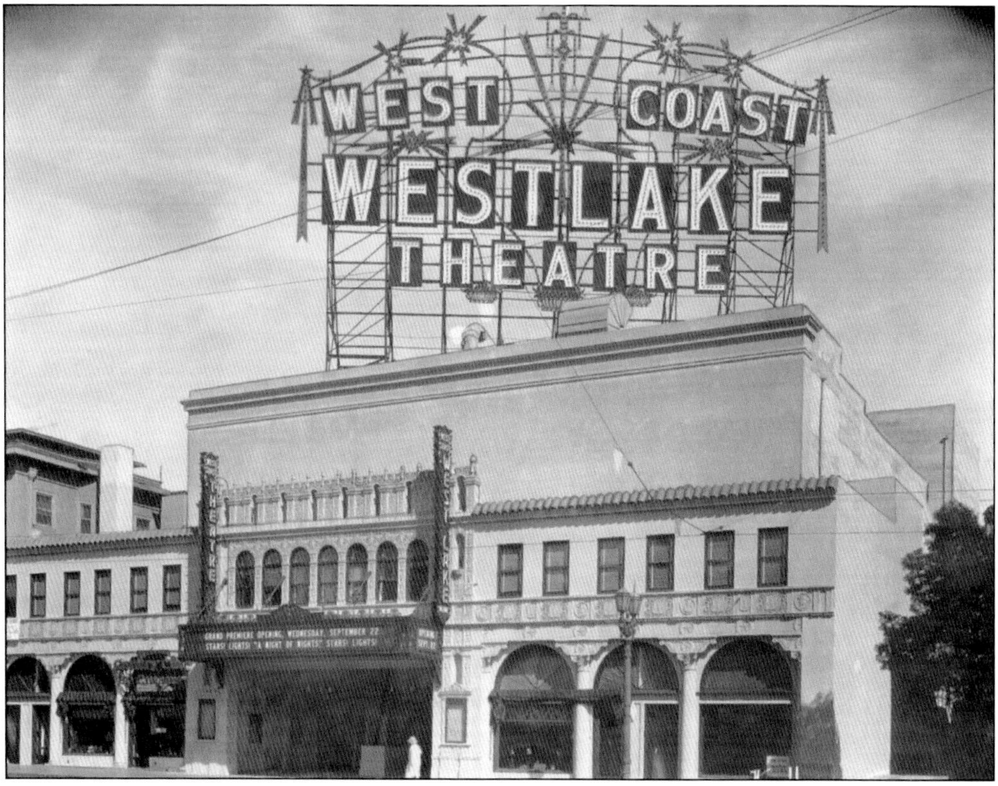

In September 1926, the Westlake Theatre celebrated its grand opening. Located on Alvarado Street just south of Sixth Street, the theater was the neighborhood's first-run movie facility. Designed by architect Richard M. Bates, the theater was a grand space. The exterior rooftop sign was a landmark on its own account and continues today as a key community marker. As single-screen theaters began to fail over the last 30 years, the Westlake Theatre was no exception to the inevitable. It closed in 1991. (Courtesy of Cinema Treasures.)

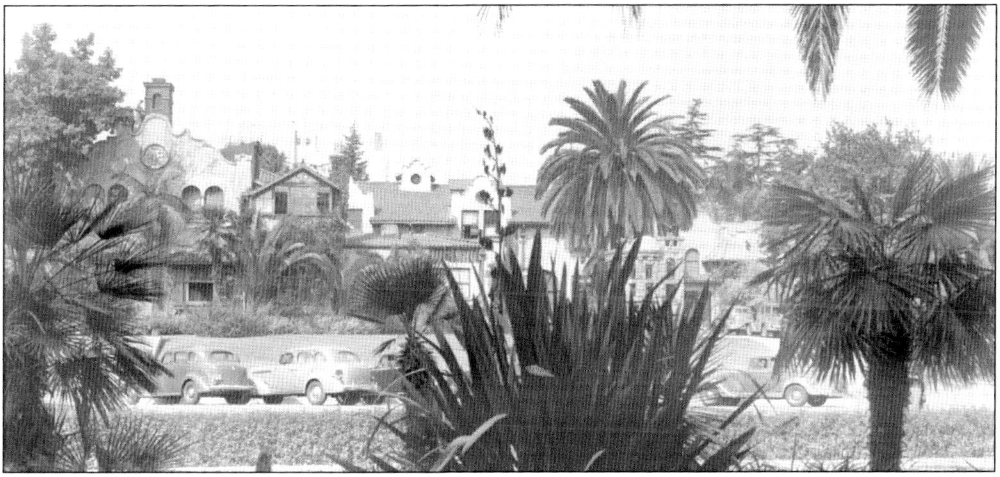

Otis Arts Institute, pictured here in 1939, was located on Wilshire Boulevard. The original house that served the art school was donated by Harrison Gray Otis, the second publisher of the *Los Angeles Times*. Along with the Chouinard Art Institute, originally located on Seventh Street, it created a vibrant arts scene in the area, which mirrored a growing art culture citywide. The schools brought students from around the world. The park became the campus quad and a source of artistic inspiration. But, as the area's public safety became problematic, the Otis Arts Institute closed in the 1990s. (Courtesy of the Los Angeles Public Library Photo Collection.)

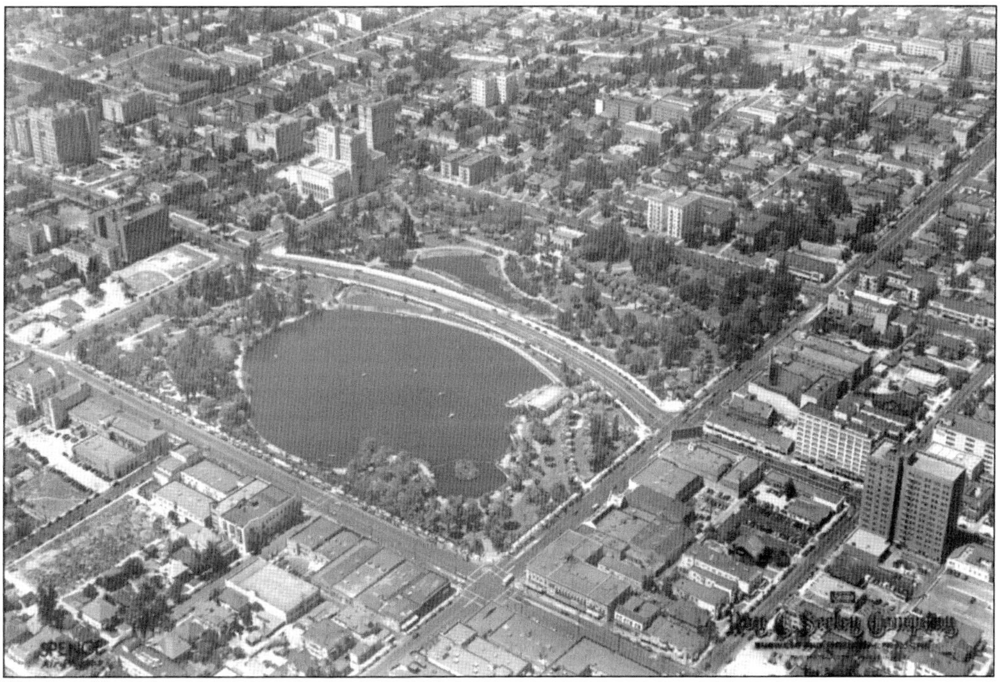

By the late 1930s, the winds of change had already blown through the neighborhood and the park by creating the Wilshire Viaduct. The infamous detour had been corrected. The lake, a place of miniature boats, ever-breeding ducks, and strolling couples, was now torn into two pieces, like the broken heart that many locals surely experienced. Commerce could now transport straight to the sea. Note the continuing vertical development to the west of the park (left side). The future was here. (Courtesy of the Los Angeles Public Library Photo Collection.)

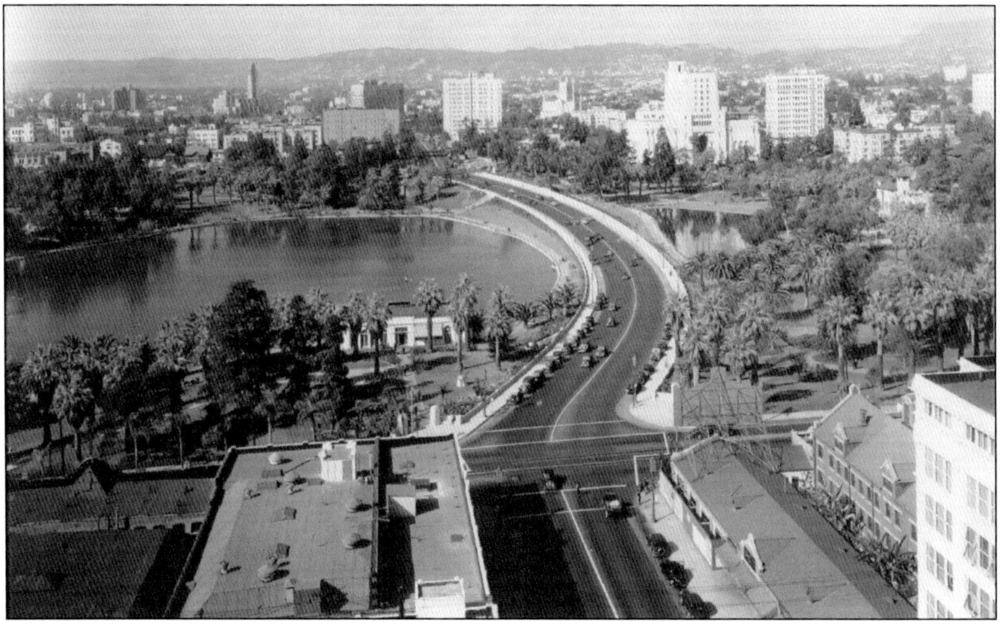

For the city of Los Angeles, the future stretched towards the western horizon. Seen from a high-rise just east of the corner of Wilshire Boulevard and Alvarado Street, the skyline was growing along Wilshire Boulevard and Sixth Street. Church spires, apartment buildings, department stores, and office towers are all captured in this optimistic rendering of the growing metropolis. (Courtesy of the Natural History Museum of Los Angeles County.)

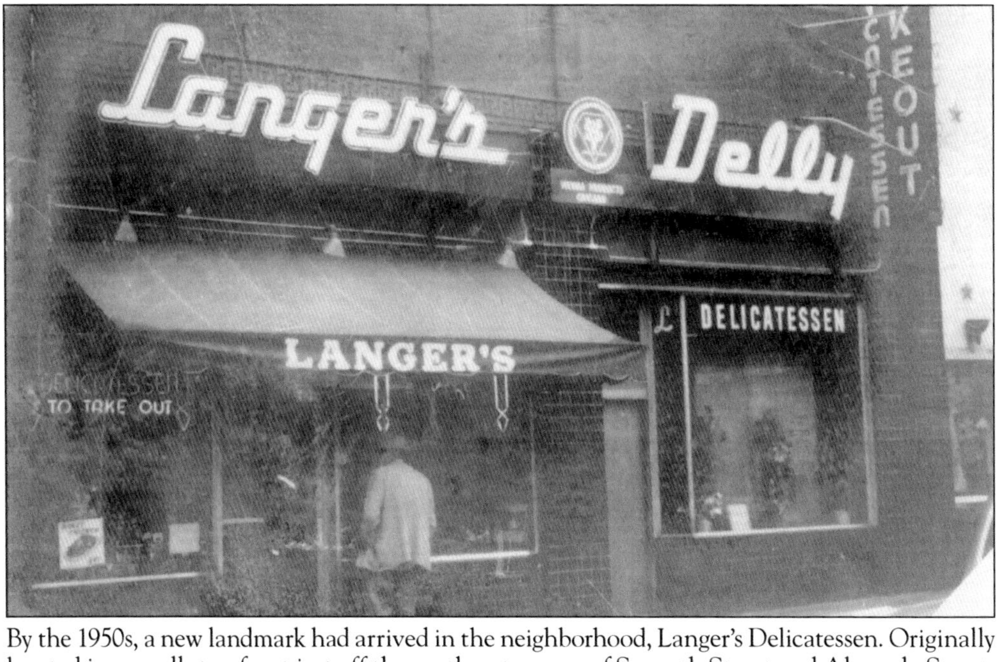

By the 1950s, a new landmark had arrived in the neighborhood, Langer's Delicatessen. Originally located in a small storefront just off the southeast corner of Seventh Street and Alvarado Street, Langer's became a popular eatery owing to the large Jewish and Eastern European population that called Westlake home. The delicious shouts of "pastrami on rye" became synonymous with Westlake Park. (Courtesy of the Langer family collection.)

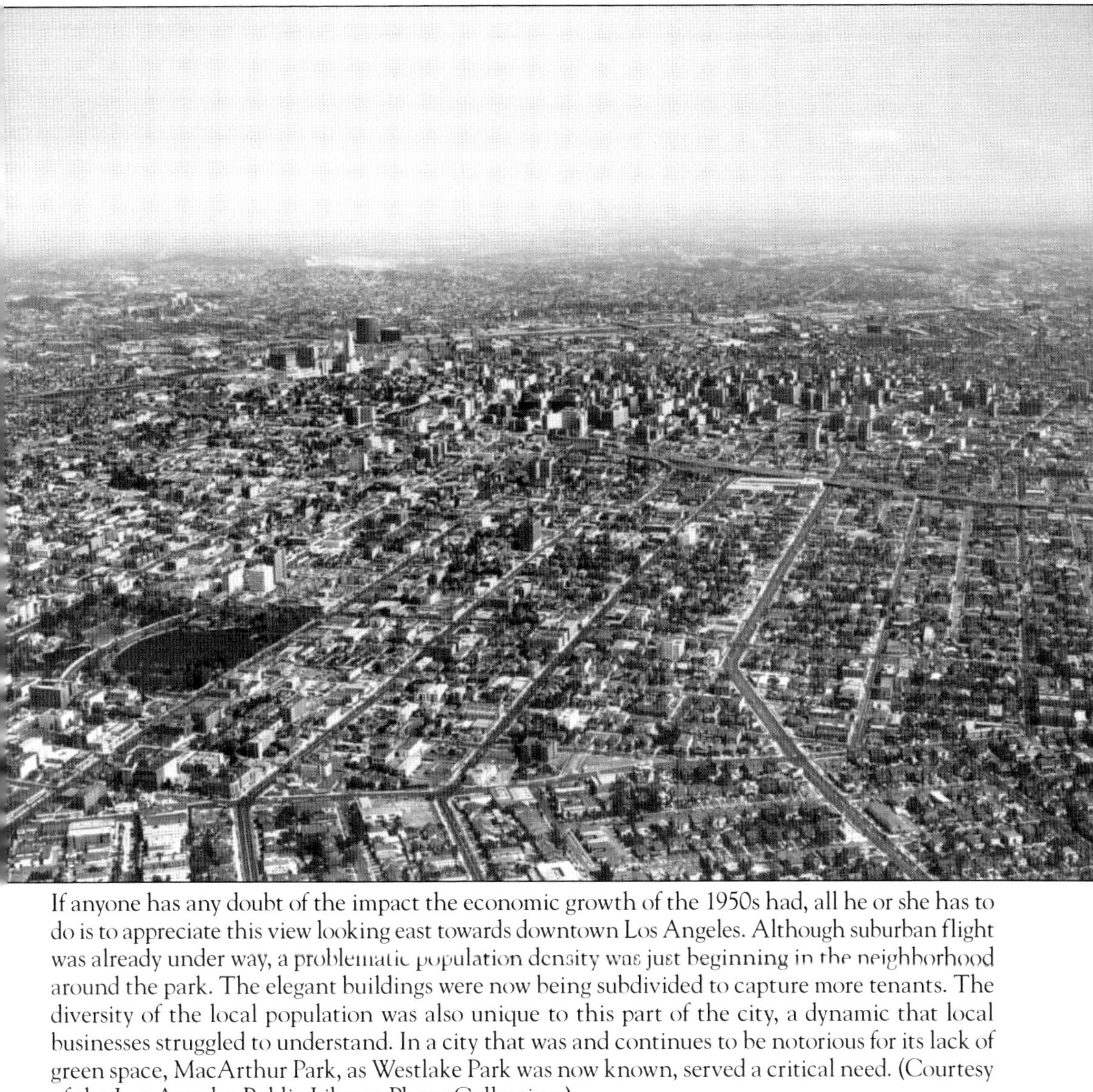

If anyone has any doubt of the impact the economic growth of the 1950s had, all he or she has to do is to appreciate this view looking east towards downtown Los Angeles. Although suburban flight was already under way, a problematic population density was just beginning in the neighborhood around the park. The elegant buildings were now being subdivided to capture more tenants. The diversity of the local population was also unique to this part of the city, a dynamic that local businesses struggled to understand. In a city that was and continues to be notorious for its lack of green space, MacArthur Park, as Westlake Park was now known, served a critical need. (Courtesy of the Los Angeles Public Library Photo Collection.)

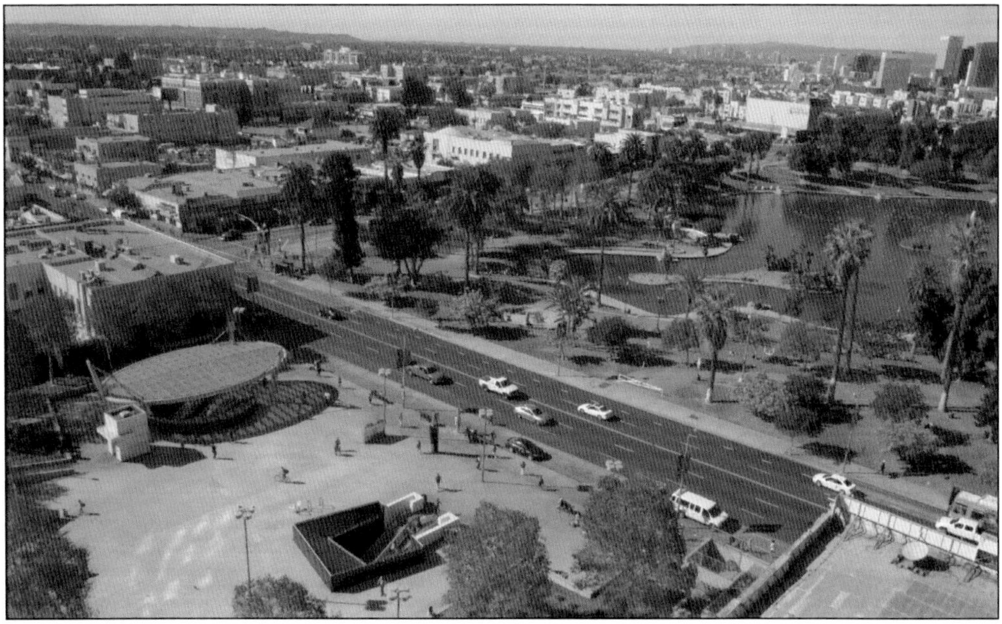

With the completion of the Metro Red Line subway, the Los Angeles County Metropolitan Transportation Authority (Metro), in partnership with a local affordable housing developer, erected a mixed-use building across the from the park on Alvarado Street. The second phase will be directly in front of the park and is expected to activate the subway portal (pictured here) and perhaps connect directly with the park during special events. (Author's collection.)

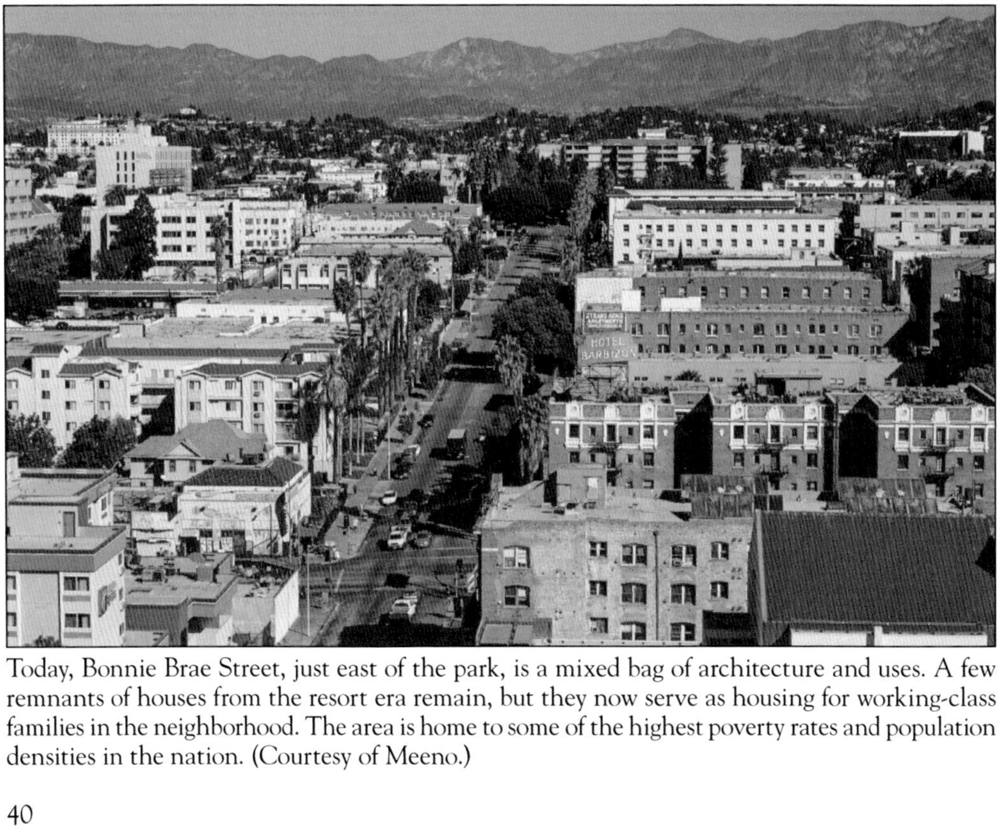

Today, Bonnie Brae Street, just east of the park, is a mixed bag of architecture and uses. A few remnants of houses from the resort era remain, but they now serve as housing for working-class families in the neighborhood. The area is home to some of the highest poverty rates and population densities in the nation. (Courtesy of Meeno.)

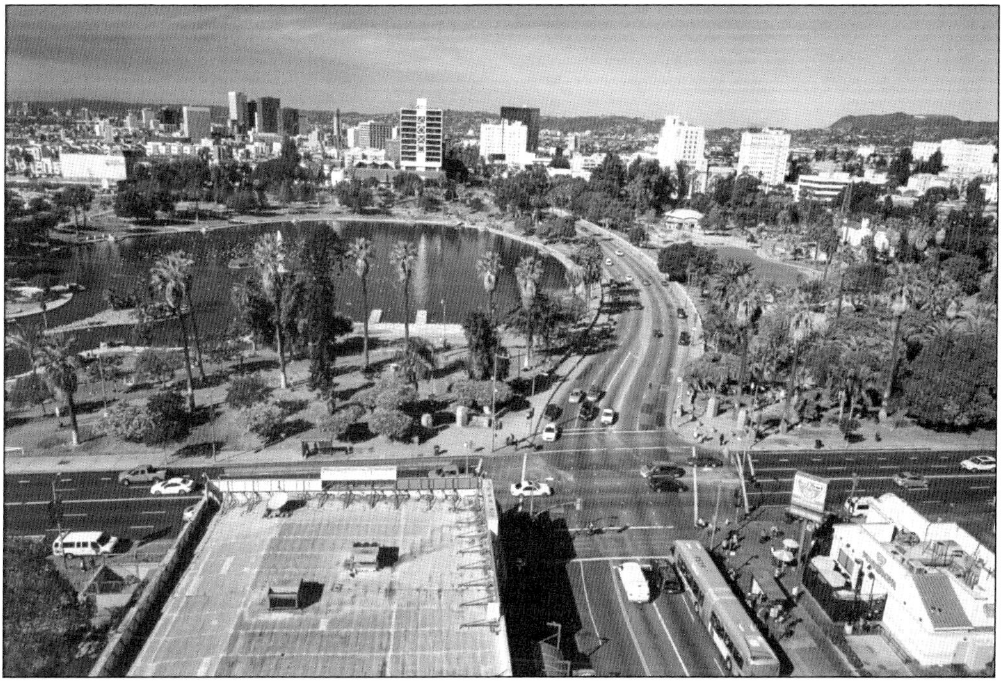

The corner of Wilshire and Alvarado Streets is a beehive of activity. Heavy traffic travels in all directions, regardless of rush hour patterns. The commercial vibrancy of Alvarado Street is evident for both established merchants and unlicensed street vendors, while Wilshire Boulevard contains several medical clinics. (Courtesy of Meeno.)

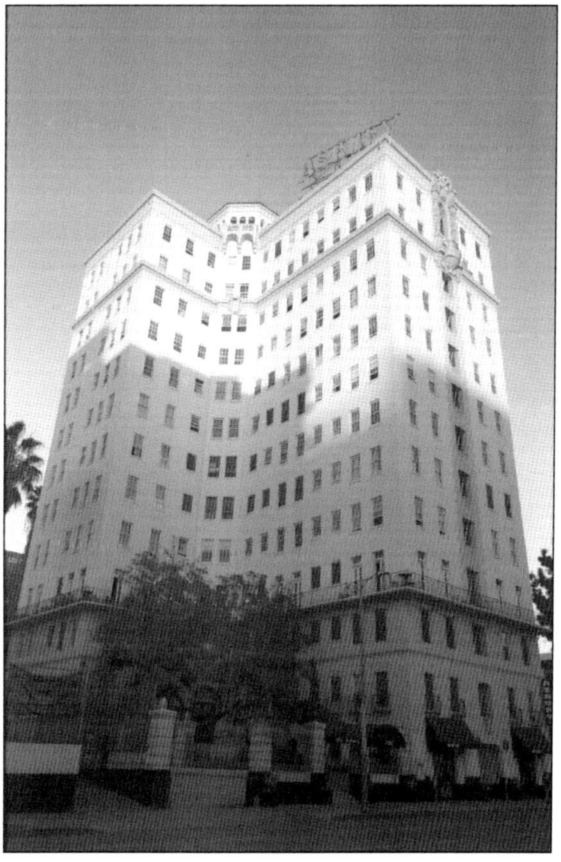

The grandfather of the architectural golden era continues to be the Asbury Building. Longtime residents will assert that the edifice was never in decline like other nearby buildings from that era. They attribute this fact to the elegant and sturdy design of the structure. The scenery from the penthouse is one of the most breathtaking panoramic views anywhere in the city. Unlike the top floor, the ground floor commercial space has seen off-and-on success with various restaurant ventures. (Author's collection.)

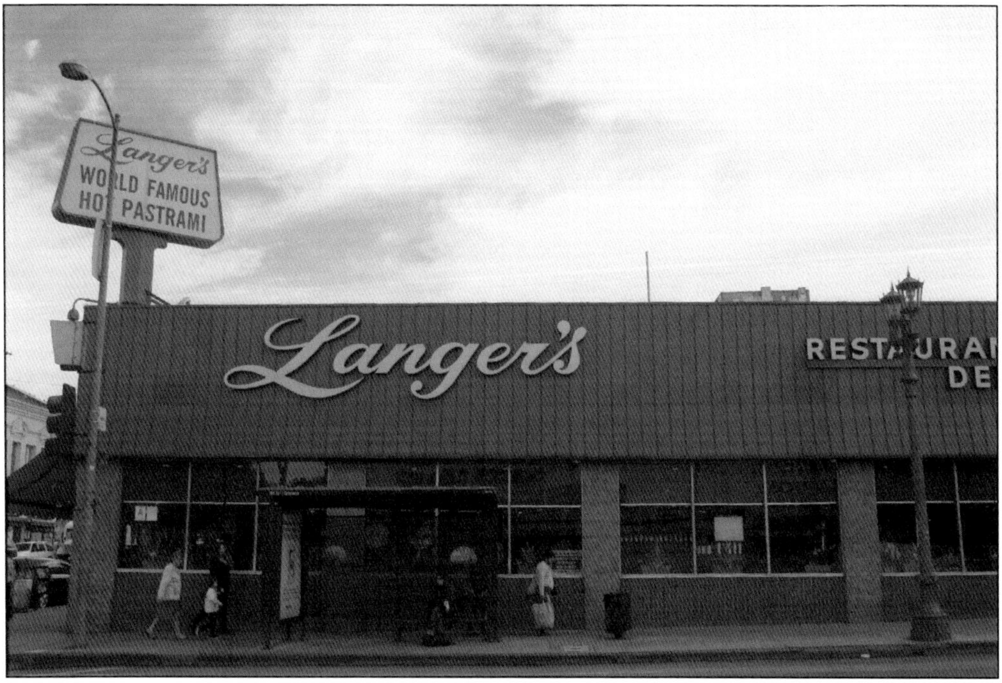

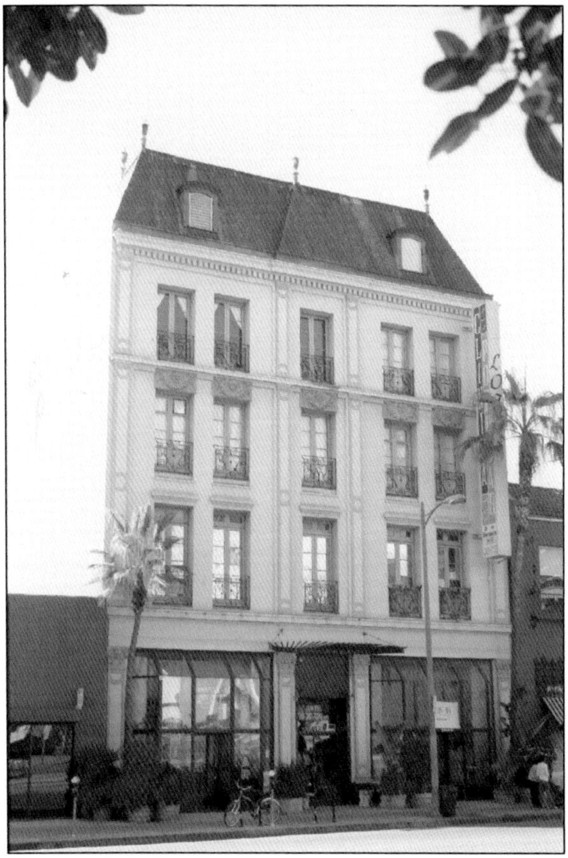

Most people will say that Langer's Deli continues to serve the best pastrami on rye in the city. Now run by Norm Langer, the son of the original owner, the deli is one of the few restaurants that offer a glimpse into the recent past of the neighborhood. Norm has witnessed the dramatic demographic changes of the area; he has also been at the forefront of the recent revitalization efforts for the park. (Author's collection.)

This structure, known locally as the Clínica Popular building, is from the prewar era and was recently restored by its owner into loft spaces. Many neighborhoods around downtown are experiencing the effects of gentrification. The Westlake area has not seen the same development forces—although real estate experts are forecasting that this neighborhood will begin to see the land valuation forces that have impacted other pockets. (Author's collection.)

The future of the Westlake Theatre is unclear. Up until a few years ago, a local redevelopment agency and the city had a plan to fully restore the theater into a community performing arts center, but the plan has been defunded. In the interim, the swap-meet vendors that for many years preserved the space have been displaced. The only bright light for the property is the rooftop sign itself, which is still a landmark reference point for the neighborhood. (Author's collection.)

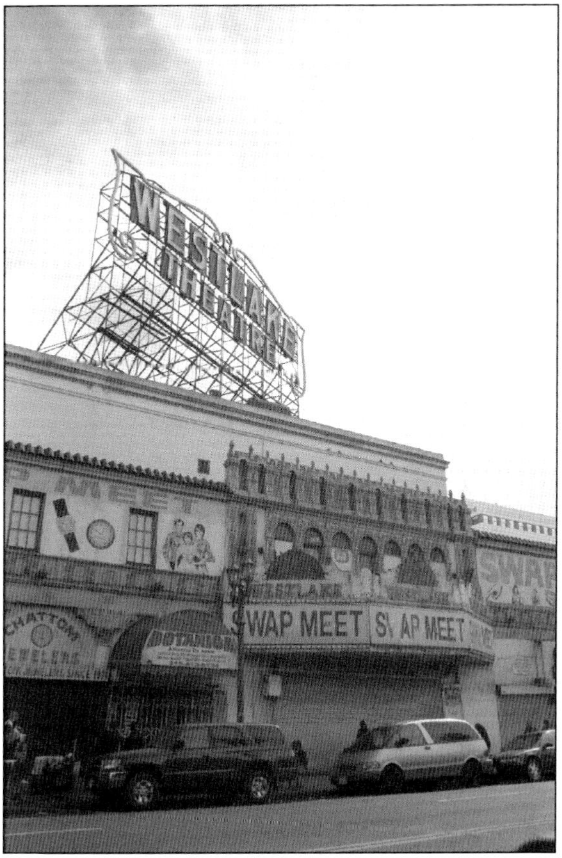

The former Otis Arts Institute is now the Charles White Elementary School. In the 1990s, when the art school departed for the west side of the city, local parents and educational advocates pushed for a local elementary school to alleviate school overcrowding. The school district has preserved most of the design motif of the original art school, and the school offers an art-based curriculum for children. (Author's collection.)

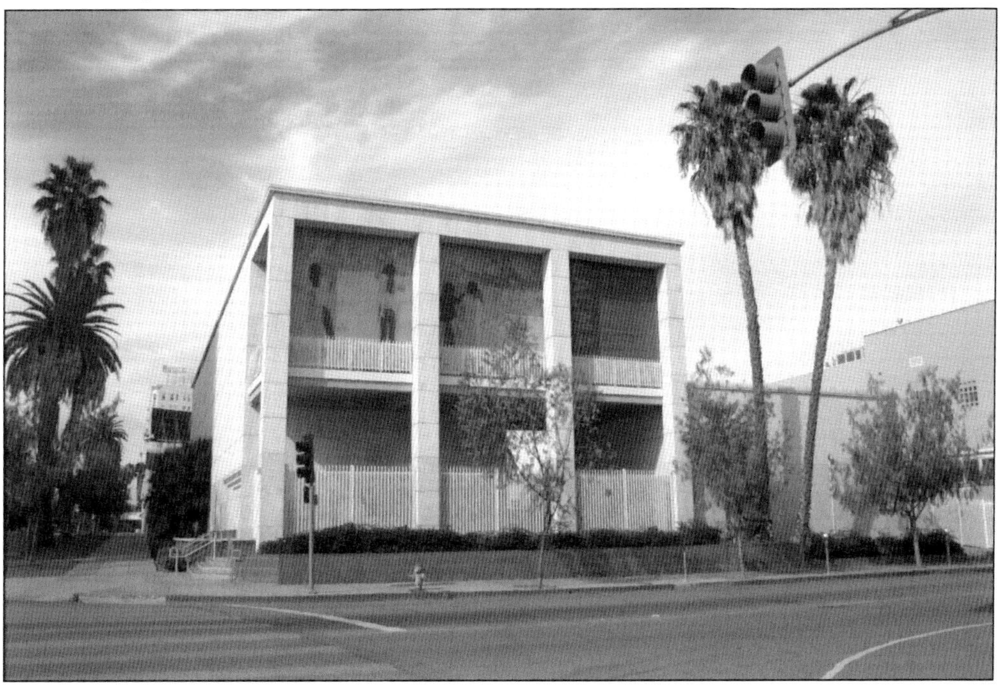

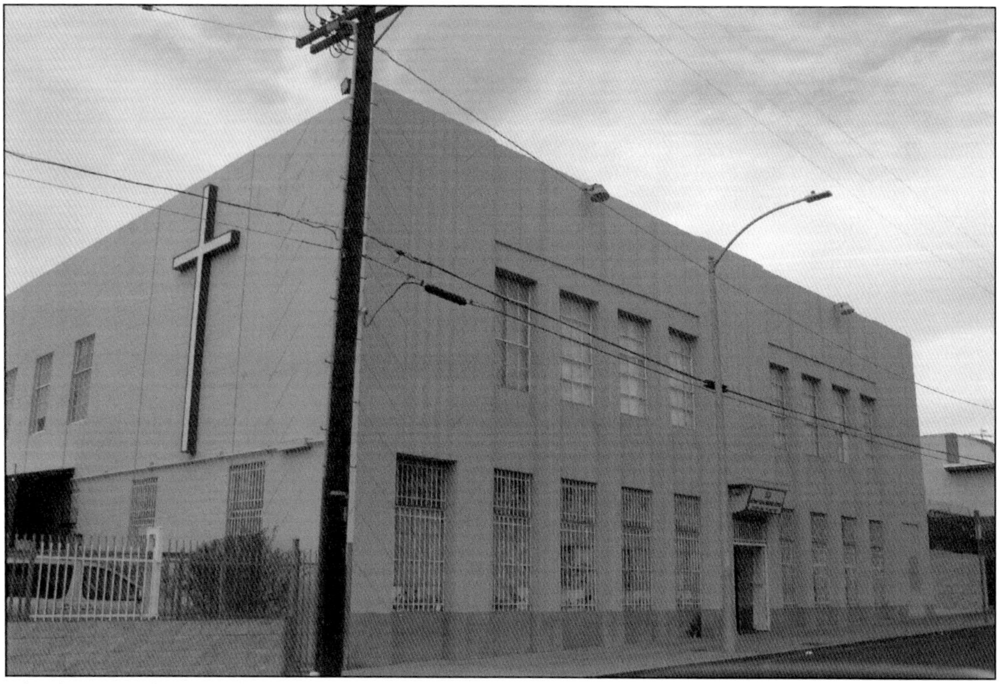

The former Chouinard School, which moved out to the suburbs, is now a Korean church and school. Owing to its proximity to the new Koreatown, the property provides religious education to young people from the region. The only artifact that remains from the art school is a painted-over mural by Mexican muralist David Alfaro Siqueiros that spans two floors of the main building. Local art aficionados are beginning to organize to restore the valuable mural. (Author's collection.)

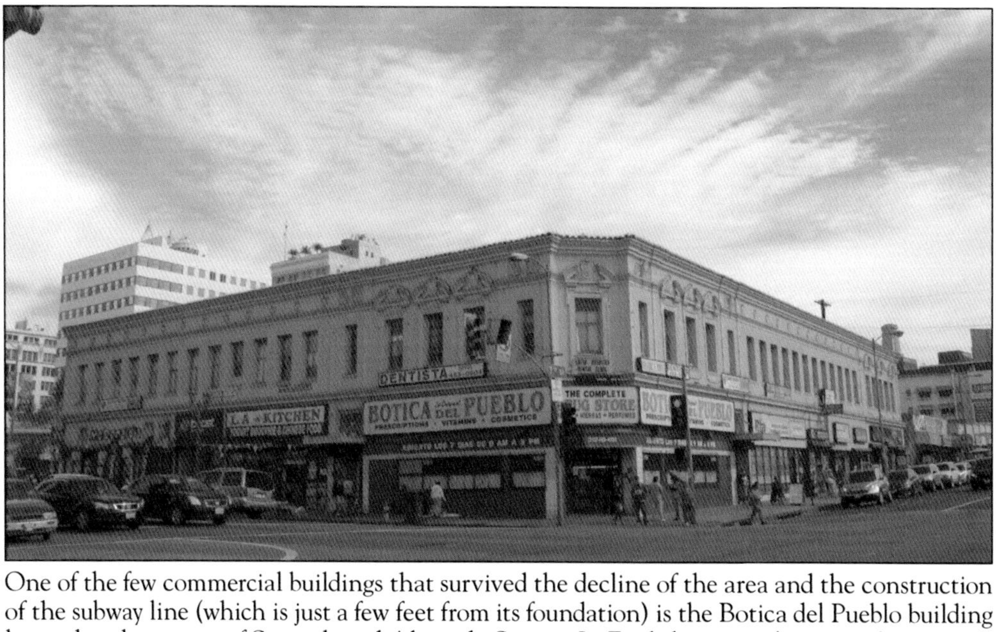

One of the few commercial buildings that survived the decline of the area and the construction of the subway line (which is just a few feet from its foundation) is the Botica del Pueblo building located at the corner of Seventh and Alvarado Streets. In English, it translates as "pharmacy of the people." The historic pharmacy has served its name and local residents well for many decades. (Author's collection.)

Three

The Architecture of the Park

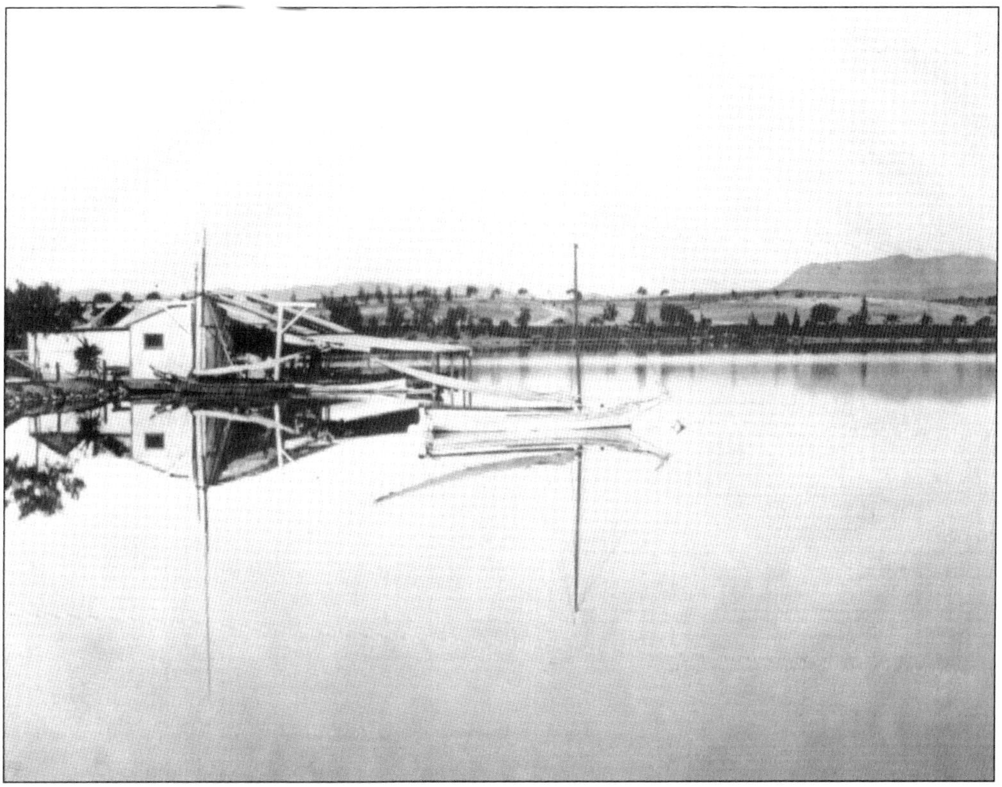

From its inception, Westlake Park was a water retention reservoir to serve the needs of the growing city. Considering that the lake was one of the largest bodies of water in the area, watercraft recreation became the primary activity for visitors to the park. As such, the city quickly built (perhaps without much thought to long-term quality) the necessary boating facilities. Seen here is one of the early boathouses for the park. (Courtesy of the Los Angeles Public Library Photo Collection.)

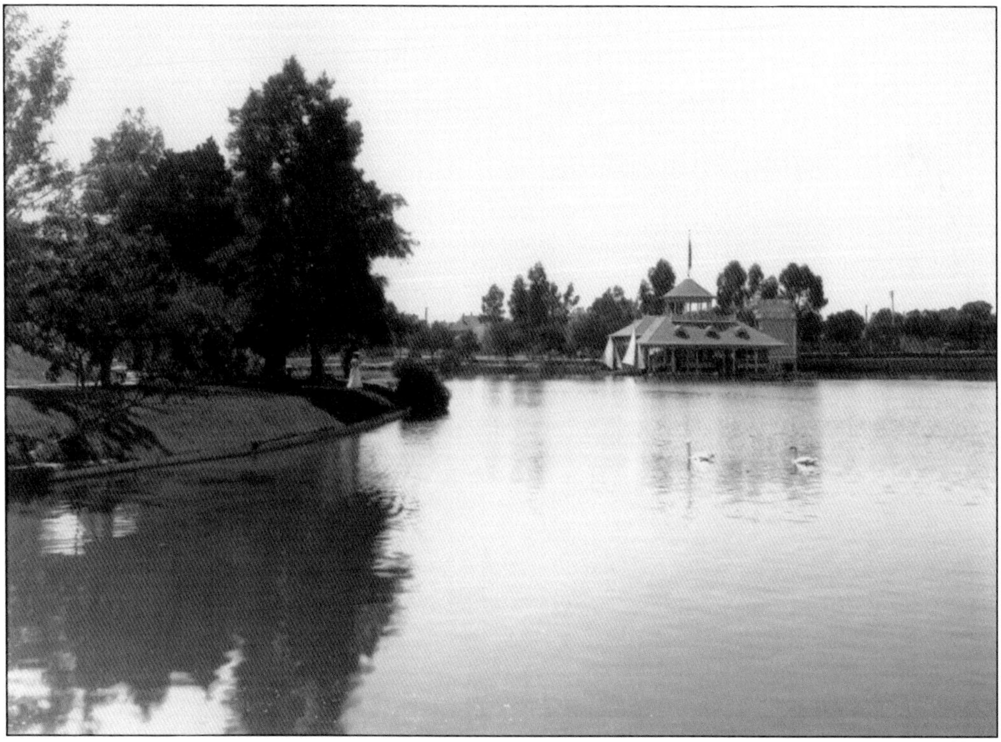

By 1898, the board of park commissioners recognized that the current facilities in the park were inadequate and in "disagreeable conditions." By the 1920s, a new and improved boathouse became a showcase facility for the new park. The design clearly reflected the architectural style that was emerging in the neighborhood. The refined design reinforced the resort aesthetic for visitors. (Courtesy of the Natural History Museum of Los Angeles County.)

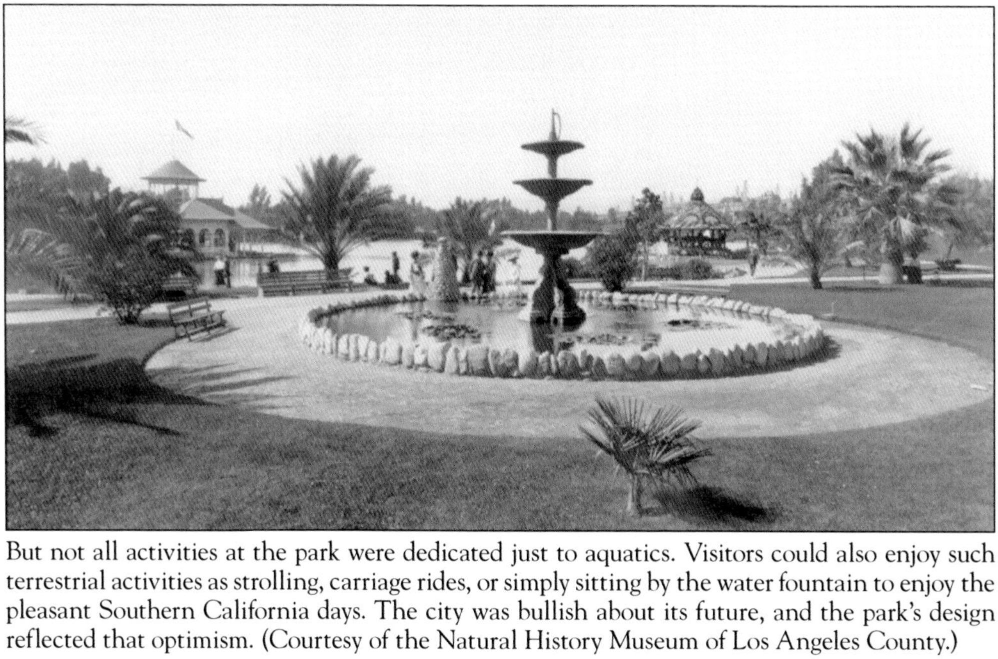

But not all activities at the park were dedicated just to aquatics. Visitors could also enjoy such terrestrial activities as strolling, carriage rides, or simply sitting by the water fountain to enjoy the pleasant Southern California days. The city was bullish about its future, and the park's design reflected that optimism. (Courtesy of the Natural History Museum of Los Angeles County.)

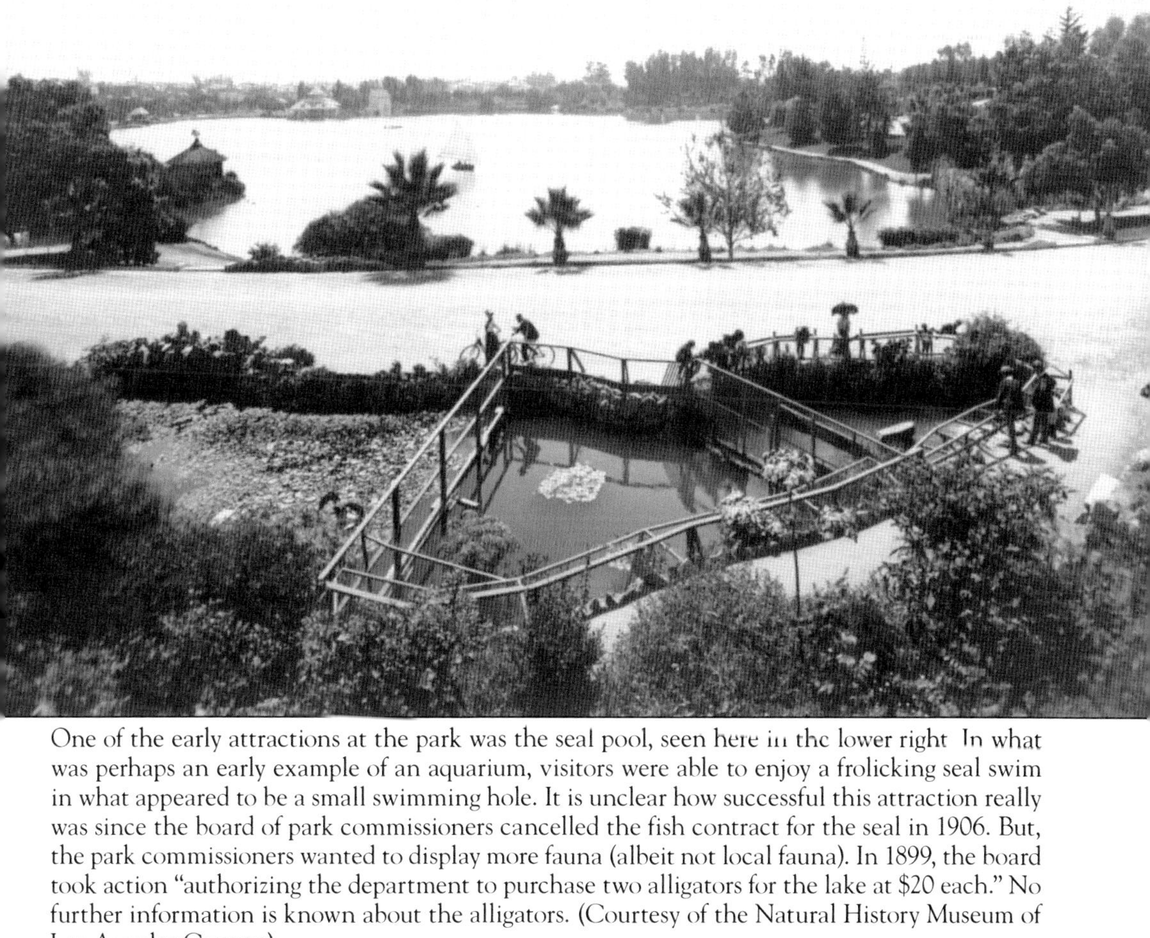

One of the early attractions at the park was the seal pool, seen here in the lower right. In what was perhaps an early example of an aquarium, visitors were able to enjoy a frolicking seal swim in what appeared to be a small swimming hole. It is unclear how successful this attraction really was since the board of park commissioners cancelled the fish contract for the seal in 1906. But, the park commissioners wanted to display more fauna (albeit not local fauna). In 1899, the board took action "authorizing the department to purchase two alligators for the lake at $20 each." No further information is known about the alligators. (Courtesy of the Natural History Museum of Los Angeles County.)

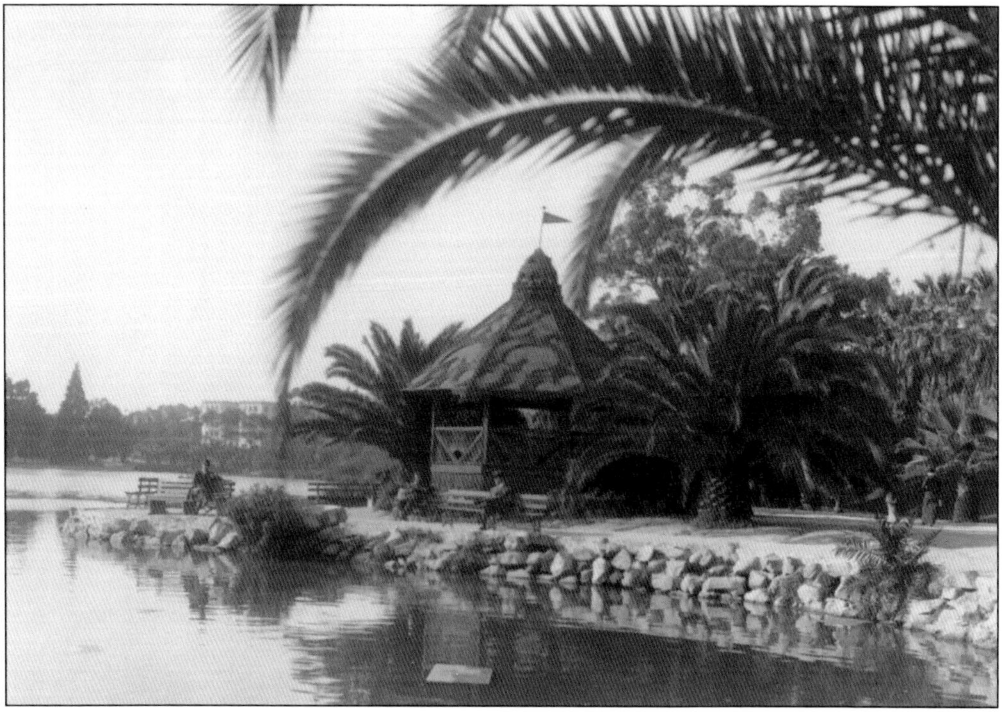

The recreation hut was another early example of the fabricated environment for the young park. It served as a place for visitors to congregate, sit, or perhaps picnic. There were a few versions of the structure over the decades. The design for the most part remained the same, but the quality of the construction improved. (Courtesy of the Natural History Museum of Los Angeles County.)

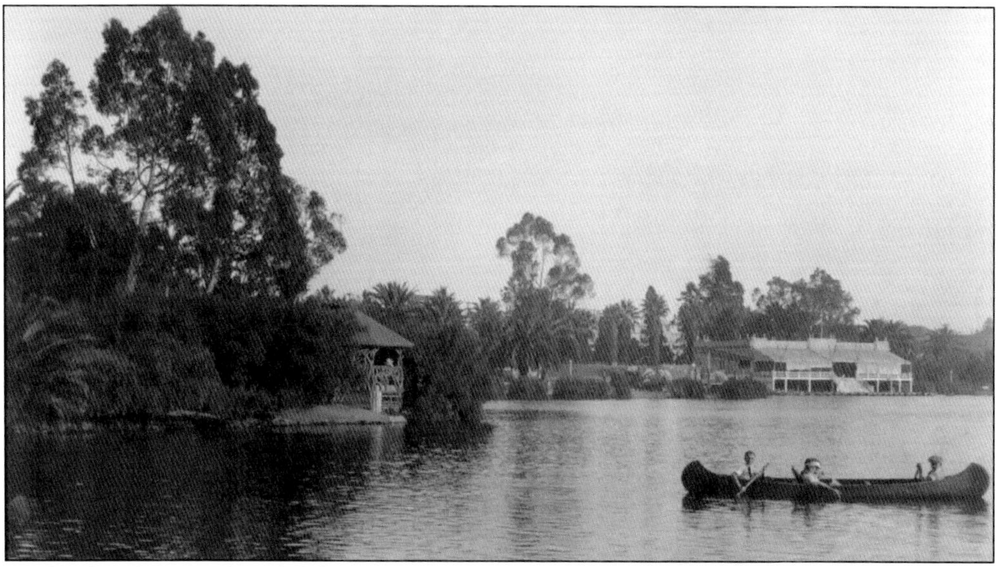

As the decades passed, so did the size of the facilities. This is an early photograph of the elegant pavilion built in the 1920s. As a result of this addition to the park, the city approved a concession for "boating, canoeing, luncheon, and refreshments" to D.J. Daze and Son. This lessee maintained a long presence at the park over the coming decades. (Courtesy of the Natural History Museum of Los Angeles County.)

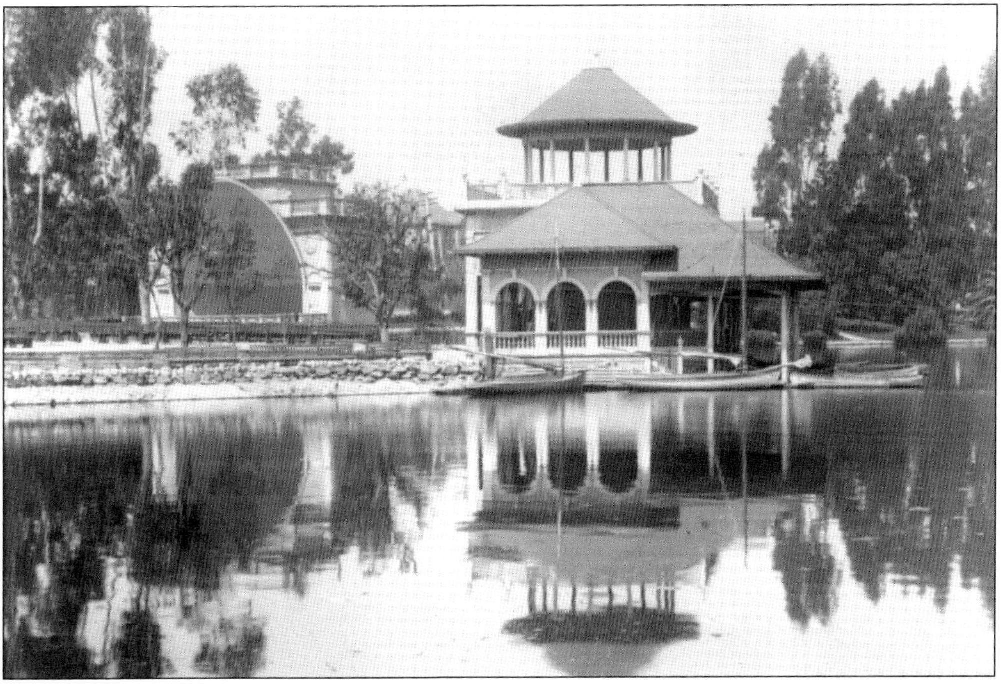

Started as the 19th century was coming to a close, the band shell, seen here in the background, was a majestic structure for the park. It stood almost two stories tall and had a performing area big enough for a large band or orchestra. Throughout the early part of the new century, many concerts were held here, garnering attention throughout the region. As a result, audiences of up to 10,000 attendees were reported. (Courtesy of the Los Angeles Public Library Photo Collection.)

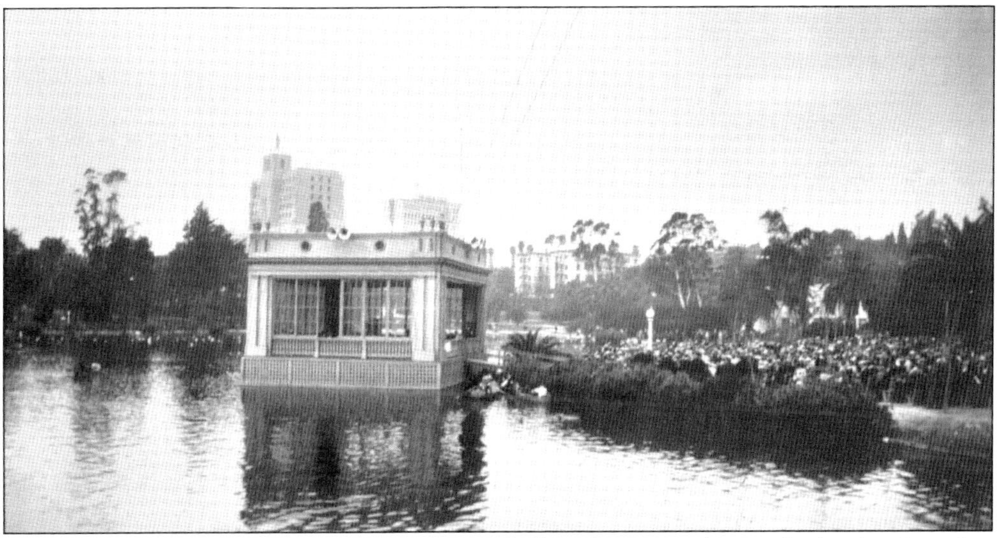

Soon after the demolition of the original band shell in the 1920s, the city built a bandstand to accommodate bands and concerts. Although the location along the edge of the lake of this boxy structure was unique, the facility was clearly not designed with large crowds in mind. In later years, additional seating was provided, but it never matched the seating capacity of the original band shell. The bandstand was later removed to make room for the Wilshire Viaduct. (Courtesy of the Watson Family Photography Archives.)

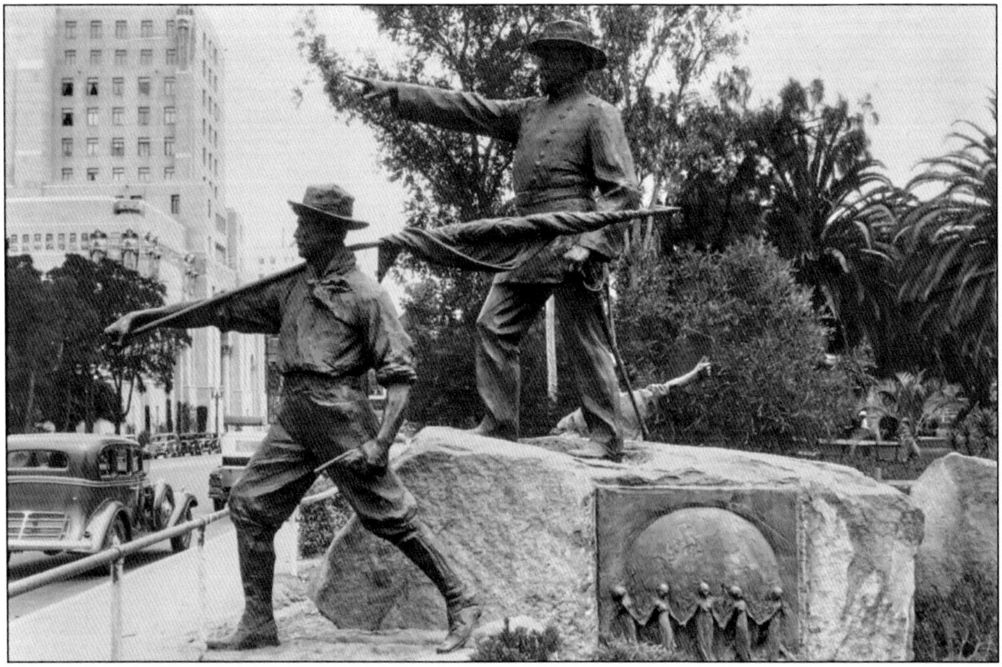

One of the oldest sculptures in the park is referred to as the *Otis Group*. The group includes a soldier; Gen. Harrison Gray Otis, a *Los Angeles Times* publisher; and below General Otis, a newspaper boy. The plaque reads: "Soldier, journalist, friend of freedom, stand fast, stand firm, stand sure, stand true." Is it a coincidence that the Otis figure is pointing to the house that he owned across the street from the park? (Courtesy of the City of Los Angeles Archives.)

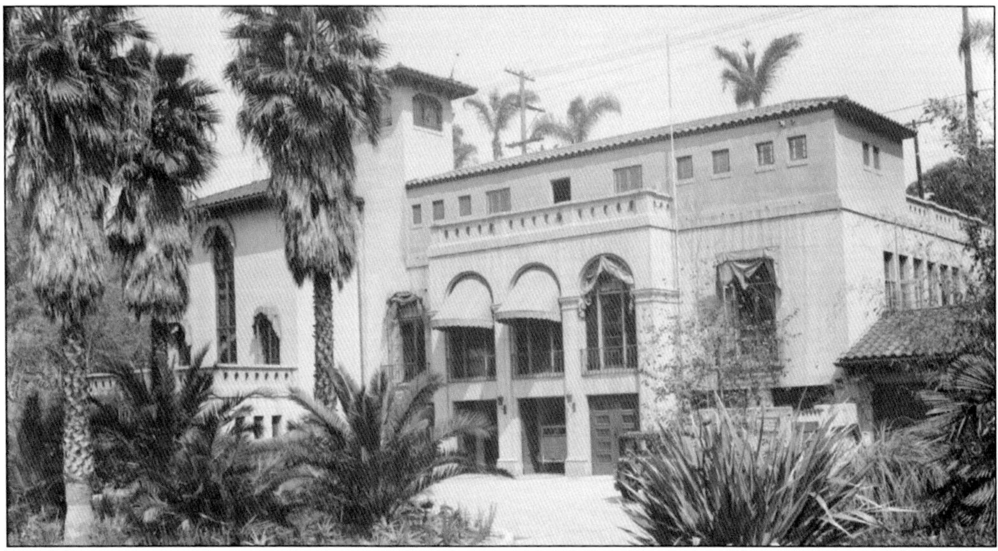

In the mid-1920s, the city built the switching station to serve as a communication center for the city's fire department. It was the first structure within the park that did not serve a recreational activity, a fact that engendered community tension when the building was first proposed. By the 1960s, the strategic function of this facility was rendered unnecessary, and as a result, the space was converted to provide storage space for the department. (Courtesy of the Los Angeles Public Library Photo Collection.)

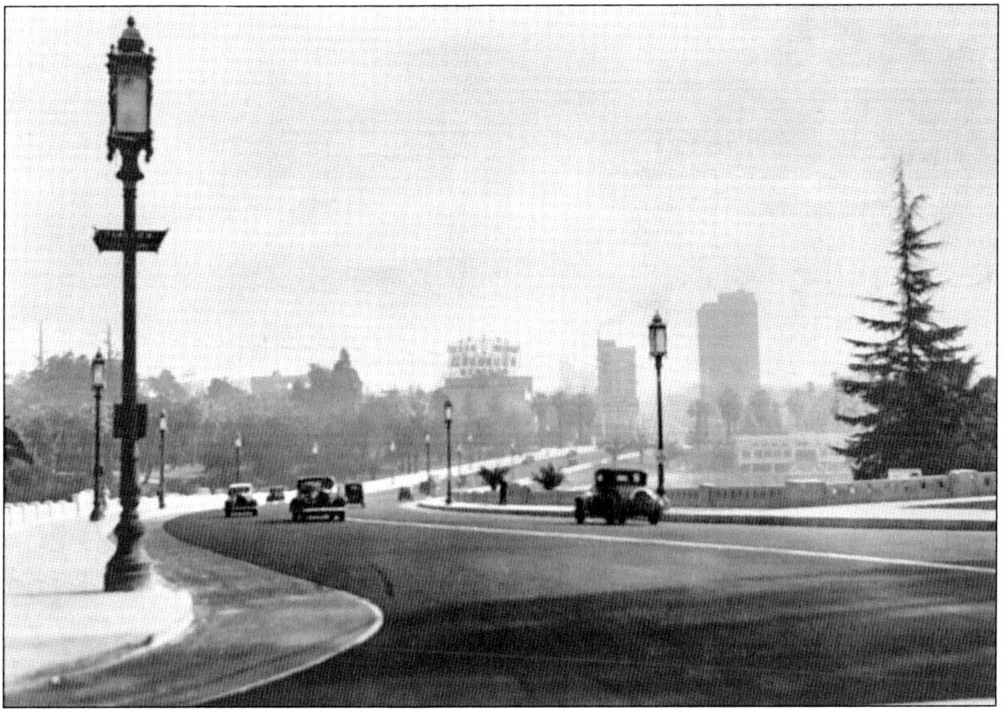

One cannot ignore the fact that the Wilshire Viaduct itself was a form of architecture for the park. Perhaps the most controversial of all the built spaces within the park, the viaduct's design aesthetic was both utilitarian and grand. It may have torn Westlake Park in two, but it united diverse parts of the city with its "river of concrete." (Courtesy of the City of Los Angeles Archives.)

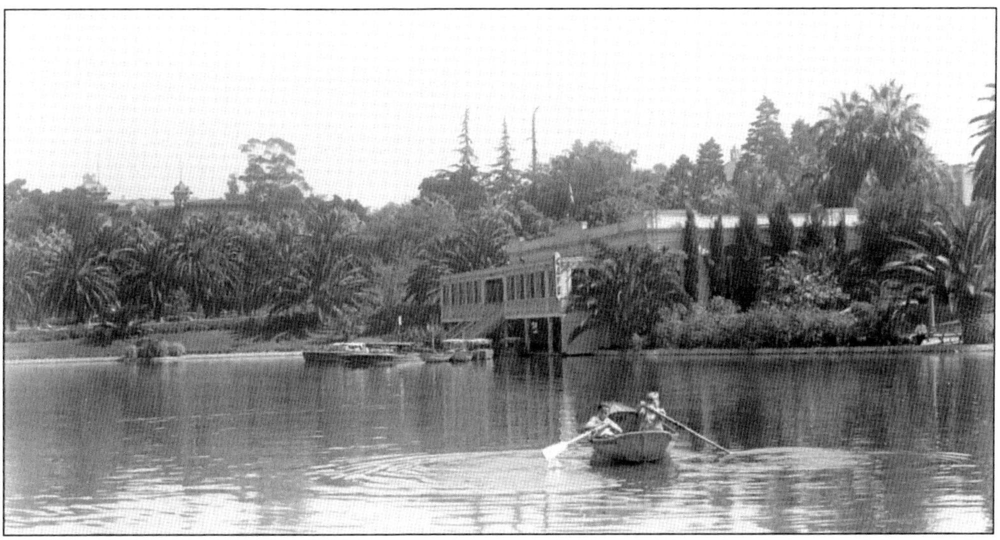

The second boathouse was perhaps the most democratic structure built inside the park. The design was inviting and engaging for the general public. There was an open porch area in the front that encouraged gatherings. On the lakeside, a "mansion-style staircase flowed all the way to the water level." This element connected visitors uniquely to the water and allowed them to touch the lake. This beautiful structure was replaced by the 1960s. (Courtesy of the Los Angeles Public Library Photo Collection.)

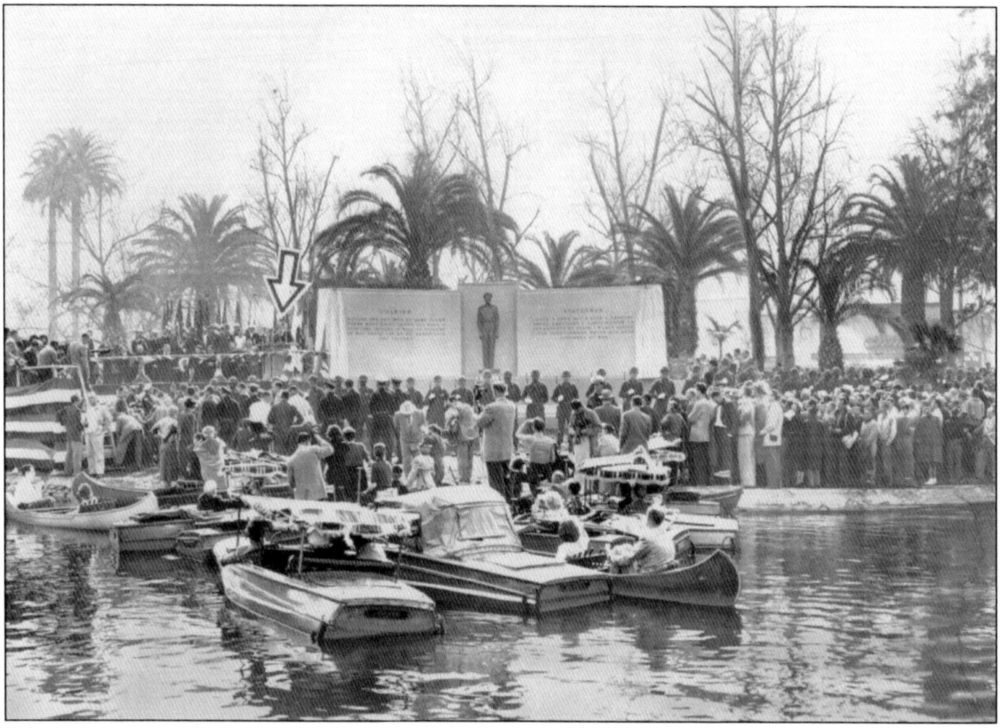

In recognition of the park's name change, the city installed the Gen. Douglas MacArthur statue near the park entrance at Seventh and Alvarado Streets. A big crowd gathered for the dedication; however, not all visitors were impressed. A local resident remembers her visit as a child to the dedication and recalls that the guest of honor did not interact with the public and made a quick getaway from the ceremony. (Courtesy of the Los Angeles Public Library Photo Collection.)

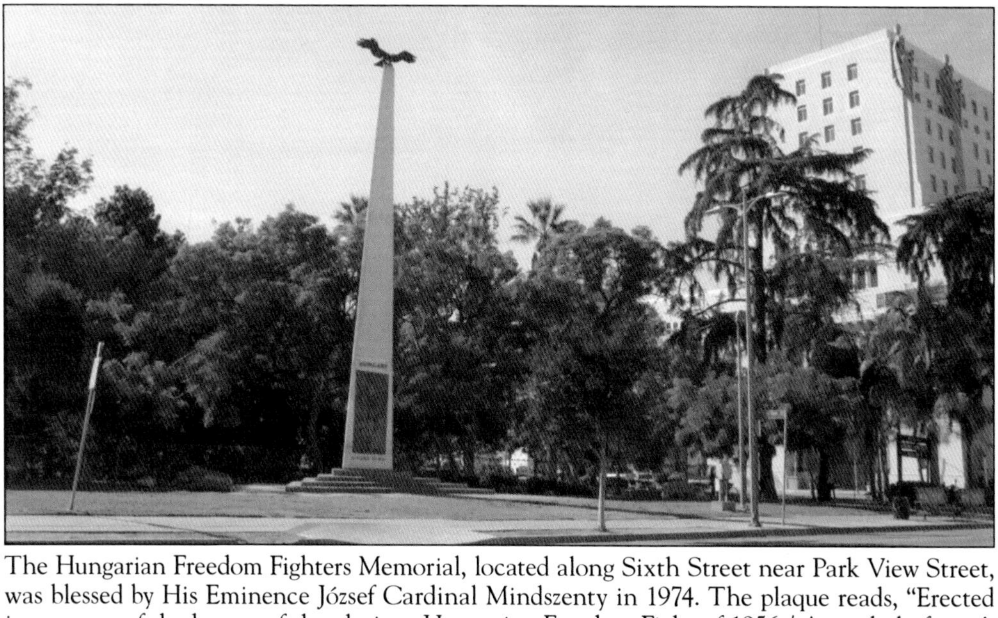

The Hungarian Freedom Fighters Memorial, located along Sixth Street near Park View Street, was blessed by His Eminence József Cardinal Mindszenty in 1974. The plaque reads, "Erected in memory of the heroes of the glorious Hungarian Freedom Fight of 1956 / A symbol of man's earning for freedom everywhere." (Author's collection.)

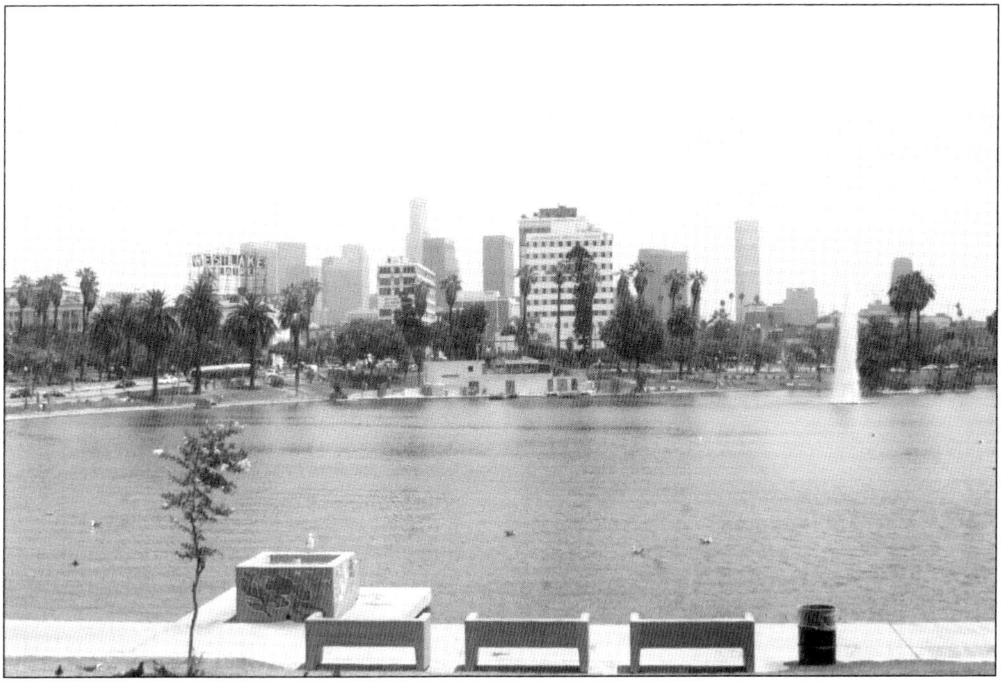

Perhaps not as sophisticated as the original park fountain, the new jet fountain was built as part of the aeration system for the lake. Like an aquatic geyser, the fountain shoots water several hundred feet into the air. Several years back, when the cleanliness of the lake's water was in question, park visitors purposely avoided the fountain's spray (especially on windy days) to prevent any possible contamination. (Courtesy of Meeno.)

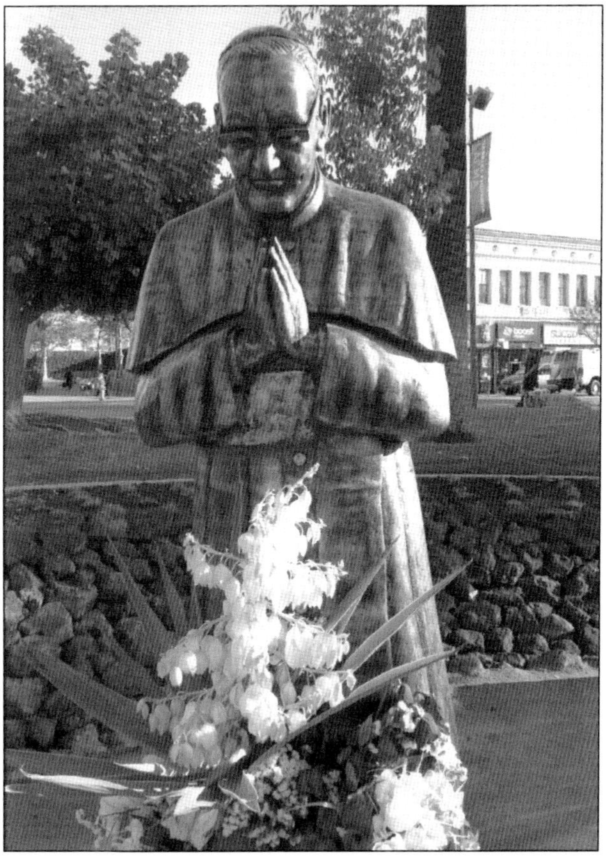

One of the more recent sculptures to be built in the park, the Monseñor Óscar Romero Monument was installed to honor and recognize the people's sacrifices during the Central American civil wars of the 1970s and 1980s. The monument is located at the exact spot in the park where countless peaceful marches were held by Central American political refugees. (Courtesy of Carlos Vaquerano.)

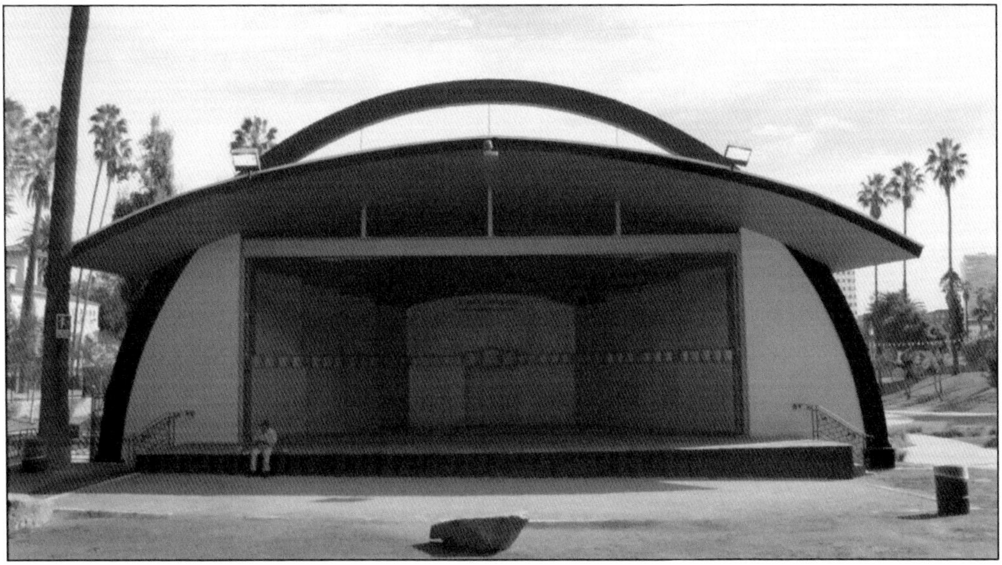

The most recent band shell was built in the 1950s, near the northwest corner of the park. It was constructed directly on top of what was the old lakebed. Owing to the high water table in this section of the park, the band shell was built atop several dozen wood piers that were buried deeply into the wet soil. After many years of deferred maintenance, the city, along with the Levitt Foundation, restored the band shell and brought back concerts in the park. (Author's collection.)

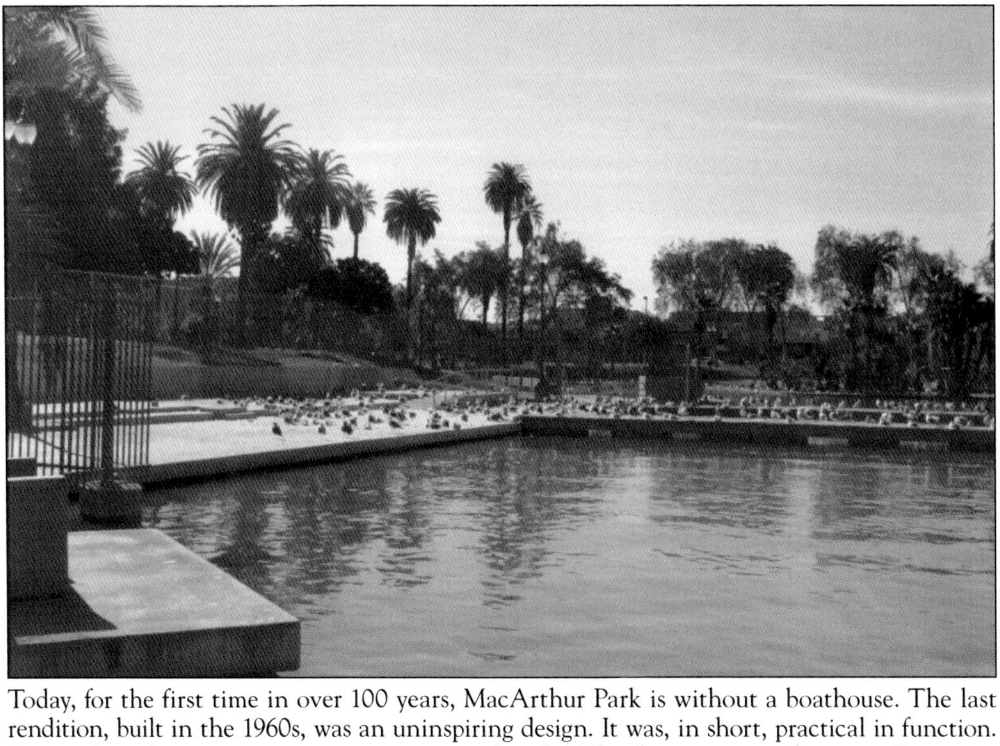

Today, for the first time in over 100 years, MacArthur Park is without a boathouse. The last rendition, built in the 1960s, was an uninspiring design. It was, in short, practical in function. It served as a boat operation, a concession, and an LAPD substation over the years. Due to its low construction quality, the building deteriorated relatively quickly over the last decades. The empty site in the park awaits the future. (Author's collection.)

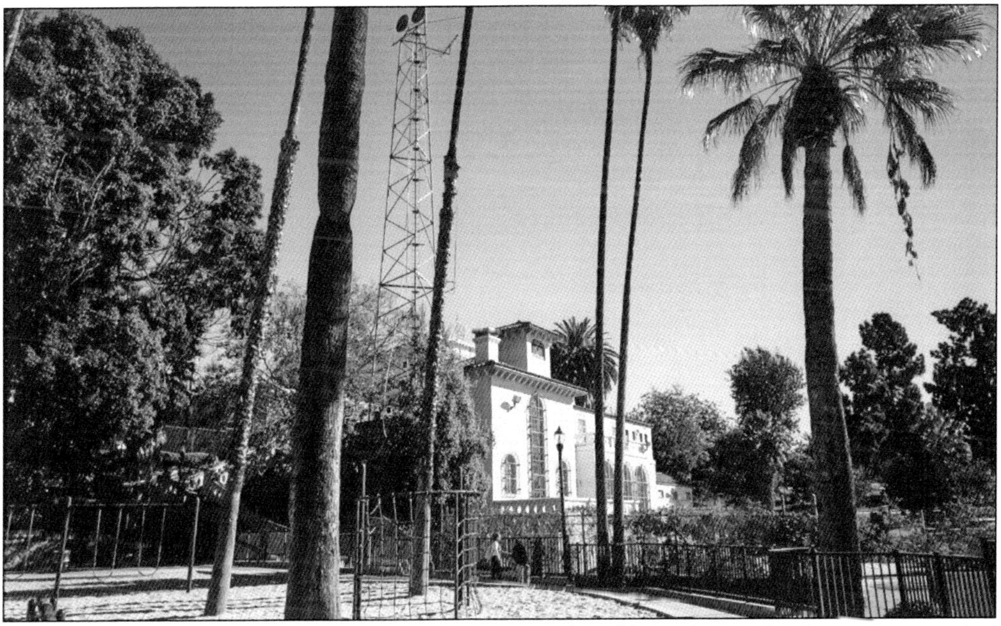

The old switching station is now known as the Signal Building, due to the large antenna that has sat in the parking lot for many decades. The city's recreation and parks department now runs the facility as a multipurpose center that serves local young people and seniors. The only strategic communication that occurs in the building now is between local park advocates that meet regularly to discuss the future of the park. (Courtesy of Meeno.)

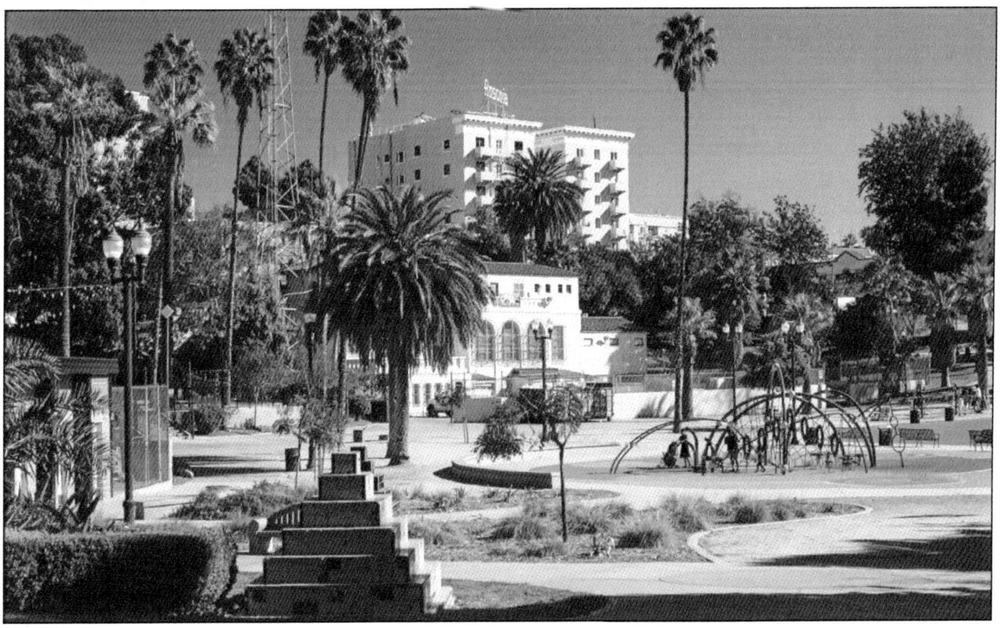

The children's playground is one of the most popular sites now within the park. The city built the space as the 21st century was arriving. It was a fitting start to the new century in that it reflected the dire need for active recreational space for children in this heavily populated neighborhood. Toward the background is what is left of the modern-day Rockery, which also featured a waterfall. (Courtesy of Meeno.)

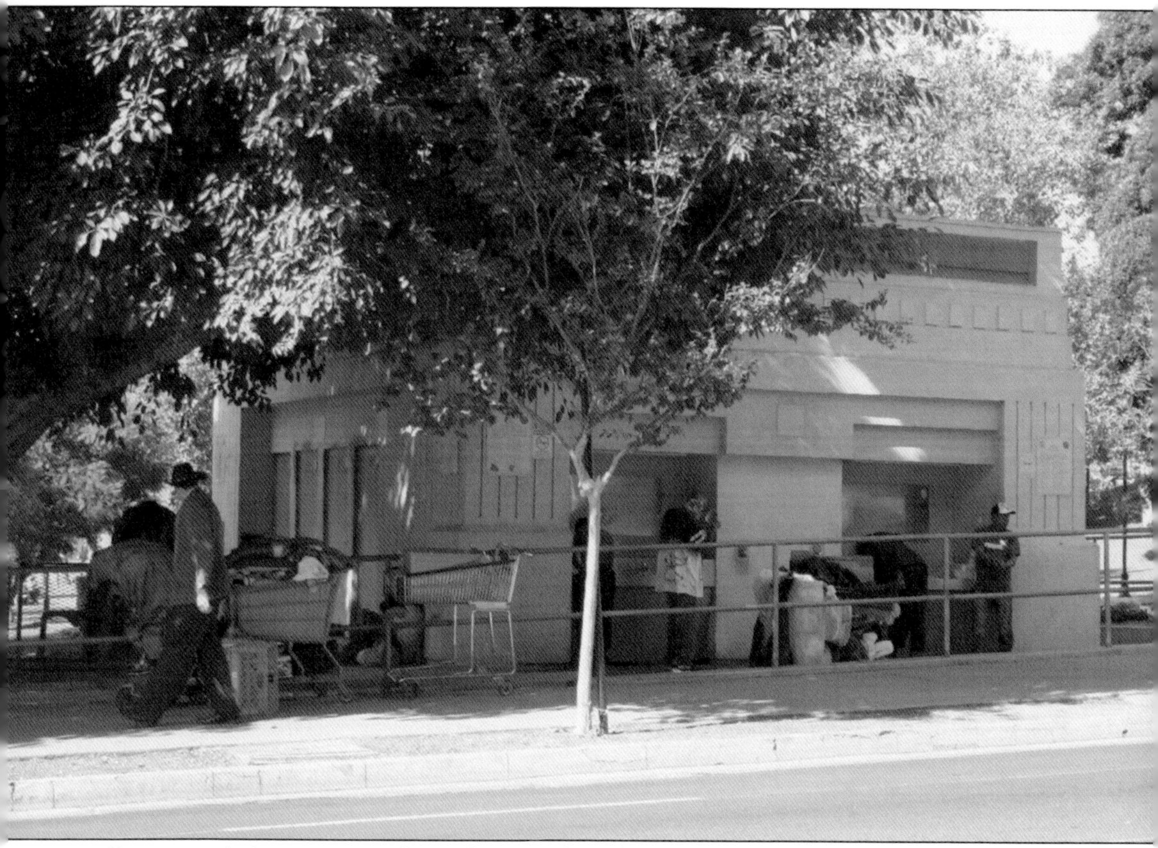

From a park favorite to perhaps the most hated spot within the park today—the Alvarado restrooms—there is always room for improvement in the park. The city, in an attempt to provide more sanitary facilities for visitors on the east side of the park, built the restrooms at a time when this section of the park was severely impacted by drug sales. As a result, the restrooms were only used by transients and drug addicts. The external nature of the design only amplified the criminal problem. (Author's collection.)

Four

CONSTRUCTION AND CHANGE

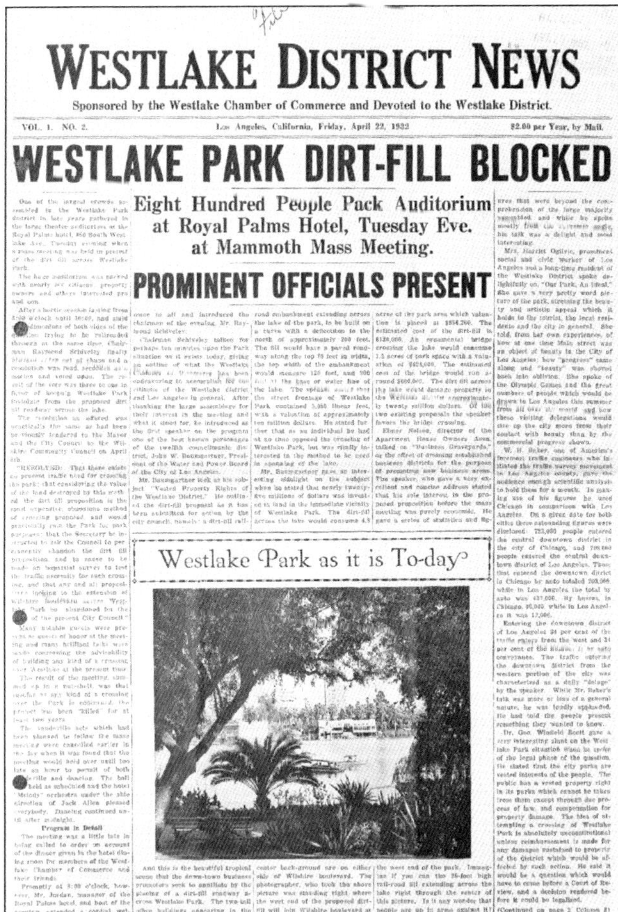

WESTLAKE DISTRICT NEWS

Sponsored by the Westlake Chamber of Commerce and Devoted to the Westlake District.

VOL. 1. NO. 2. Los Angeles, California, Friday, April 22, 1932 $2.00 per Year, by Mail

WESTLAKE PARK DIRT-FILL BLOCKED

Eight Hundred People Pack Auditorium at Royal Palms Hotel, Tuesday Eve. at Mammoth Mass Meeting.

PROMINENT OFFICIALS PRESENT

Westlake Park as it is To-day

Before construction began on the transformative Wilshire Viaduct project, the local community mobilized to fight the dirt-fill option. According to the *Westlake District News*, the "mammoth mass meeting" attracted 800 local residents to the Royal Palms Hotel (the building still stands today and continues to host community events) to hear from local community and political leaders regarding their concerns with the proposal that would annihilate "the beautiful tropical scene" of Westlake Park. The dirt-fill option was described as "the most expensive, obnoxious method" proposed. Political leaders present at the meeting promised to fight the proposal until the end. (Courtesy of the City of Los Angeles Archives.)

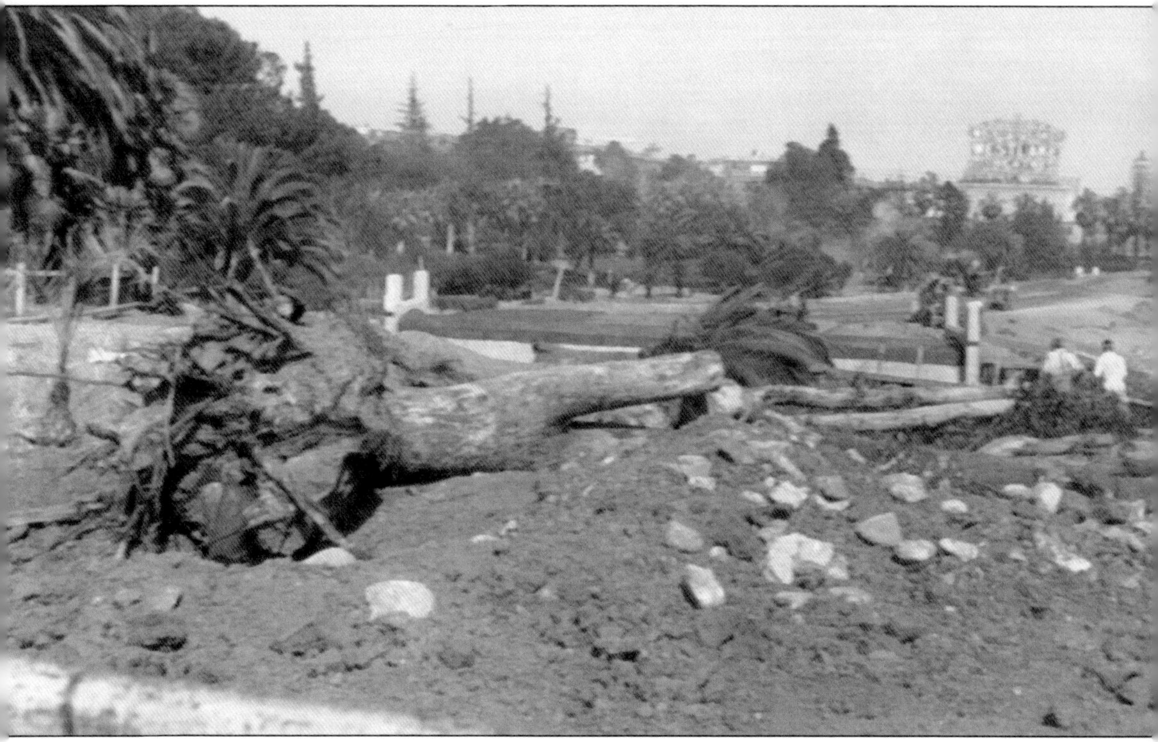

Although local community leaders were able to delay the beginning of construction by citing the original 1886 ordinance's noncommercial clause, the city council ultimately approved the low-cost alternative. With the lake drained and the mature trees felled, this view looking east from Park View Avenue clearly demonstrates the monumental change underway in the "greatest park in the center of the city" that the resolution (June 1931) from the Wilshire Community Council, in opposition to the project, predicted. (Courtesy of the Los Angeles Public Library Photo Collection.)

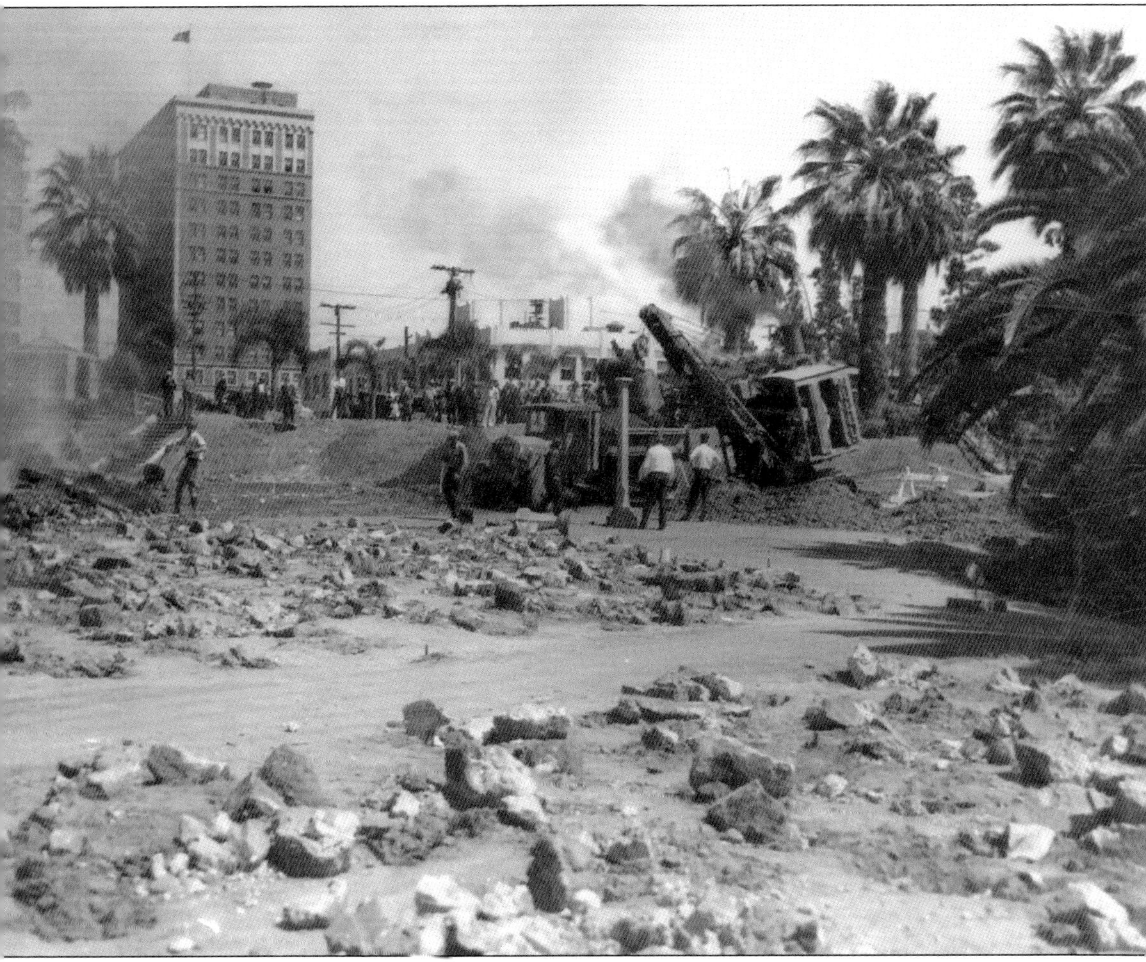

As digging ensued for the viaduct in 1933, one must not forget that the aftershock of the stock market crash and the subsequent Great Depression continued to reverberate across the desperate city. Indeed, a portion of the funding came from the federal government to stimulate job creation and growth. Interestingly, in the heat of the approval battle, a local labor union, the Brotherhood of Locomotive Engineers, submitted a letter stating that the city "refrain from taking action relative to bisecting the park." (Courtesy of Los Angeles Public Library Photo Collection.)

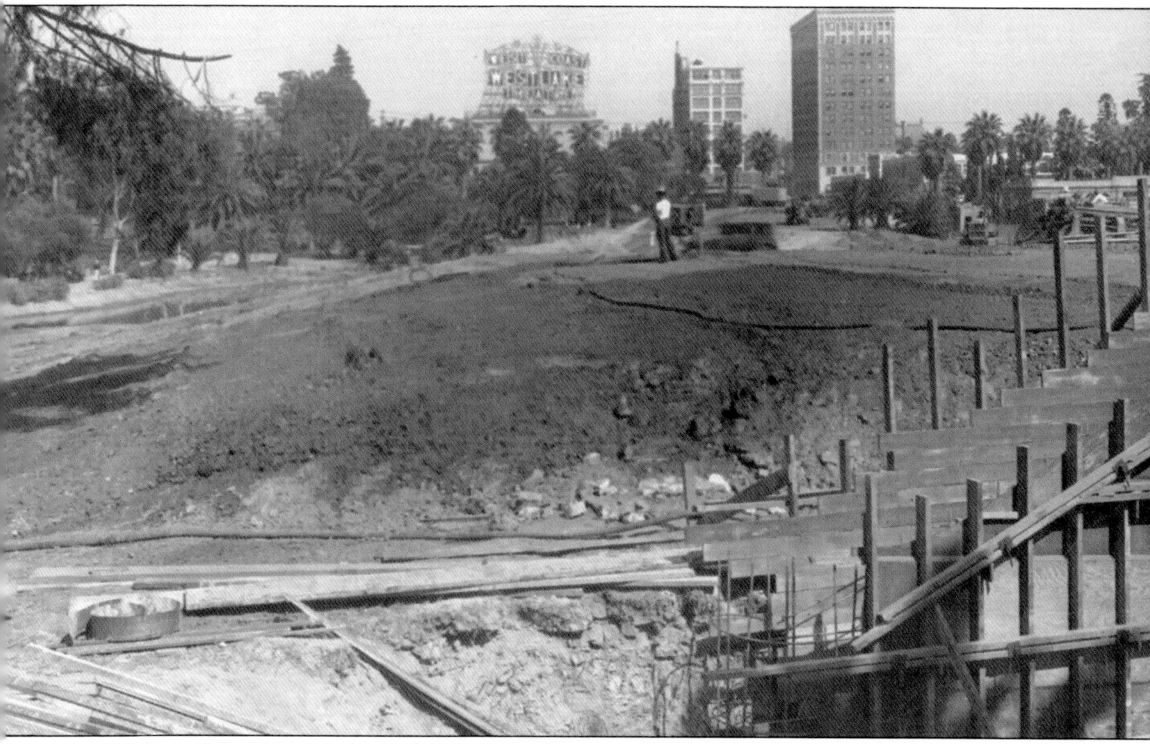

With the lake drained, the park became a construction wasteland. The "heavy turmoil of a noisy city" that local stakeholders were trying to prevent from infringing upon the park had arrived, with bulldozers, scoopers, and cranes. Concrete forms were replacing the nearly 50-year-old trees and shrubbery. (Courtesy of the Los Angeles Public Library Photo Collection.)

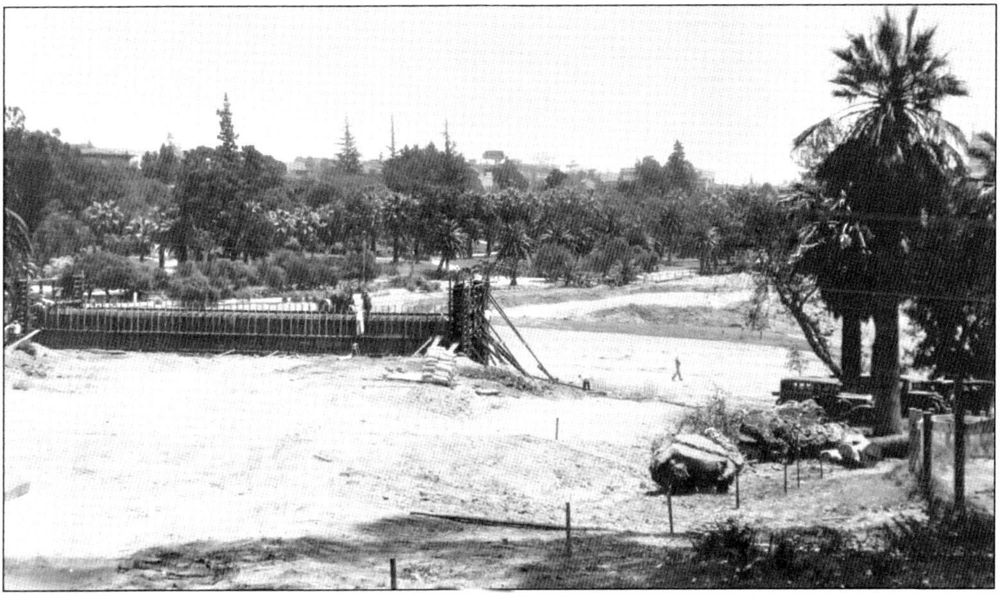

In this view looking northeast toward Alvarado Street, the first concrete foundation for Wilshire Boulevard emerges from the wet ground like a prehistoric gray whale cresting in the turbulent Pacific Ocean, heading south towards warmer waters. For commuters and business people traveling on the soon-to-be-finished Wilshire Viaduct, their journey to the cold, blue ocean would take them in a westward direction, with traffic creating the turbulence. (Courtesy of the City of Los Angeles Archives.)

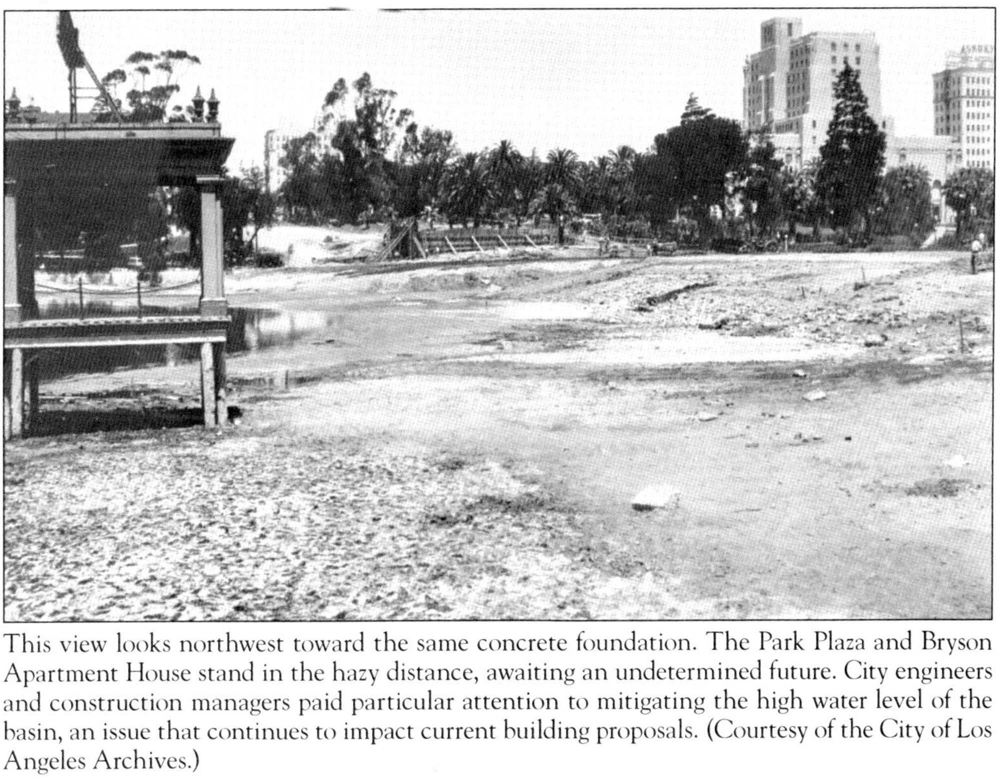

This view looks northwest toward the same concrete foundation. The Park Plaza and Bryson Apartment House stand in the hazy distance, awaiting an undetermined future. City engineers and construction managers paid particular attention to mitigating the high water level of the basin, an issue that continues to impact current building proposals. (Courtesy of the City of Los Angeles Archives.)

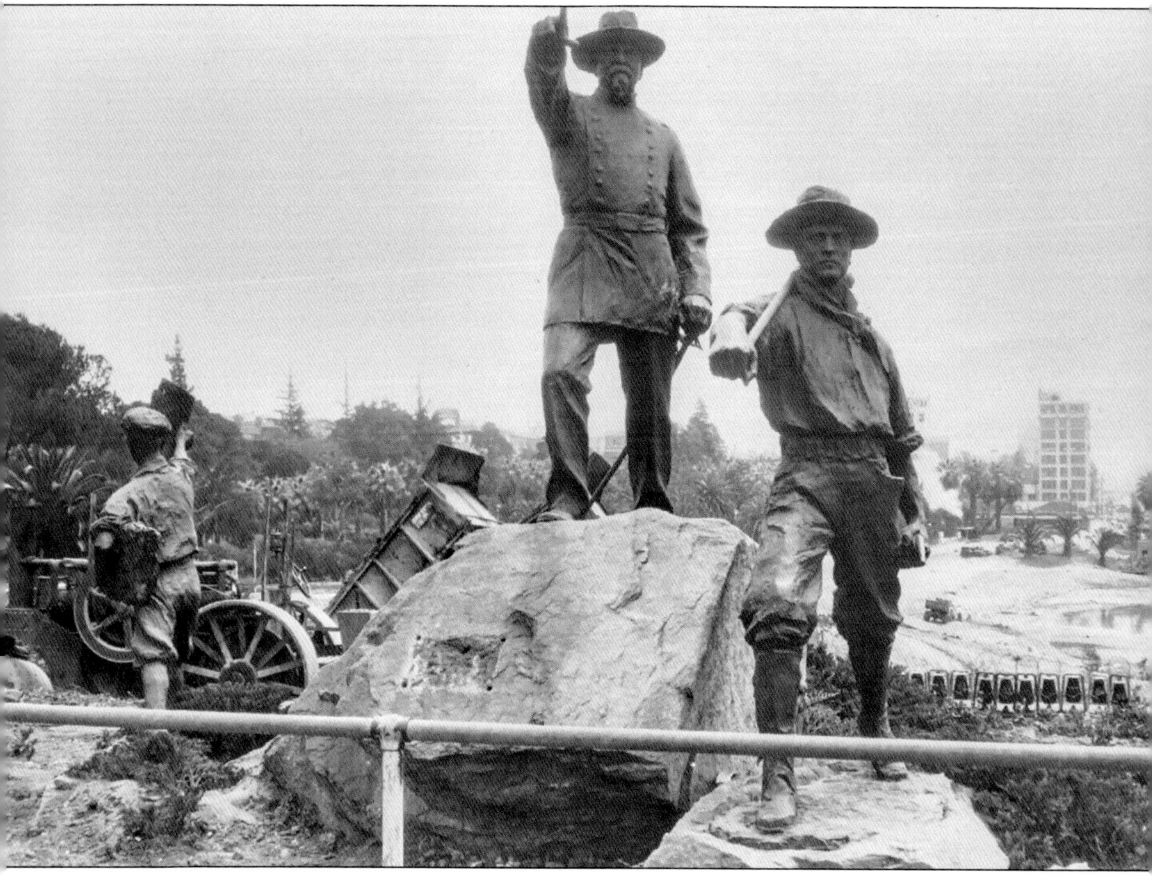

Even Colonel Otis could not stop progress, especially with heavy construction under way directly behind the statues. The memorial, originally located across the street from his former estate, was relocated to its current site near the southeast corner of Park View Street and Wilshire Boulevard. But, the colonel did not miss a beat, he continues to point in the direction of his abode from his current resting place. (Courtesy of the City of Los Angeles Archives.)

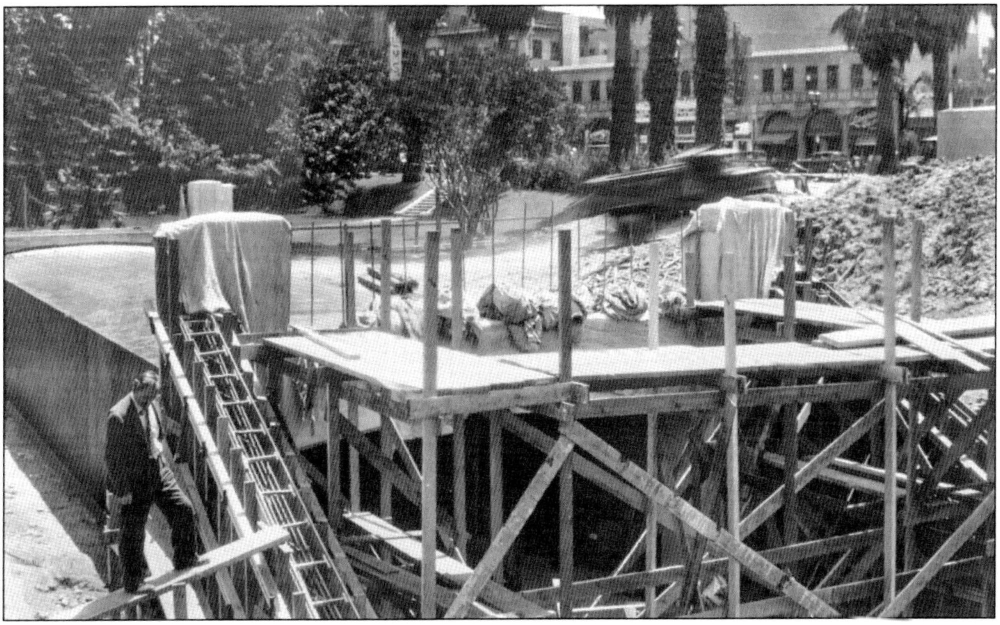

The concrete forms for the south pedestrian tunnel are well under way. The twin tunnels under the viaduct would provide critical links between the north and south side of the park. With the tunnels, pedestrians would not need to cross busy Wilshire Boulevard to enjoy either side of Westlake Park. A glimpse of the Westlake Theatre is in the upper right of the photograph. (Courtesy of the City of Los Angeles Archives.)

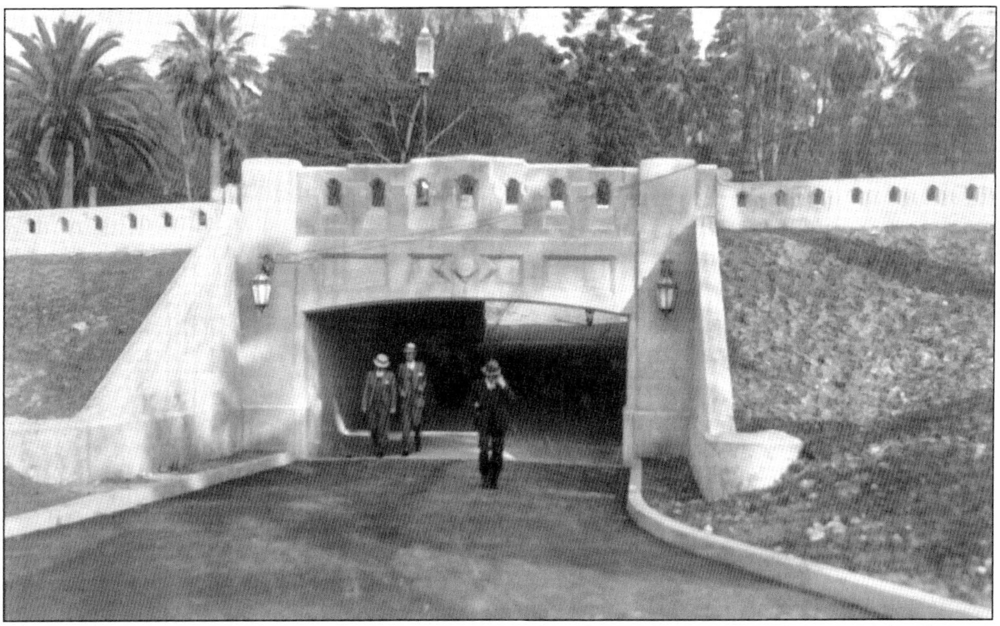

One of the tunnels nears completion. Over the decades, the tunnels became famous and infamous for their public art and criminal activity. Although each tunnel is relatively short in length, pedestrians have learned to walk quickly through the tunnels, partly out of safety concerns, but primarily because the park views on either side of the tunnels are indeed stunning. (Courtesy of the City of Los Angeles Archives.)

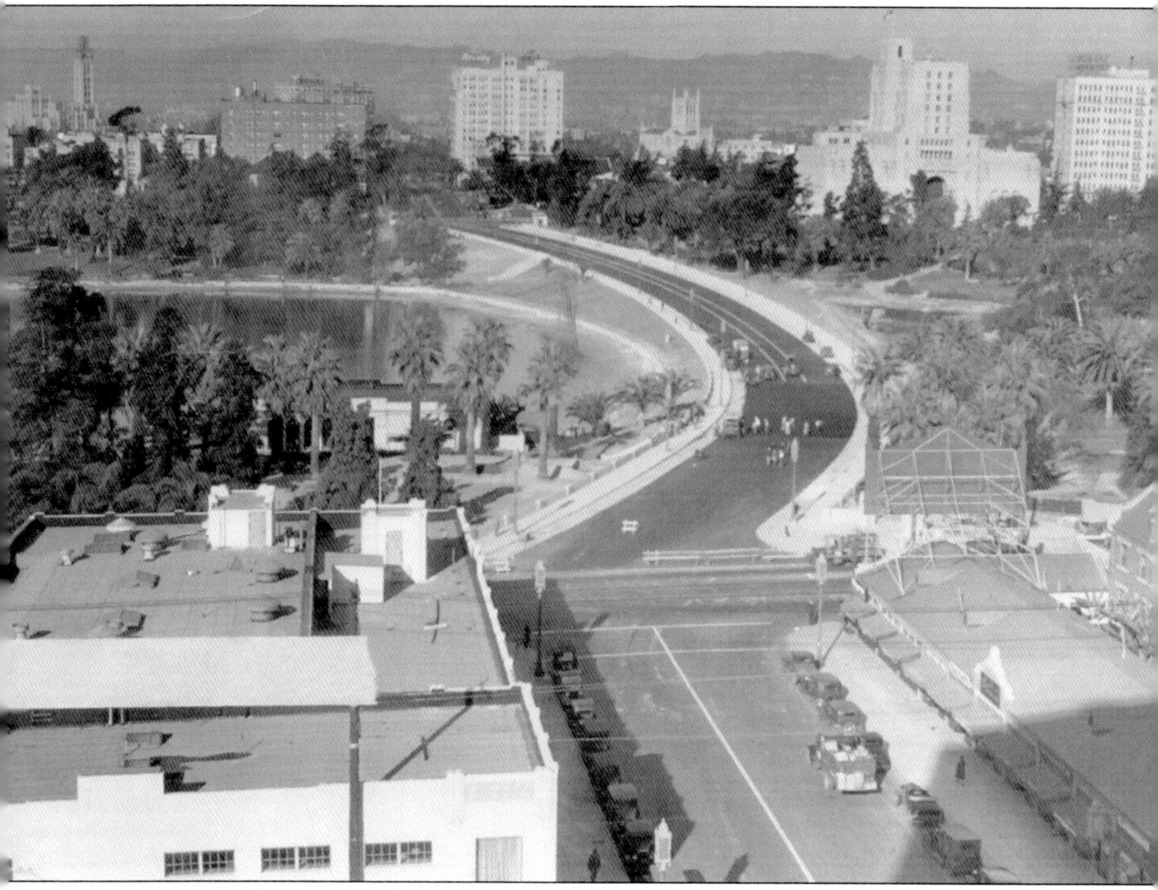

In this view looking westward, the Wilshire Viaduct has taken shape. Construction crews are laying down lane striping for the surge of vehicular traffic that would soon baptize the newest roadway of the optimistic city. Echoing amongst the surviving trees of the park were the cautionary words of the Wilshire Community Council: "Diversion of traffic . . . through this park would endanger the health of the occupants of said park . . . in as much as the expelling carbon monoxide would settle to the trees." (Courtesy of the Los Angeles Public Library Photo Collection.)

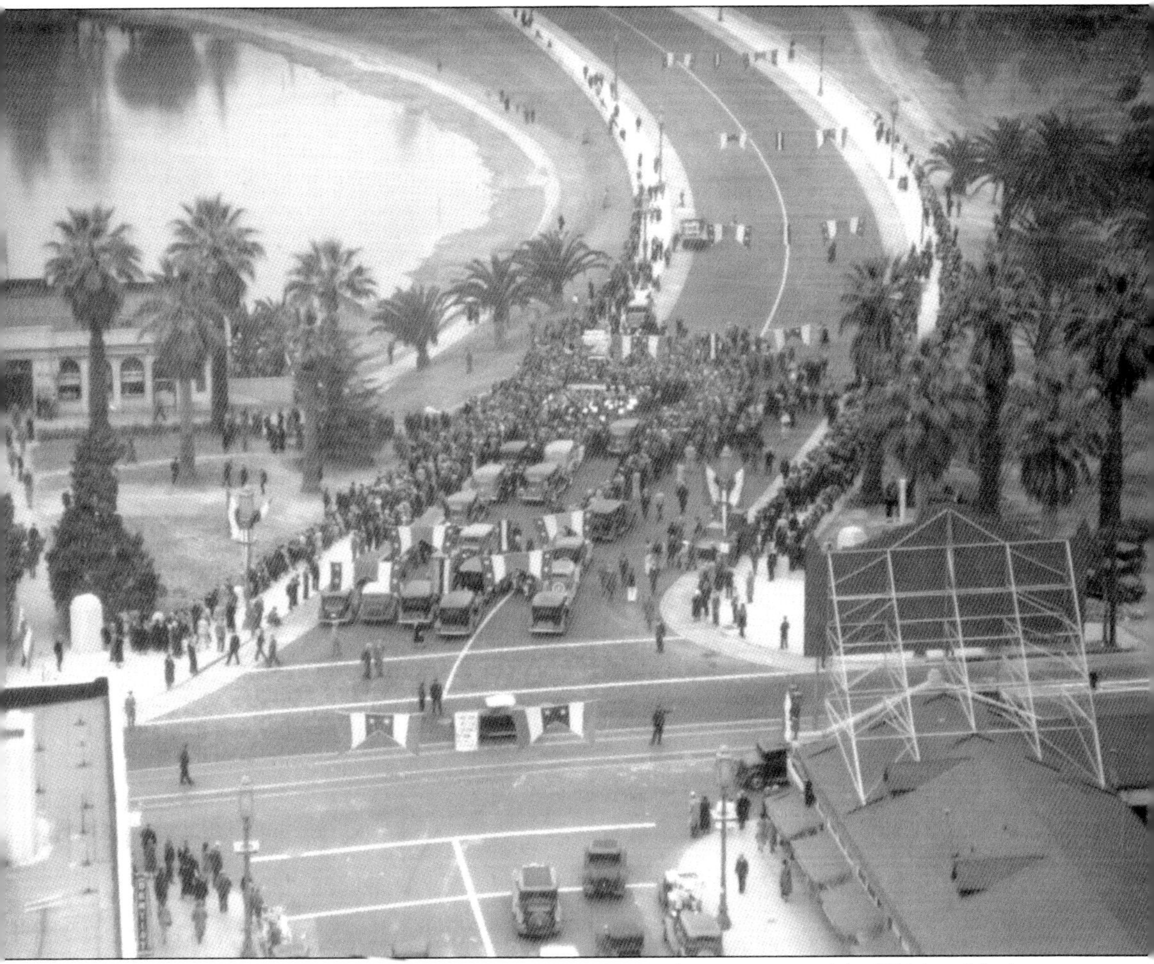

The viaduct is complete, and the street ready to open. Certainly, supporters of the Wilshire Viaduct like the Wilshire Boulevard Association, the Central Business District Association, the Downtown Business Men's Association, and, last but not least, the Los Angeles Traffic Association celebrated this momentous day for the city's growth. Westlake Park was now a pass-through park instead of a destination park. (Courtesy of the Los Angeles Public Library Photo Collection.)

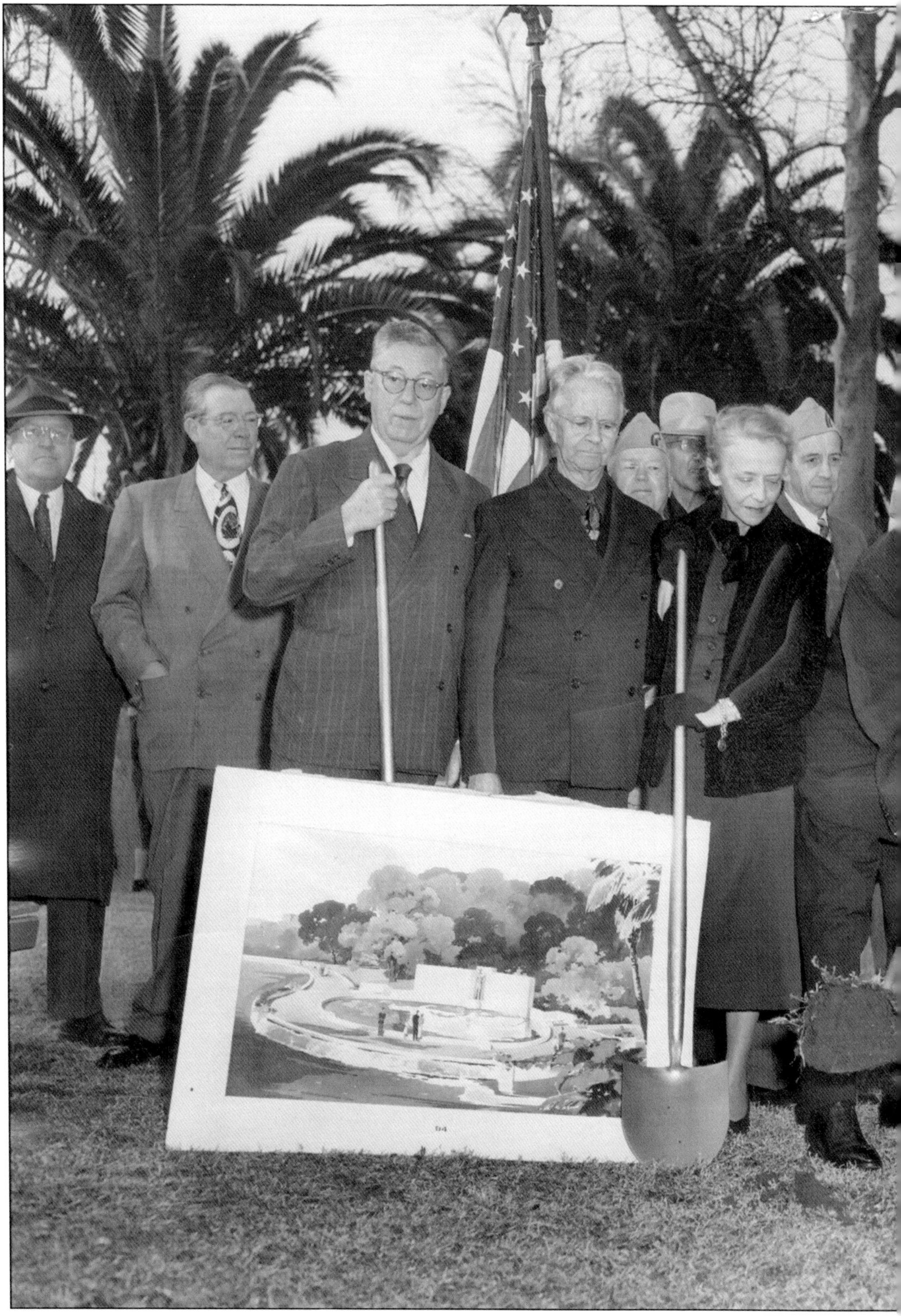

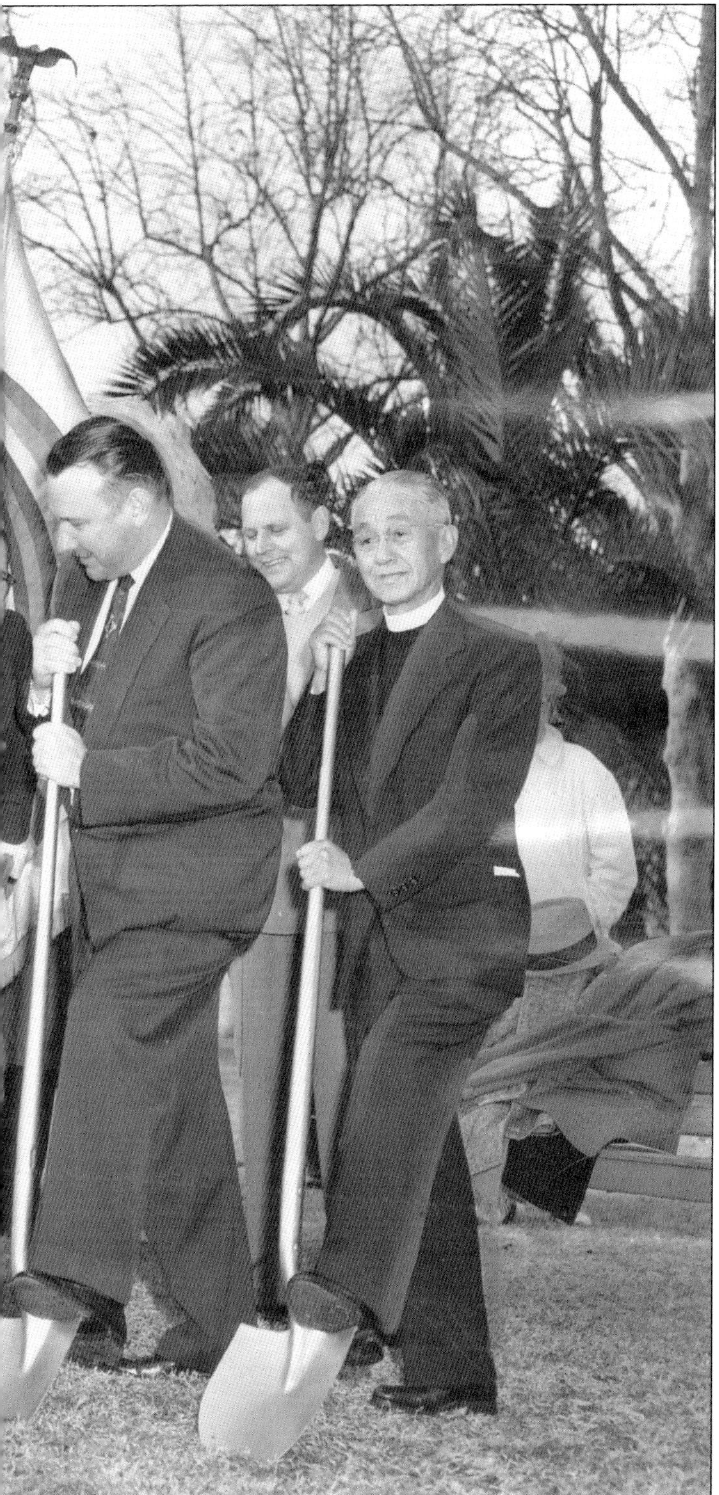

A couple of decades after the completion of the viaduct, Westlake Park, now officially called MacArthur Park, hosted city officials and other dignitaries to kick off the construction of the Gen. Douglas MacArthur Memorial near the southeast corner of the park. Over the years, countless war and veteran–related commemorations have taken place at the MacArthur statue. Today, the memorial is showing signs of decay and needs a major restoration. (Courtesy of the Los Angeles Public Library Photo Collection.)

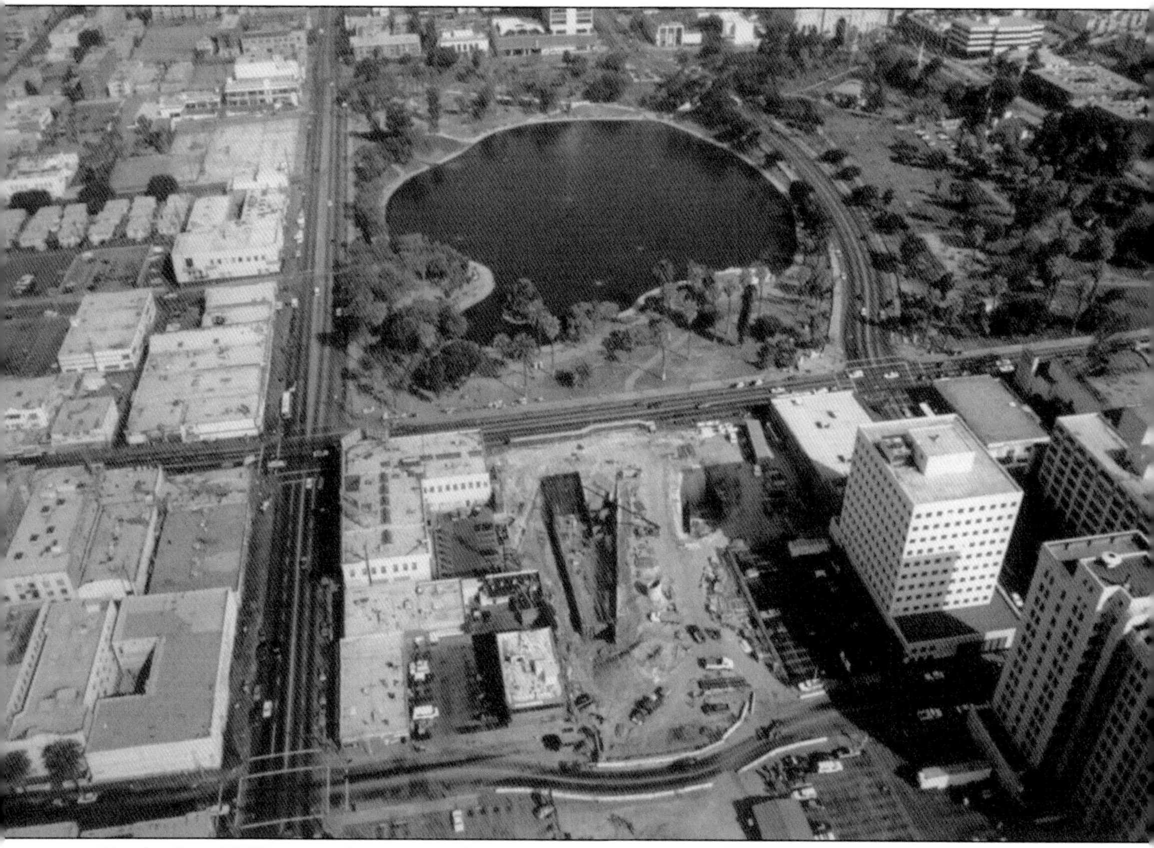

By the late 1980s, transformative change was again visiting MacArthur Park by way of the Red Line Subway system. In this aerial, the lay-down zone for the construction of the subway station across from the park on Alvarado Street is beginning to take shape in the lower center of the photograph. Construction of the Red Line would take several years and, once completed, bring thousands of new visitors into the neighborhood, especially to enjoy those Langer's pastrami sandwiches. (Courtesy of Metro.)

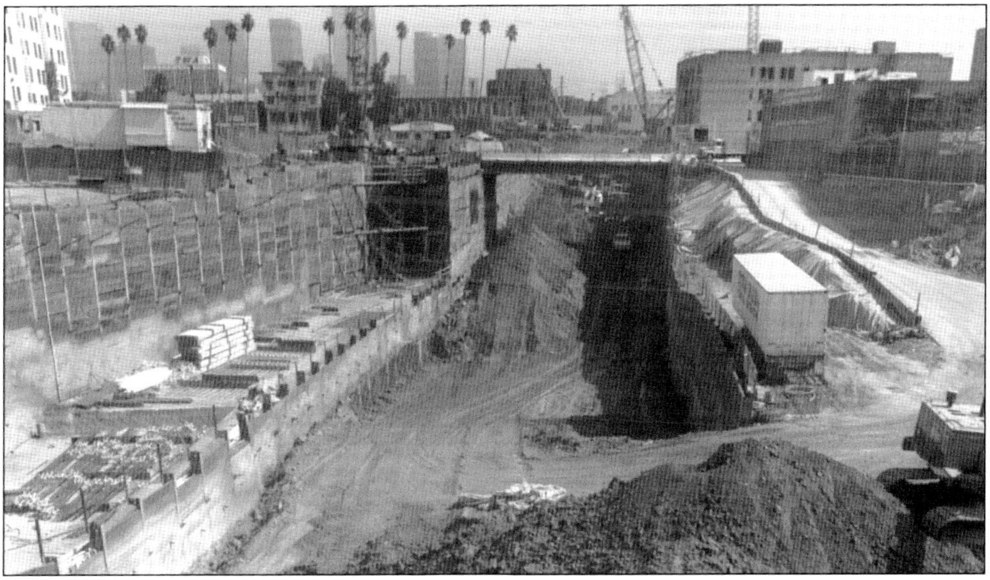

The construction trench extended several blocks eastward from the station site. In the distance is the Los Angeles skyline and the final destination for the Red Line subway. Fortunately, the alignment of the subway line did not result in the demolition of any historically significant structures. Many of these buildings have now undergone some level of restoration since the completion of the subway line. (Courtesy of Metro.)

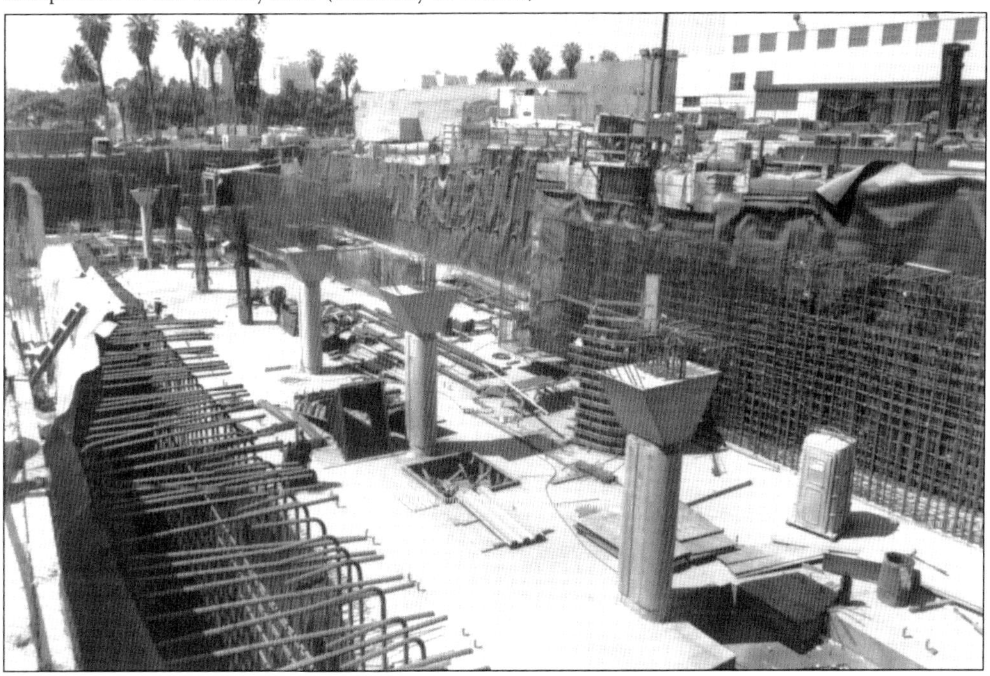

The subway station platform begins to take form between Alvarado Street and Westlake Avenue. Incredibly, the Los Angeles County Metropolitan Transportation Authority (Metro) originally contemplated bypassing the park for a station. Fortunately, attentive elected officials and aggressive community organizing led to a more enlightened system alignment that resulted in a MacArthur Park station. (Courtesy of Metro.)

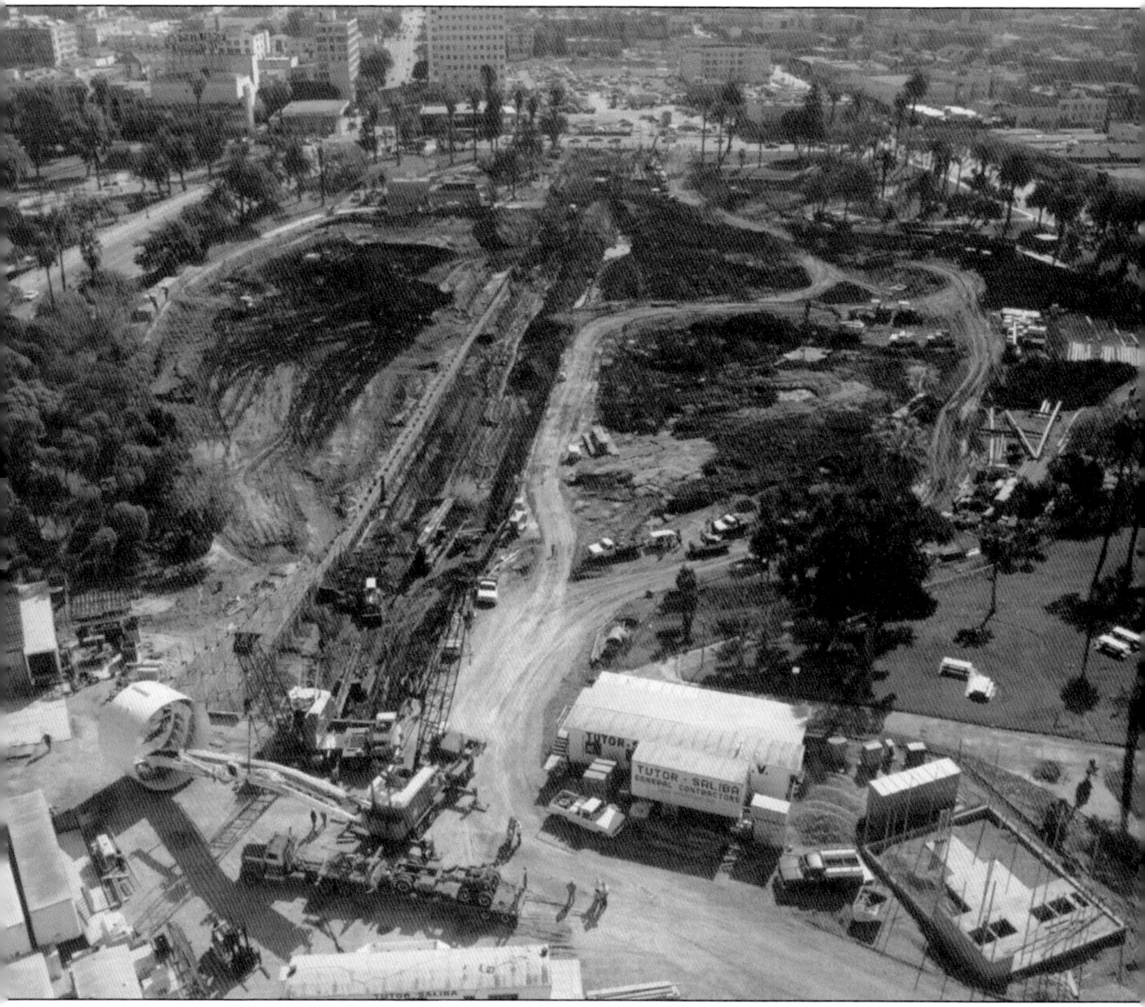

This incredible aerial demonstrates the topographical impact on the park during the subway construction. The author's nine-year-old son described it as "if Godzilla himself scratched the earth with his giant claws." In a scene looking eerily like the construction of the Wilshire Viaduct several decades ago, builders created a long scar-like corridor to facilitate the placement of the earth grinders that would continue the underground digging of the dual subway tunnels. (Courtesy of Metro.)

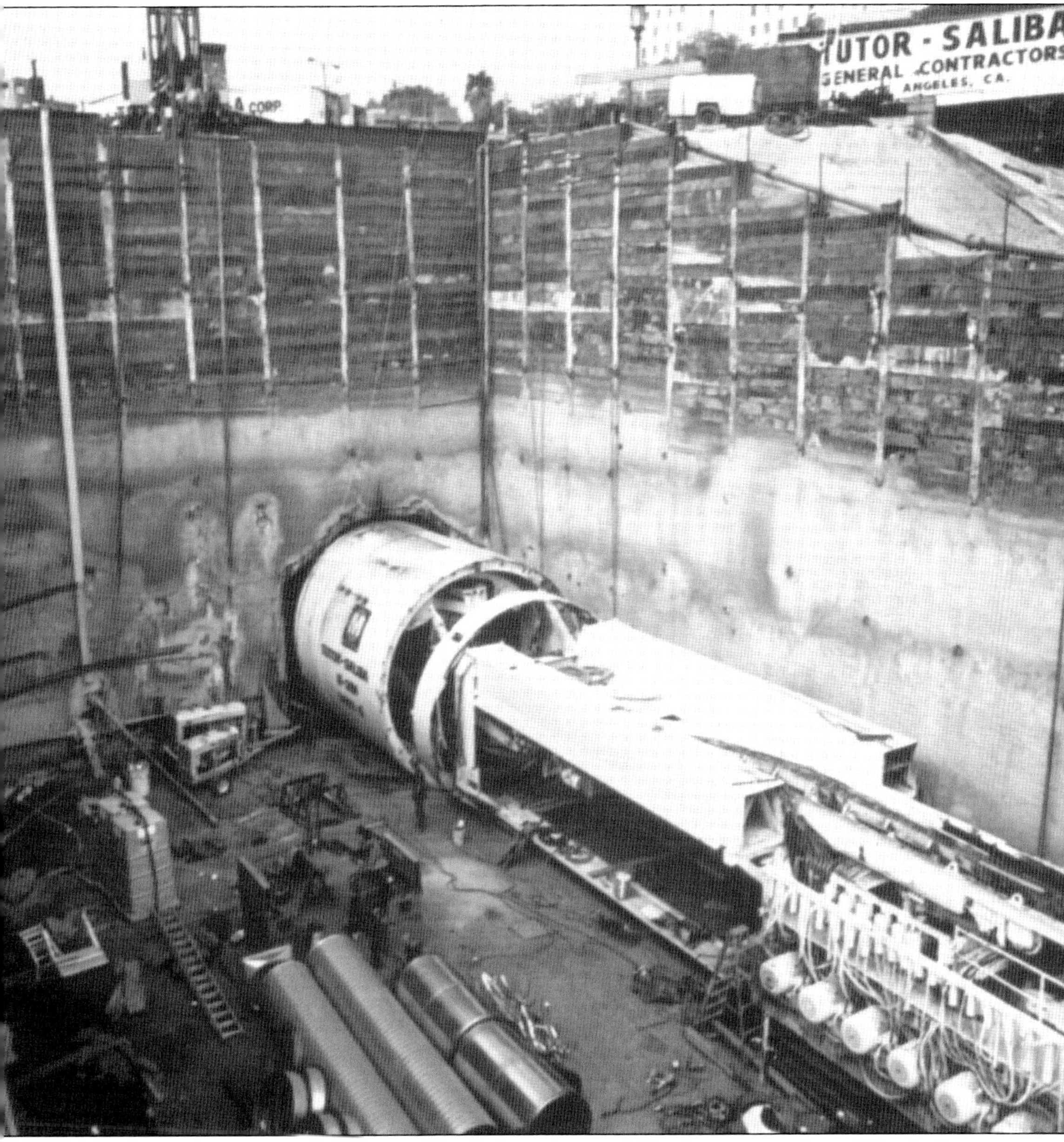

The earth grinders, pictured here several feet below what would be the water surface of MacArthur Park, prepares to bore into the earth on their westward journey, not to the ocean like Wilshire Boulevard, but to Koreatown, Hollywood, and eventually North Hollywood, the new centers of growth and development in the new century. The historic viaduct street lighting is just to the left of the construction trailer. (Courtesy of Metro.)

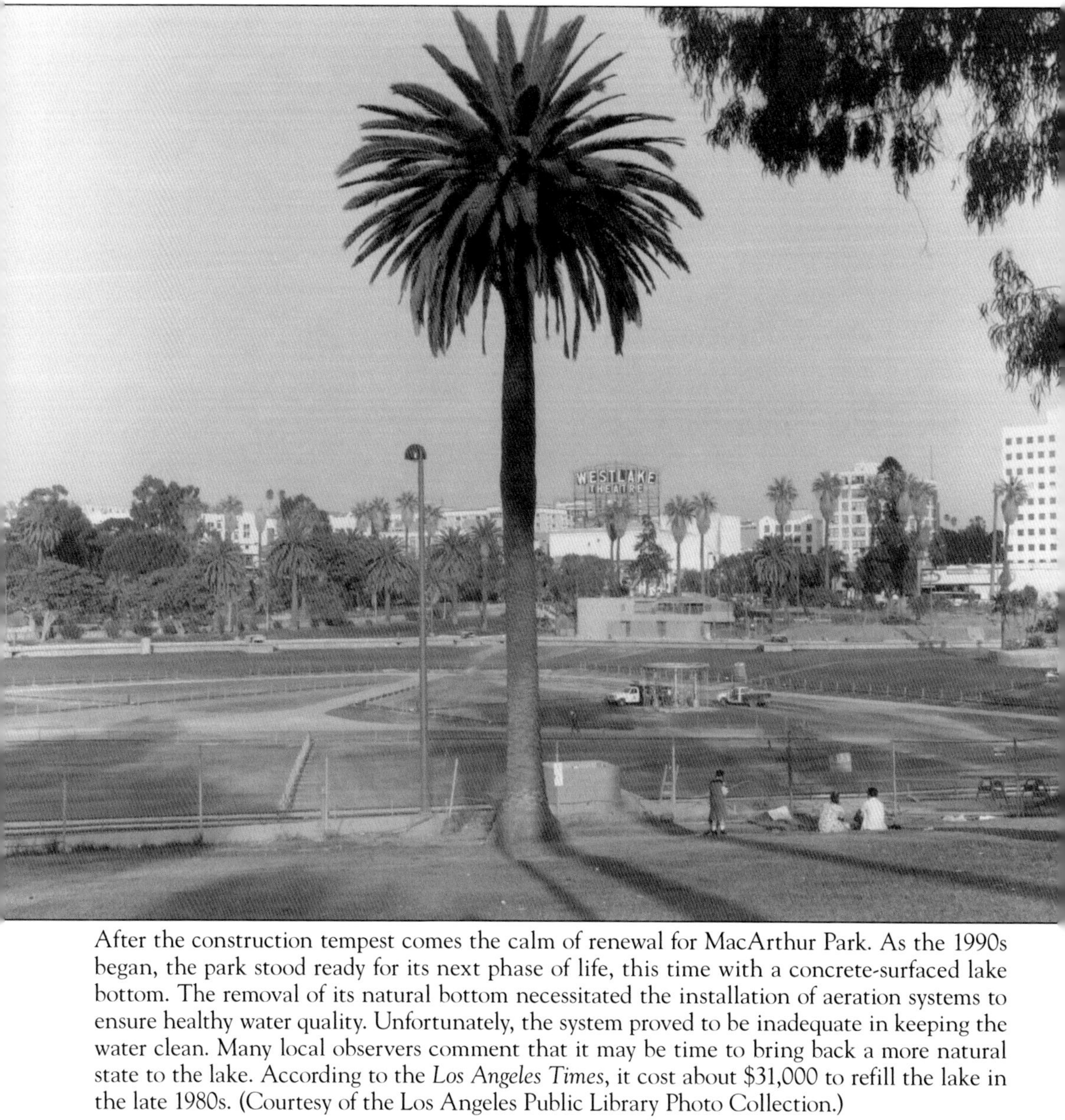

After the construction tempest comes the calm of renewal for MacArthur Park. As the 1990s began, the park stood ready for its next phase of life, this time with a concrete-surfaced lake bottom. The removal of its natural bottom necessitated the installation of aeration systems to ensure healthy water quality. Unfortunately, the system proved to be inadequate in keeping the water clean. Many local observers comment that it may be time to bring back a more natural state to the lake. According to the *Los Angeles Times*, it cost about $31,000 to refill the lake in the late 1980s. (Courtesy of the Los Angeles Public Library Photo Collection.)

Five

People at Play and Protest

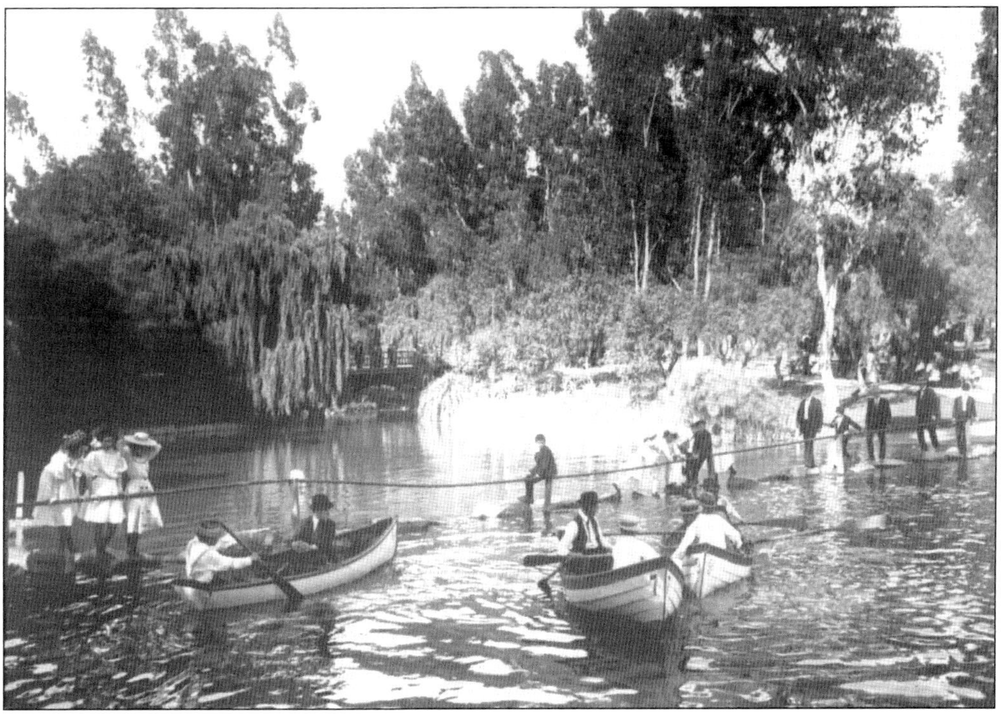

When the City of Los Angeles reluctantly purchased the land that would become Westlake Park, it intended to beautify a neighborhood, create a green urban oasis, and escalate real estate development. What city leaders in fact created was the most important democratic space within a city born of multiculturalism, free-rein economic opportunism, and foreign immigration but still struggling to find its civic foundations. Westlake Park led the way for people to play and protest. (Courtesy of the Natural History Museum of Los Angeles County.)

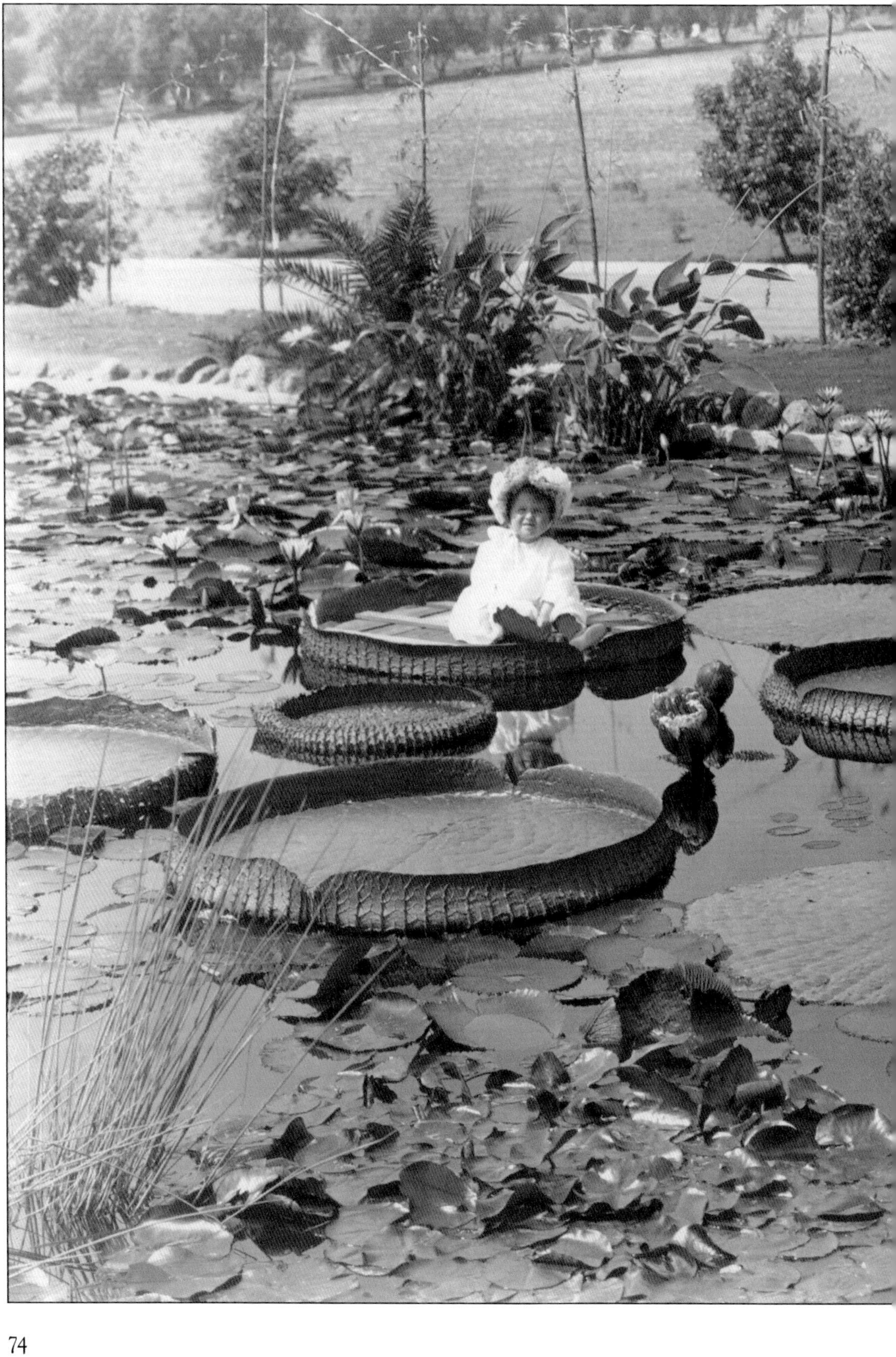

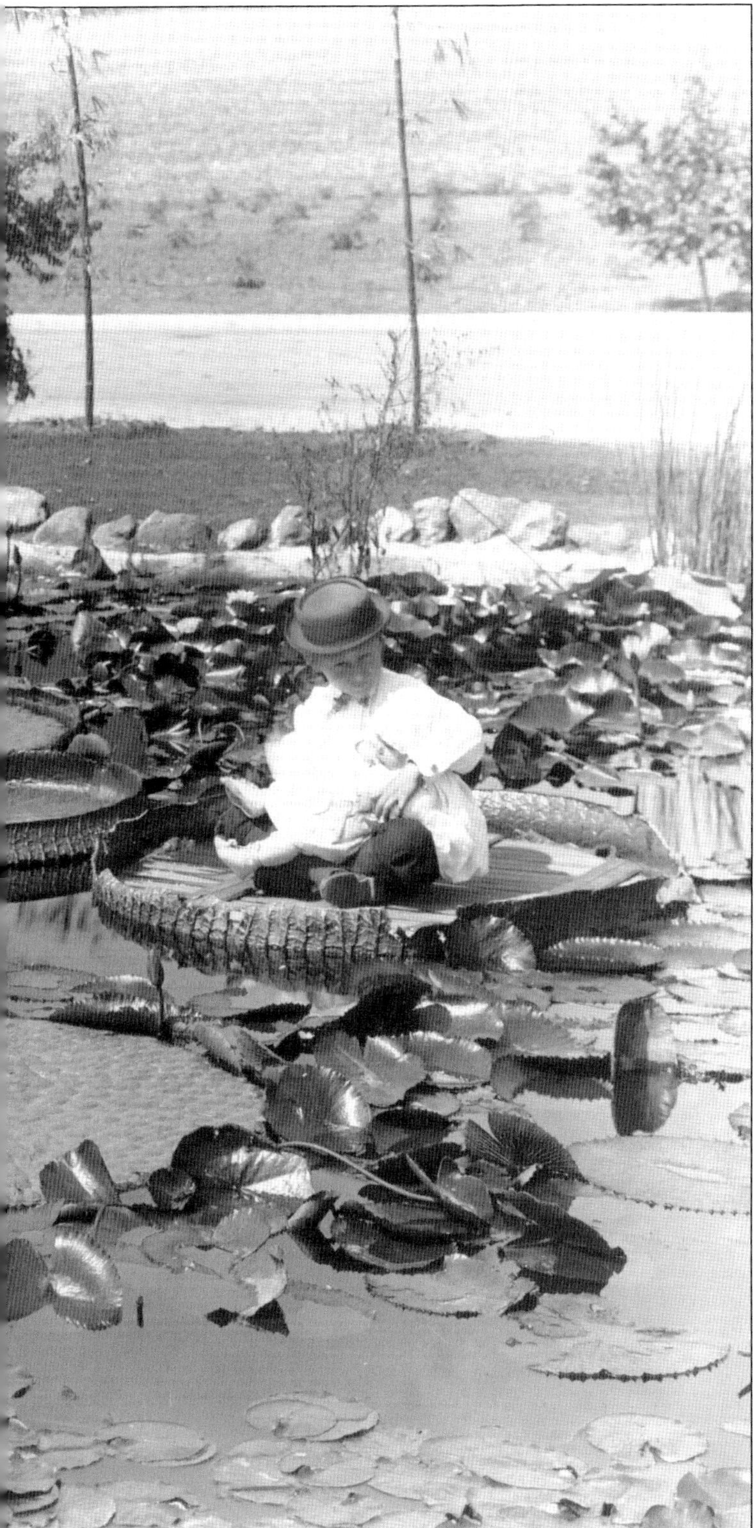

Children, water, giant lily pads, and a new urban lake make for a perfect photo opportunity at the start of the 20th century. Familial scenes like this one informed and motivated city leaders to ensure that the new park and reservoir's water quality was maintained at healthy levels. City records from the first few decades of the park contain many letters from concerned visitors stating their observations about the water quality and, more importantly, the water level within the reservoir. (Courtesy of the Natural History Museum of Los Angeles County.)

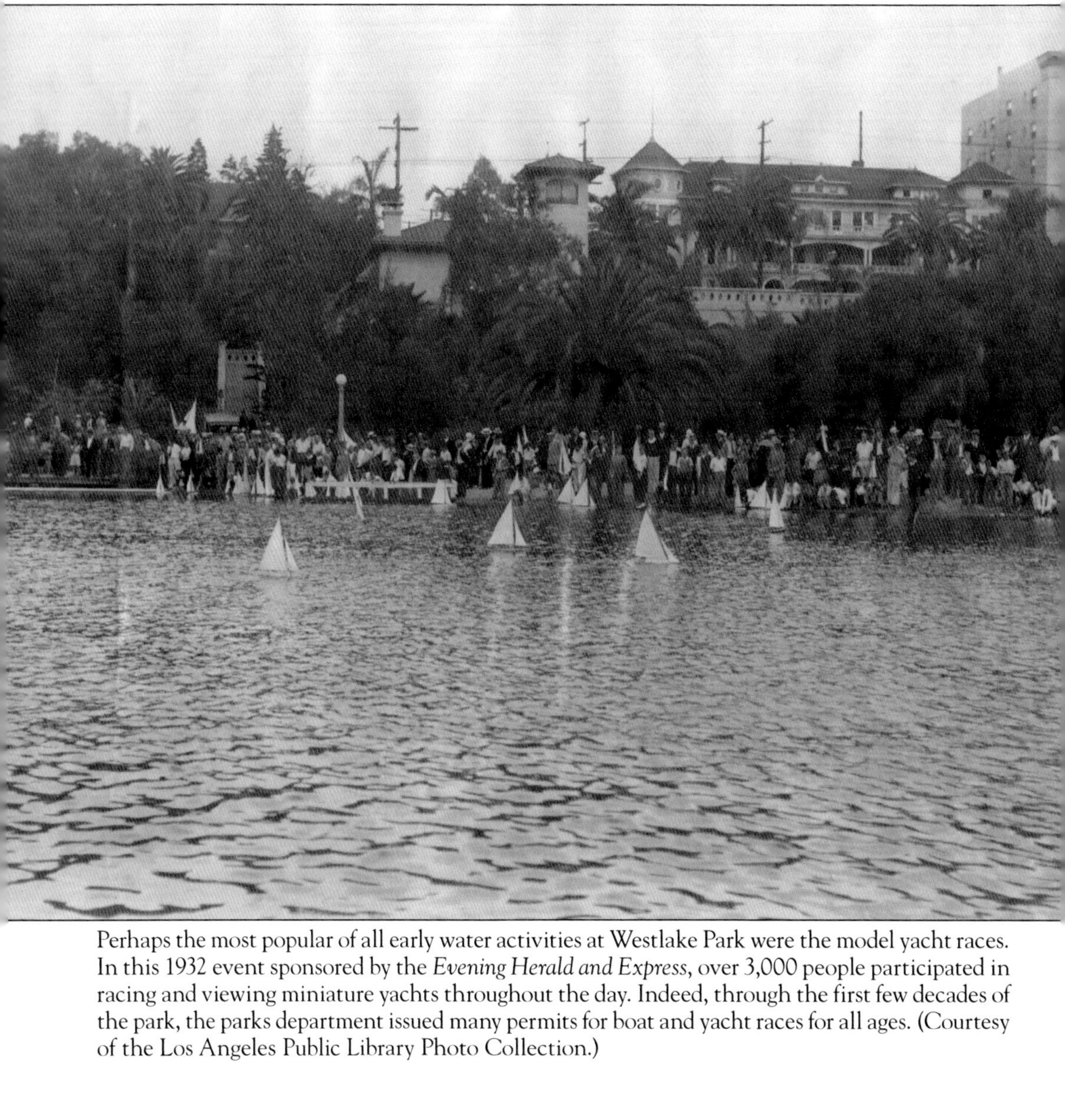

Perhaps the most popular of all early water activities at Westlake Park were the model yacht races. In this 1932 event sponsored by the *Evening Herald and Express*, over 3,000 people participated in racing and viewing miniature yachts throughout the day. Indeed, through the first few decades of the park, the parks department issued many permits for boat and yacht races for all ages. (Courtesy of the Los Angeles Public Library Photo Collection.)

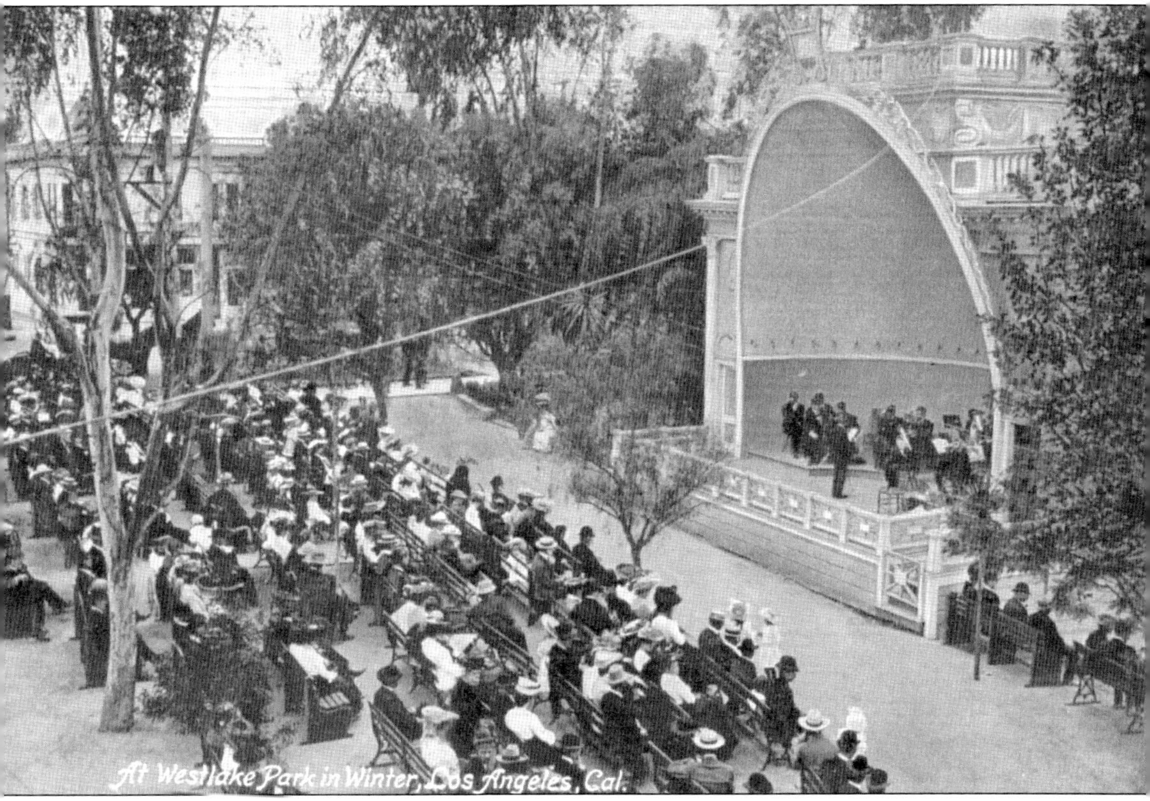

Along with water-related activities, musical performances became a popular pastime for families and visitors to the park. This is a scene from the late 1890s of the newly opened band shell at the park. In the spirit of egalitarianism, local civic organizations sponsored concerts and performances for all age groups at no charge. Local boosters frequently made reference to the large crowds of patrons that attended the concerts. (Courtesy of the Los Angeles Public Library Photo Collection.)

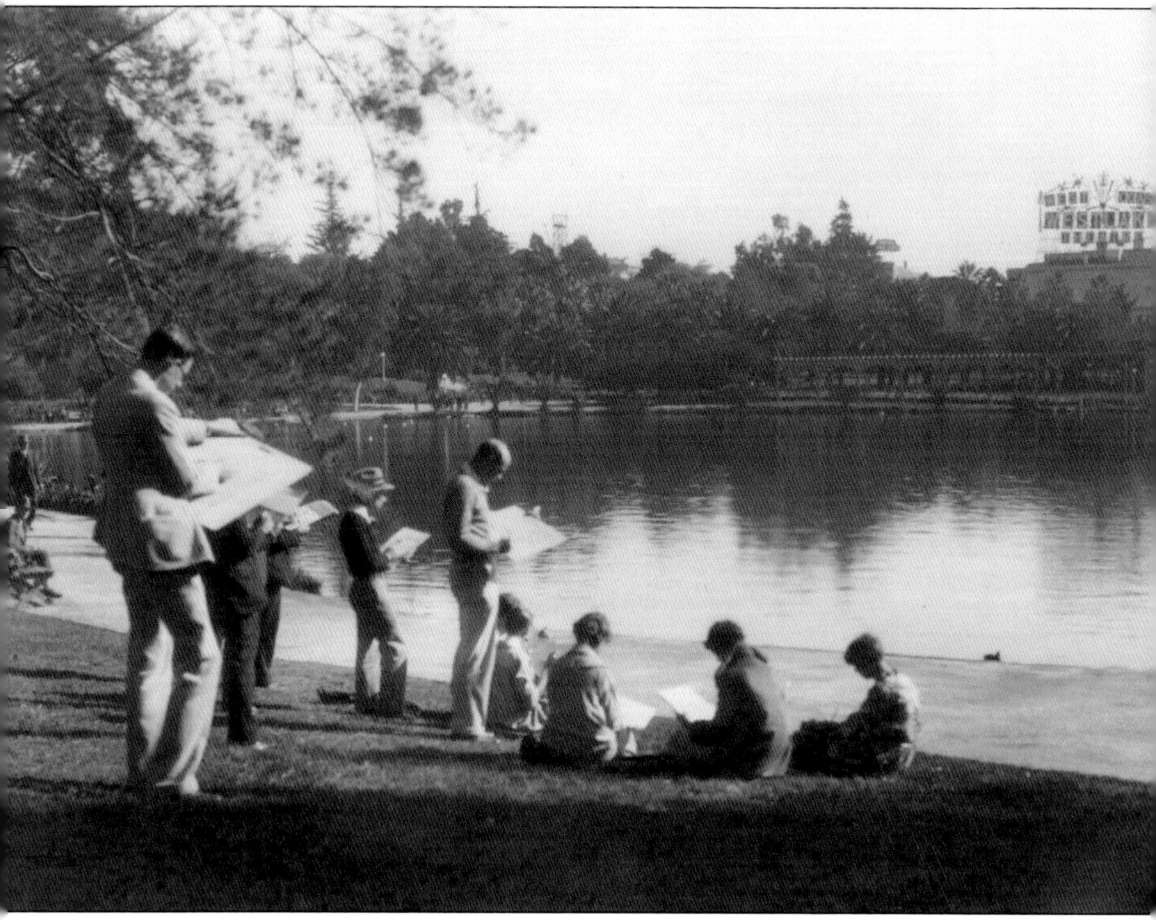

The arts extended beyond the walls of the two local art institutes and into the park. Here, art students appreciate the aesthetic beauty that the urban oasis provided for all. With the fine points of their pencils, artists would draw the gleaming lake, texturized landscape, and angular architecture to fill their sketchbooks. (Courtesy of the Los Angeles Public Library Photo Collection.)

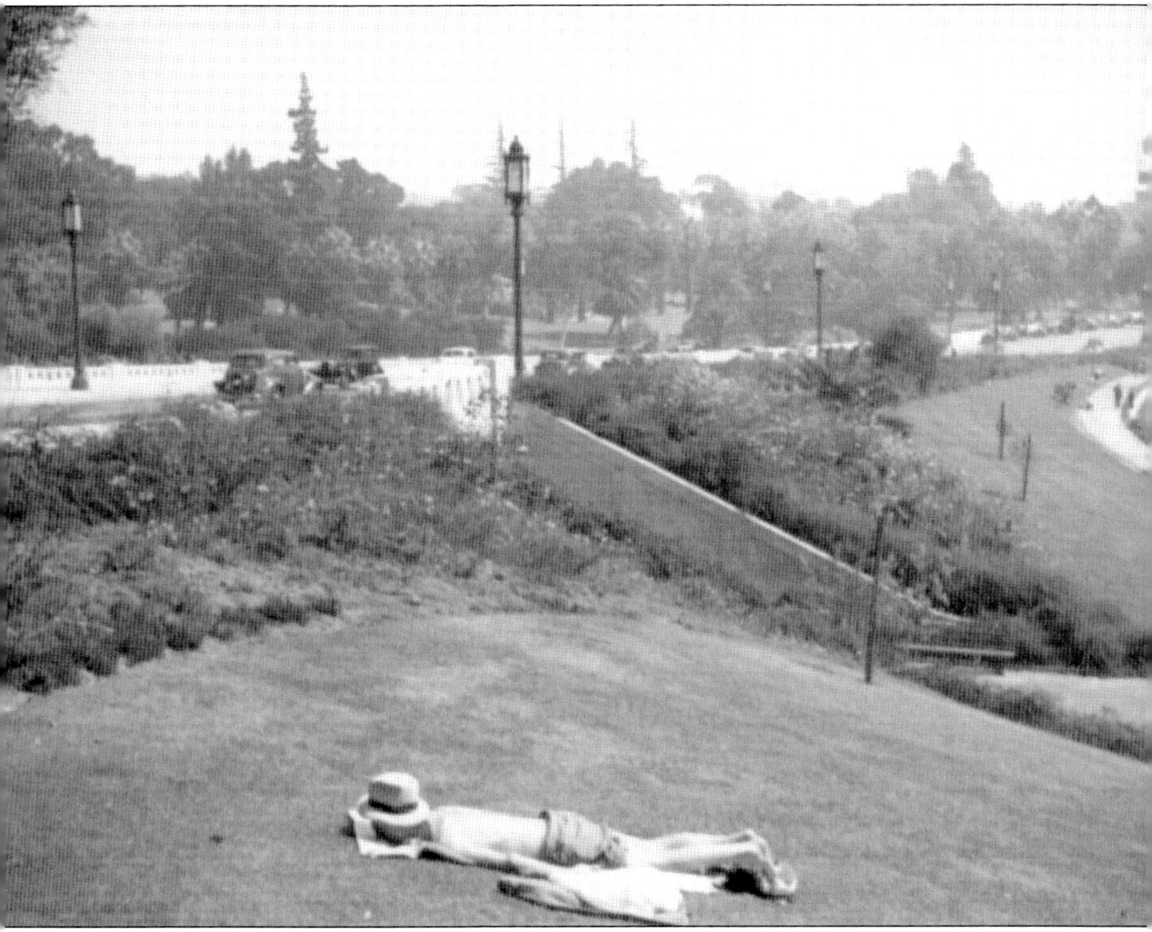

As American as apple pie, sunbathing in sunny Southern California has a long tradition. In this photograph, taken soon after the physical division of the park, the natural embankment created by the construction of the Wilshire Viaduct allows this park visitor to celebrate the sunniest of traditions. This passive activity continues today in the park. (Courtesy of the Los Angeles Public Library Photo Collection.)

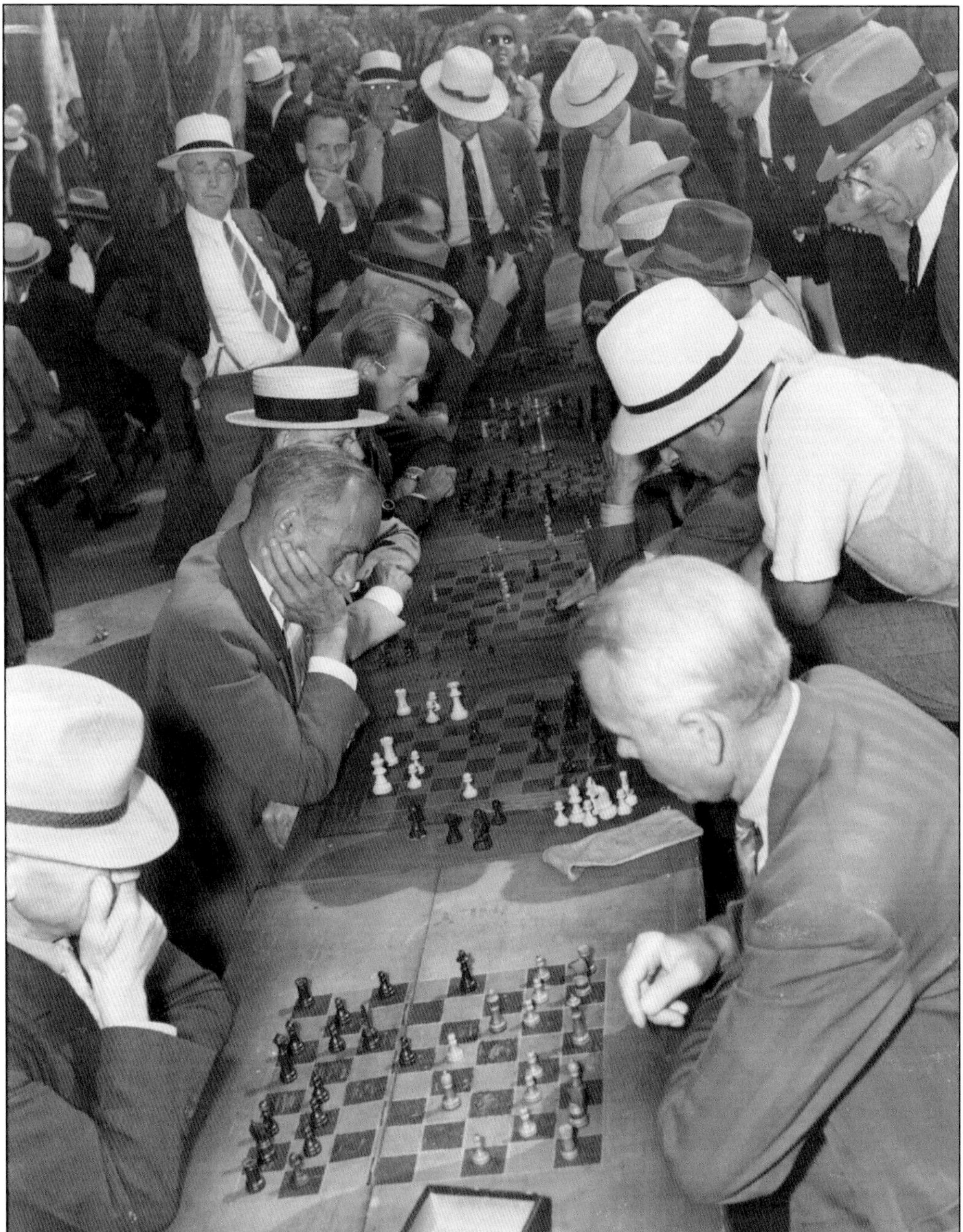

This photograph from 1939 is a testament to the fact that MacArthur Park was a public space for all age groups. In a cherished activity from its earliest days, chess players held court in the southwest corner of the park. According to a local old-timer from the neighborhood, over the years, famous chess players have secretly visited the park to compete with local talent. (Courtesy of the Los Angeles Public Library Photo Collection.)

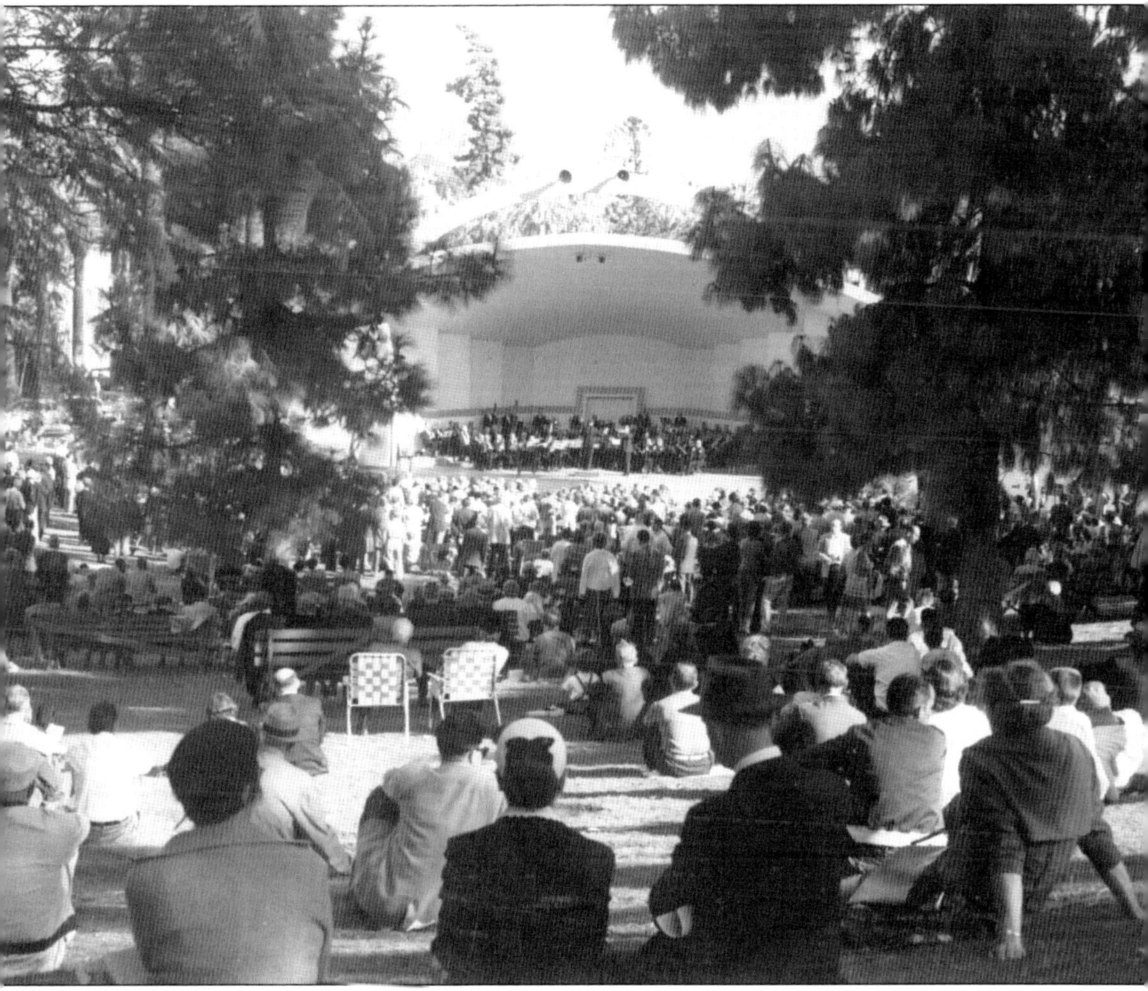

The new band shell may not have been as elegant as the original, but the facility, situated within a natural amphitheater setting, continued to host large crowds that came to the park to listen to music, enjoy a Shakespeare play, or simply be distracted from the chaotic stress of the throbbing city. (Courtesy of the Natural History Museum of Los Angeles County.)

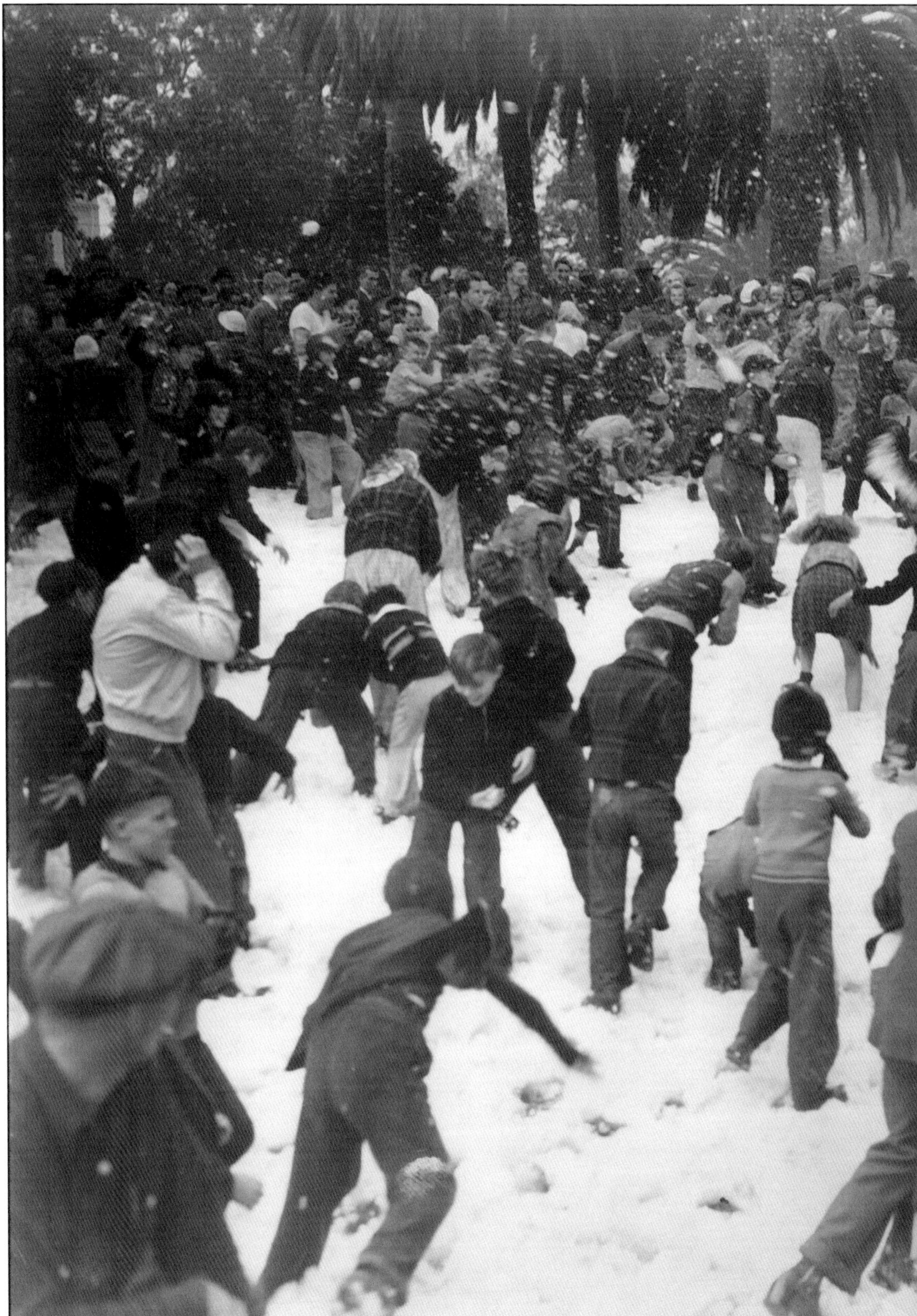

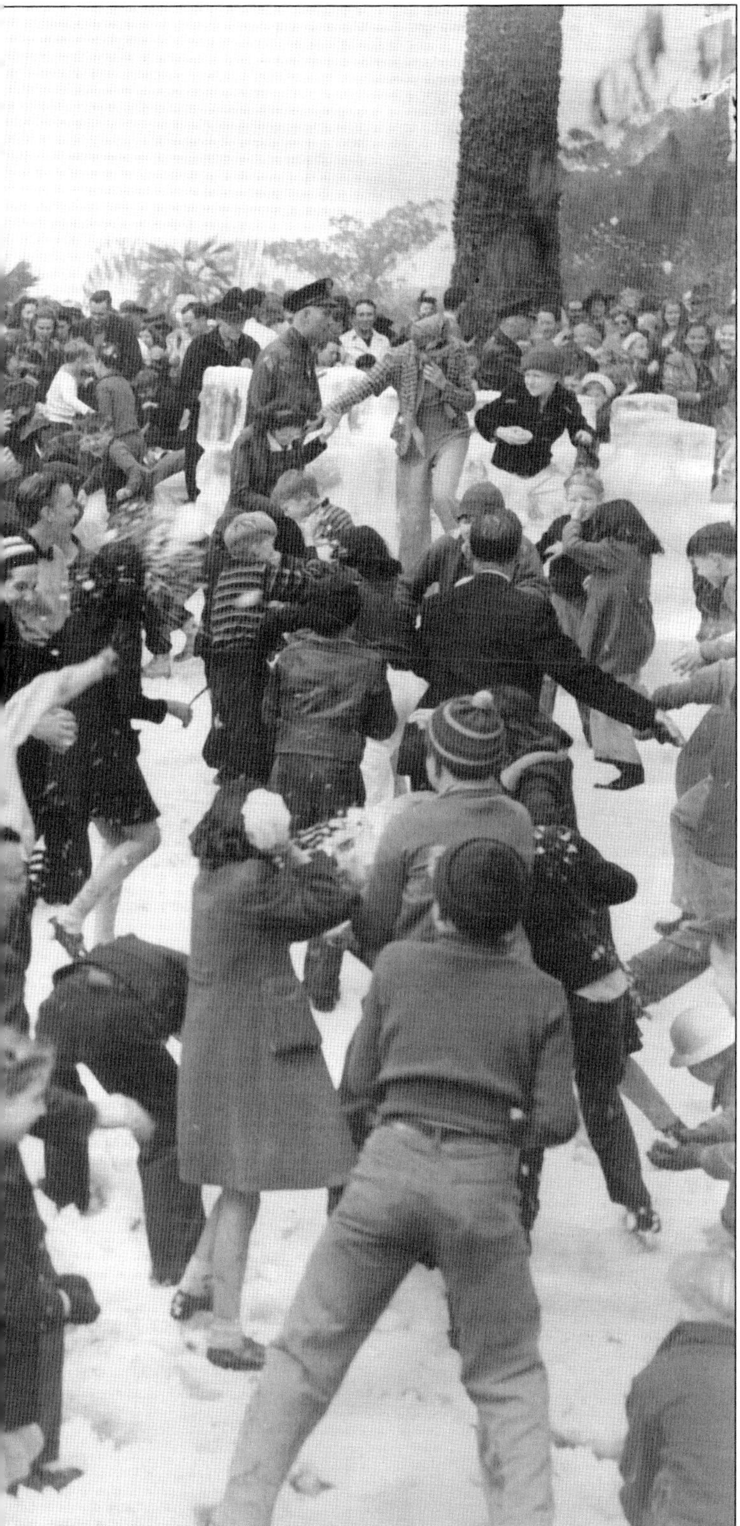

The snow seen in this photograph was proudly shipped in not by a great Pacific winter storm but by ice trucks sponsored by local media outlets. Although there have been documented snowfalls within the Los Angeles basin, no snowfall has been recorded at the park. (Courtesy of the Los Angeles Public Library Photo Collection.)

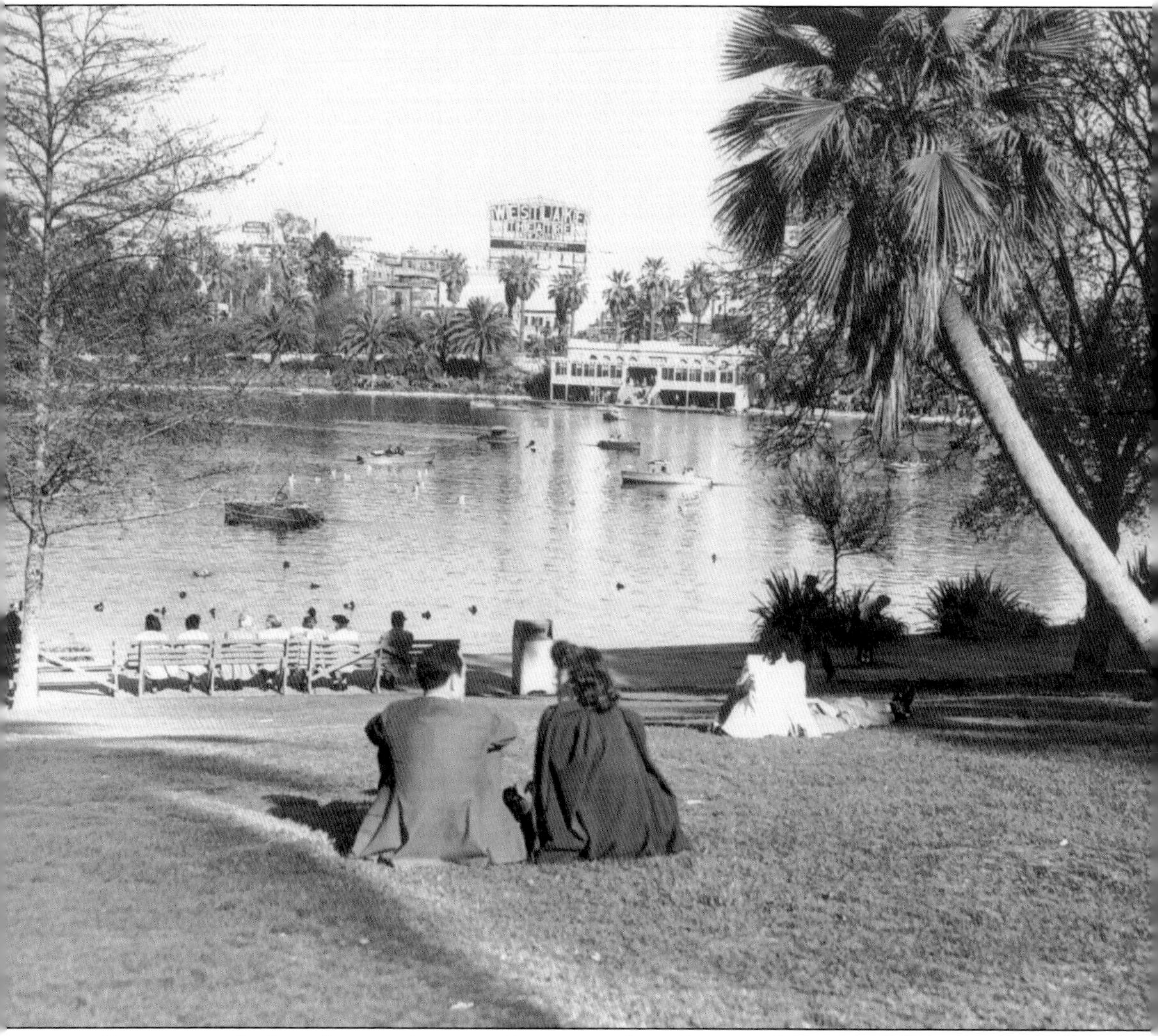

Sometimes, the best thing to do in a park is to simply sit down and appreciate one's surroundings. This couple from 1950 surely understood the special place in front of them. In a perfectly framed photograph, one can observe the best elements of the park—the lake, the tropical foliage, and the Westlake Theatre sign in the background. (Courtesy of the University of Southern California Libraries.)

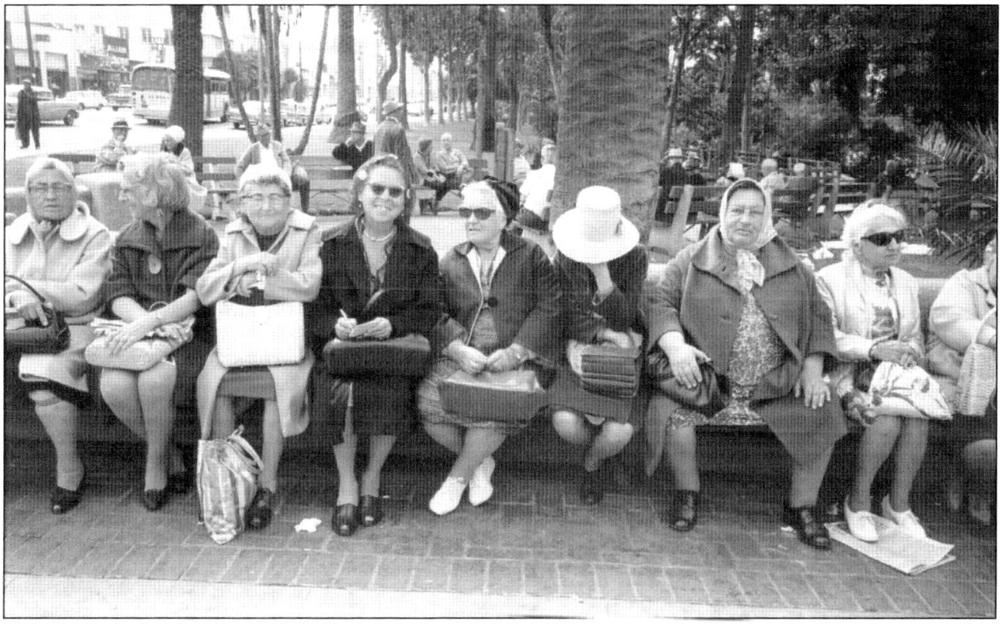

In this photograph from 1968, ladies enjoyed a fine afternoon in the city doing what humans have been doing for thousands of years and continue to do today—people watch. During this time, the park and the neighborhood were beginning a slow decline due to disinvestment, an aging population, and the beginning of the immigration wave that would change the park for the next 40 years. (Courtesy of the Los Angeles Public Library Photo Collection.)

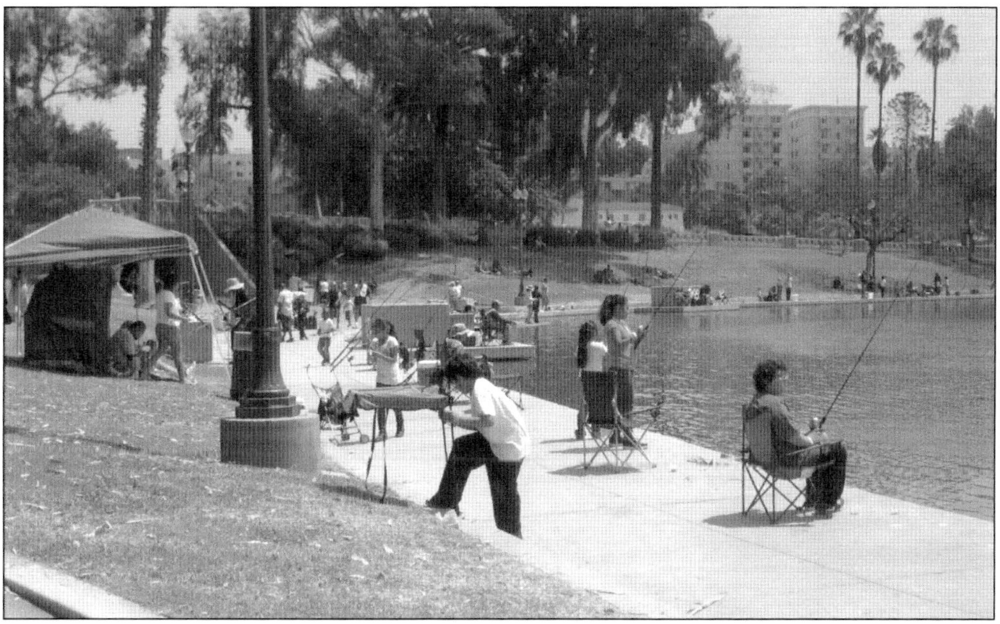

More recently, the city's recreation and parks department has returned fishing derby events to the lake. During certain weekends of the year, local children can again angle for catfish introduced into the lake a few days prior to the actual derby. As a precaution, fish and game officials recommend that the fish dumped in the lake are only healthy to eat within the first week of being in the water. (Courtesy of Andy Ho, Los Angeles Recreation and Parks.)

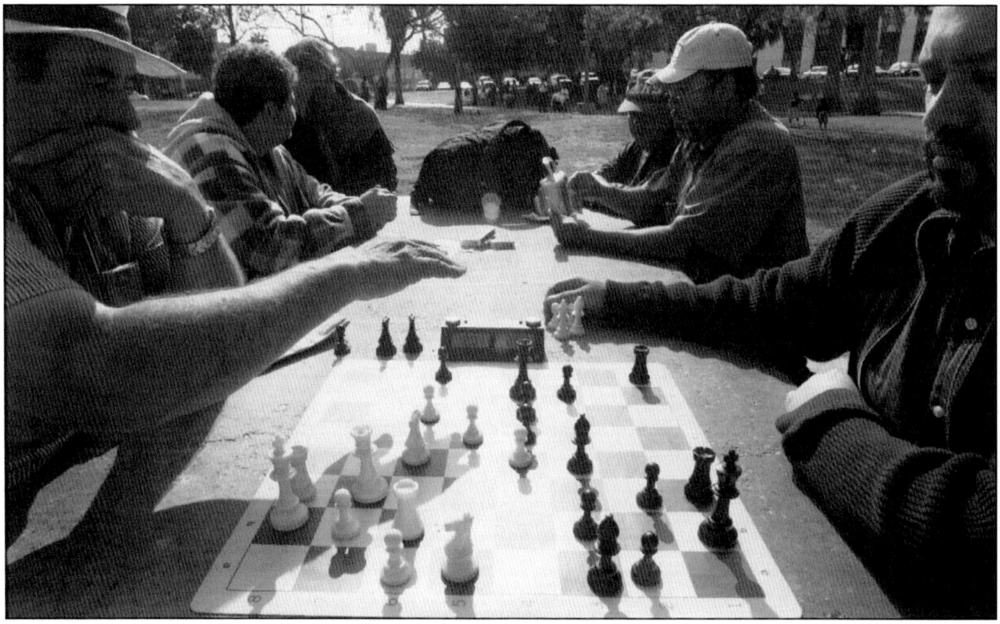

Today, the chess games continue in the park, although now players gather in the north side of the park. The crowds that come together now are more diverse in ethnicity and age, and they also play checkers and cards. Many local folks believe that the chess players were moved to this section of the park so that the LAPD could keep a better eye on the playing via the security cameras situated in the area. (Courtesy of Genaro Molina, 2009, *Los Angeles Times*.)

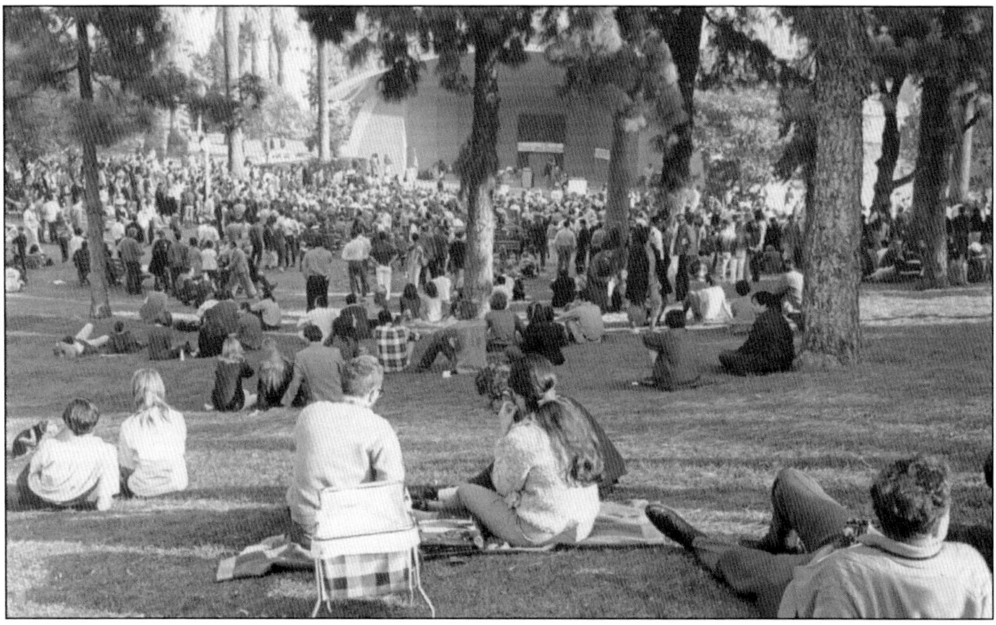

For a park to be truly public, it not only must allow for recreation, but it should also provide the space for protest and demonstration. MacArthur Park, as was the case across the city and the entire country, hosted many protest events during the 1960s. In 1967, one of the largest rallies in the city, in this case organized by the Peace and Freedom Party, occurred at the band shell. (Courtesy of the Los Angeles Public Library Photo Collection.)

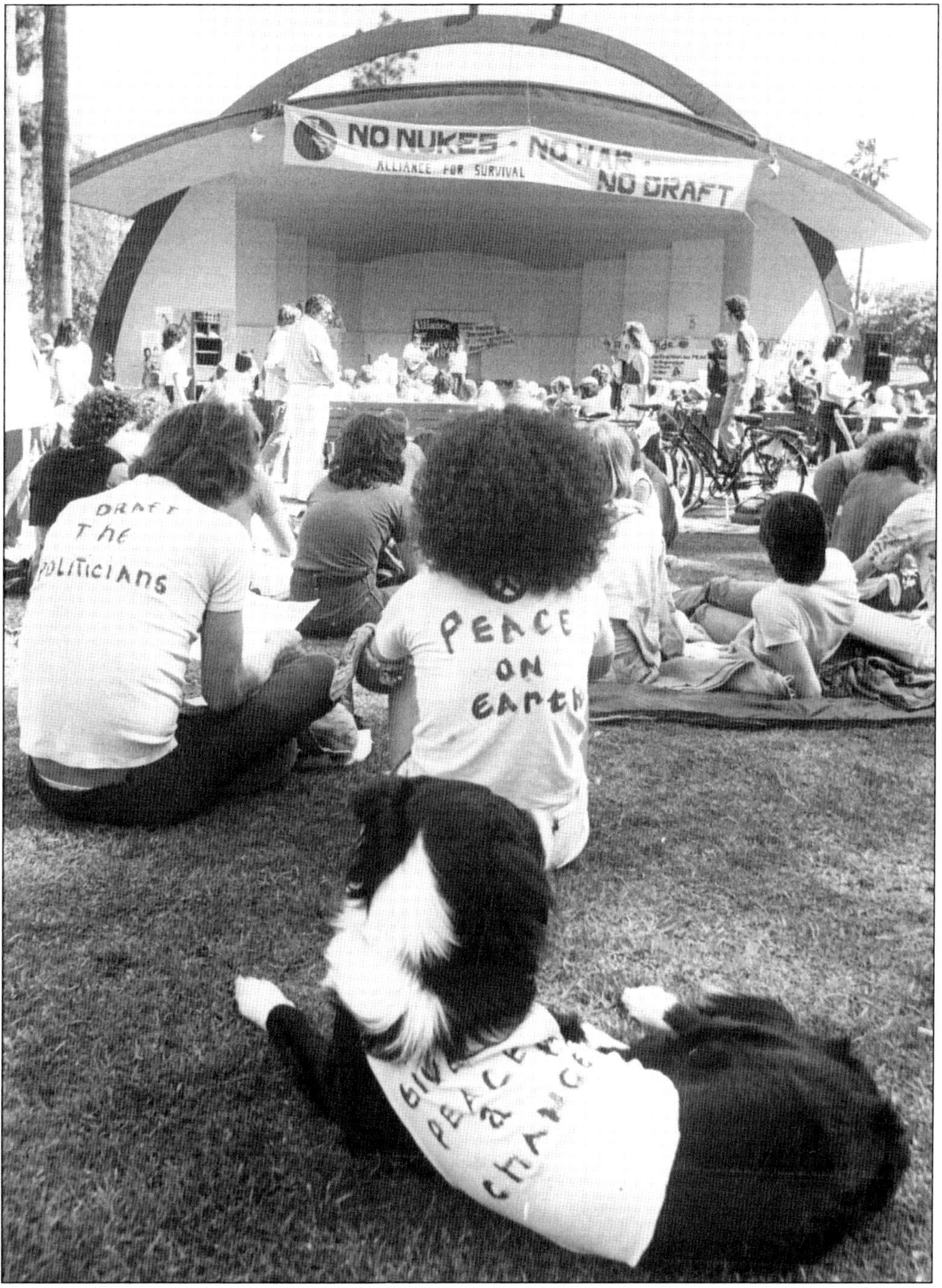

The 1980s were a particularly active decade for rallies and protests inside MacArthur Park. It was the beginning of the Reagan era and the resulting upheaval with issues revolving around labor relations, the Central American civil wars, Middle East crises, and energy usage. The "No Nukes" debate arrived at the park's band shell in 1980. (Courtesy of the Los Angeles Public Library Photo Collection.)

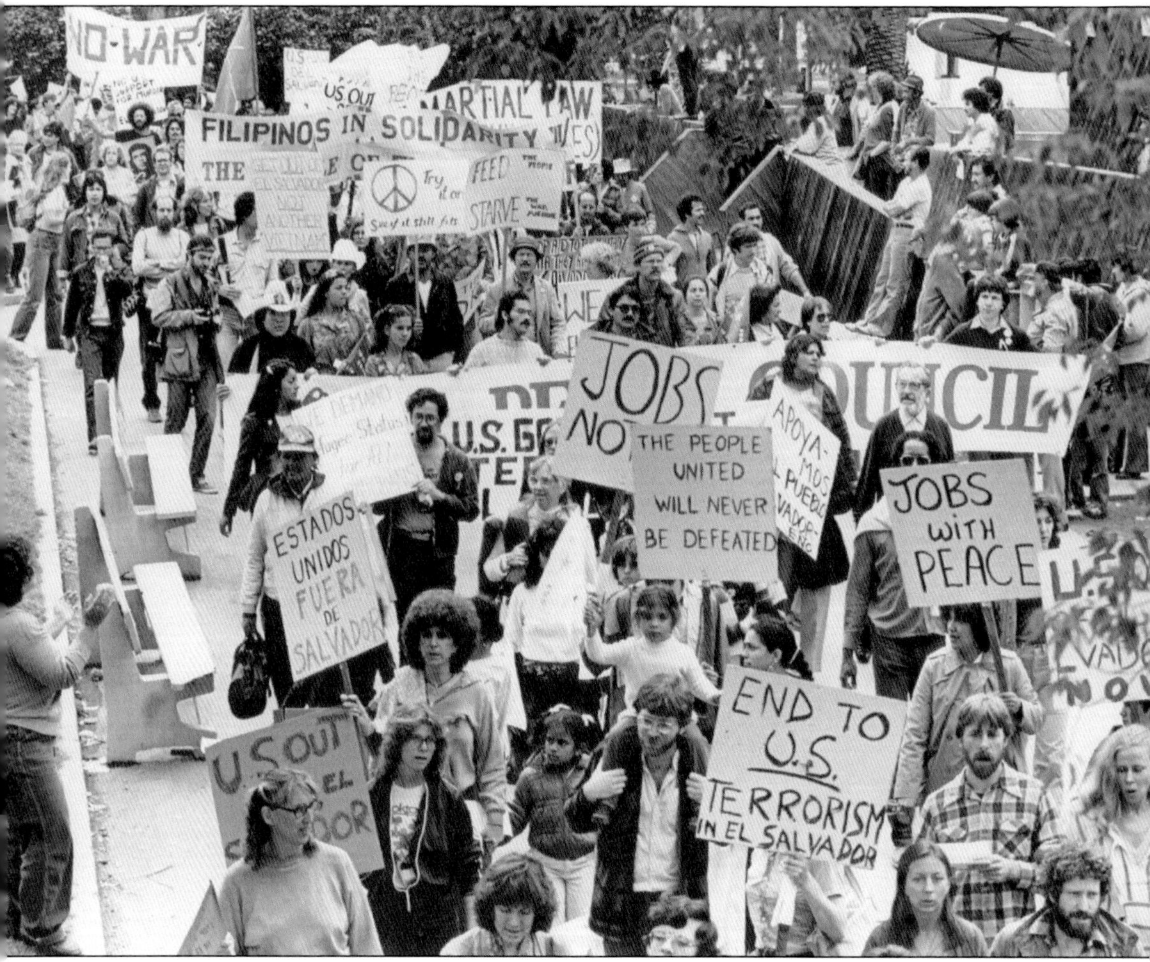

The onset of the civil war in El Salvador drove tens of thousands of political refugees to the United States. Many of the refugees were students and professionals who were escaping intense persecution. A great number of the refugees arrived in Los Angeles. Soon after their arrival, scores of Salvadoran leaders, along with American veterans of the civil rights era, began a campaign to raise awareness in this country in regards to the role of the United States in the civil wars exploding throughout Central America. In 1981, one of the largest protests occurred in MacArthur Park. (Courtesy of the Los Angeles Public Library Photo Collection.)

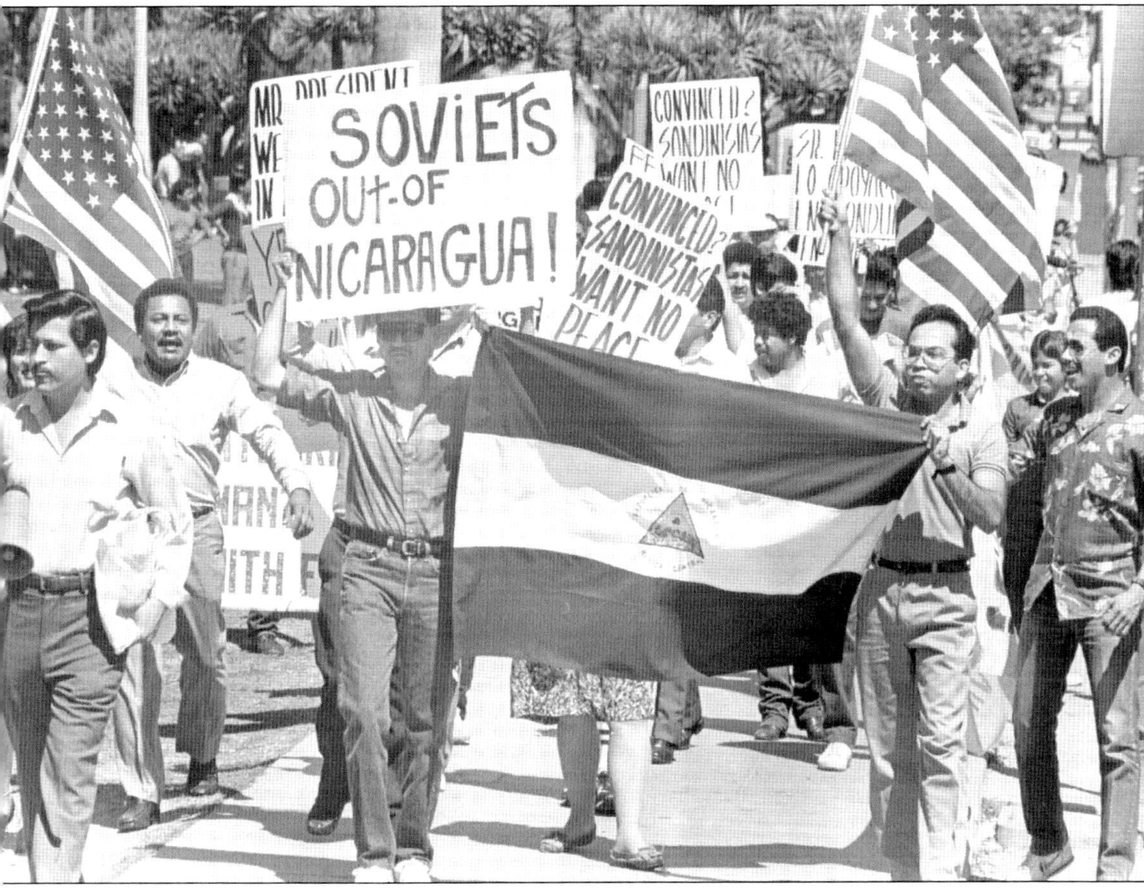

Along with the newly arrived Salvadoran community, fellow refugees from Guatemala, Honduras, and Nicaragua represented the newest group of residents in the neighborhoods around MacArthur Park. For the Nicaraguan community, the impact and consequences of the Contra War drove many of them to the streets to rally against US intervention. MacArthur Park was a safe haven for these protests. (Courtesy of the Los Angeles Public Library Photo Collection.)

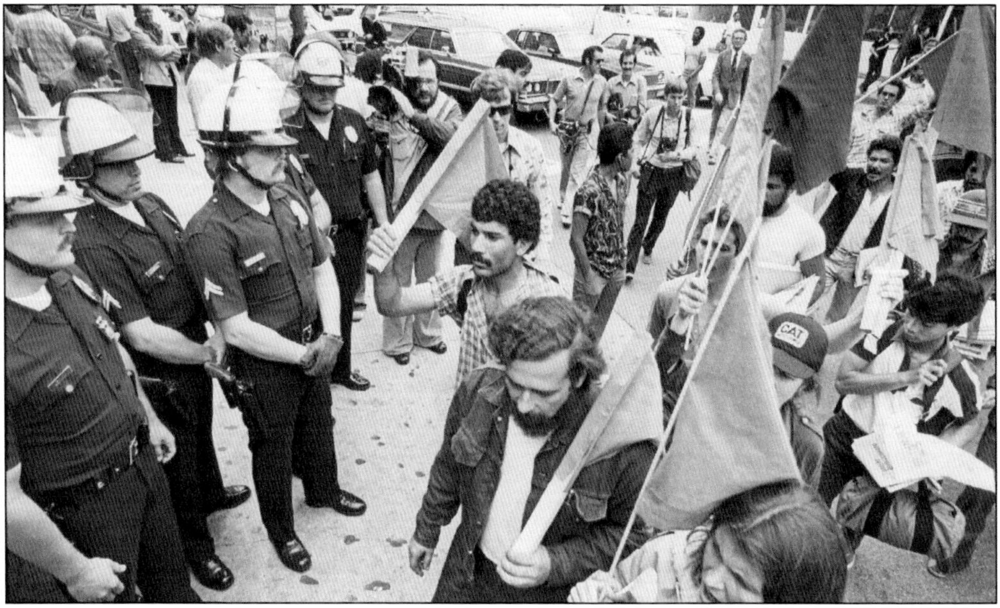

May Day rallies have been a long tradition in many cities across the country, and MacArthur Park has hosted a May Day rally for many decades. Many labor unions have had their headquarters in the Westlake neighborhood, so the park is a logical gathering point. Pictured here is the May Day parade and rally in 1981. The LAPD can be a calming presence at rallies and protests. (Courtesy of the Los Angeles Public Library Photo Collection.)

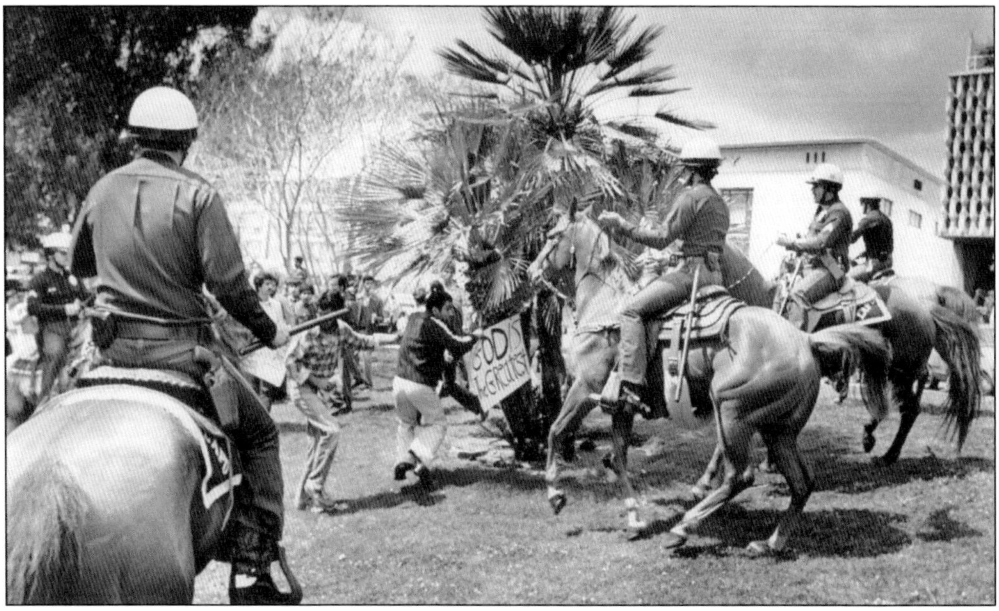

But the LAPD can also be a force of aggression, depending on one's political persuasion or perspective. During the same May Day rally in 1981, the LAPD took action to disperse the crowd within the park. Over the years, there have been frequent confrontations, sometimes violent, between protestors and police officers during May Day rallies. As one protestor said during a recent event, "Democracy is complicated." (Courtesy of the Los Angeles Public Library Photo Collection.)

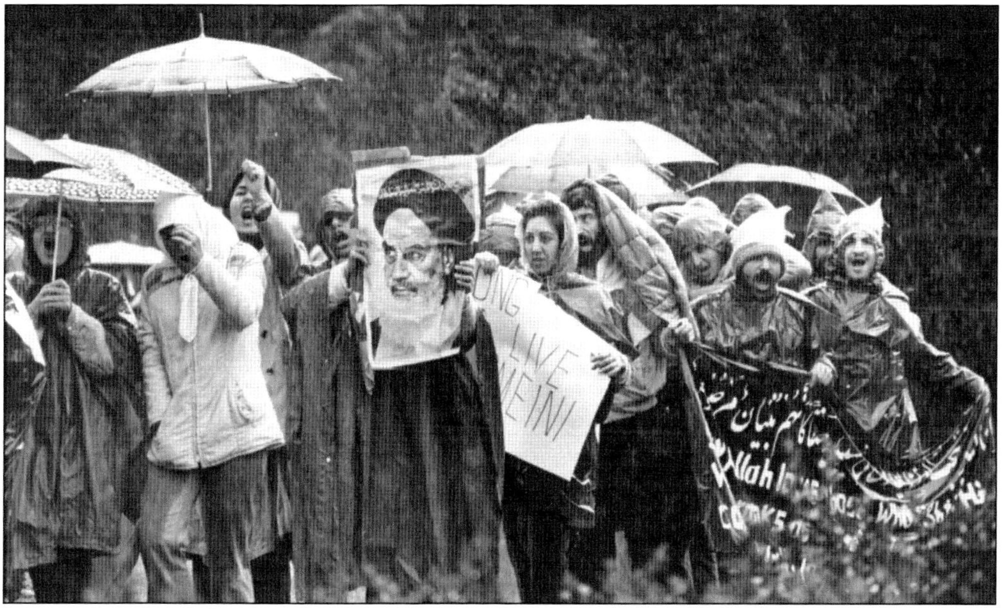

On a rainy March day in 1981, pro- and anti-Khomeini demonstrators gathered in MacArthur Park at the same protest to raise awareness of their respective points of view in regards to Iranian-American relations. Unlike the Central American community, there is not a large Iranian or Persian population around MacArthur Park. But the event is a testament to how the general public sees MacArthur Park as the democratic park for the city. (Courtesy of the Los Angeles Public Library Photo Collection.)

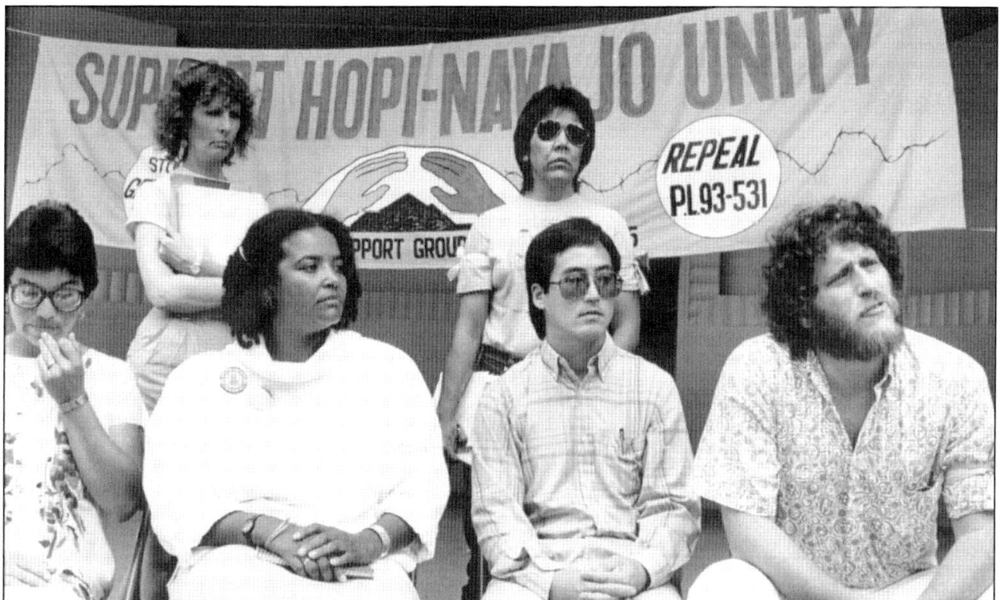

As a show of solidarity for the growing refugee community that lived around the park, a coalition of Native American groups gathered in the park in 1986 to organize a press conference in support of the Navajo and Hopi Indians in their dispute over their forced eviction from lands in Arizona. (Courtesy of the Los Angeles Public Library Photo Collection.)

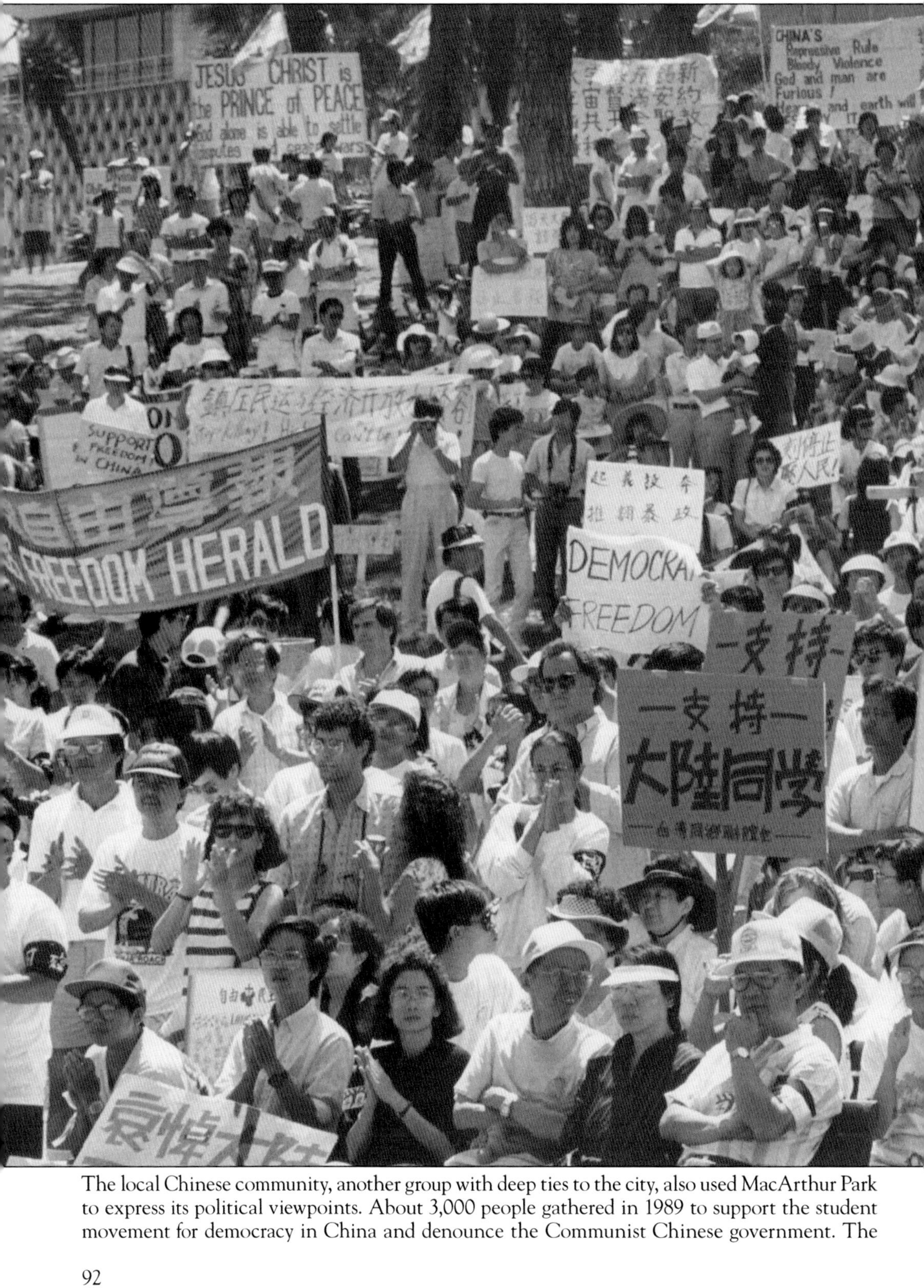

The local Chinese community, another group with deep ties to the city, also used MacArthur Park to express its political viewpoints. About 3,000 people gathered in 1989 to support the student movement for democracy in China and denounce the Communist Chinese government. The

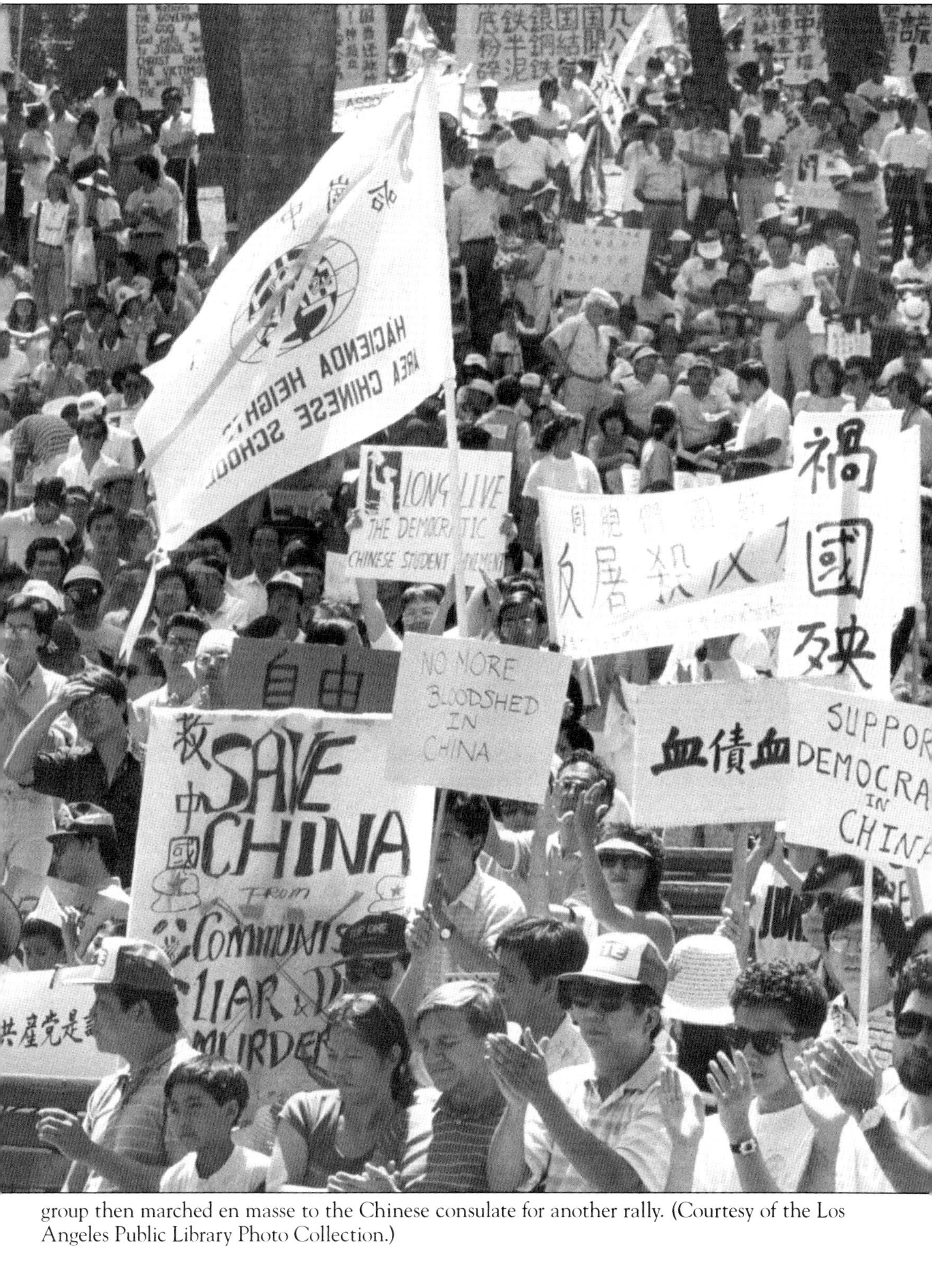

group then marched en masse to the Chinese consulate for another rally. (Courtesy of the Los Angeles Public Library Photo Collection.)

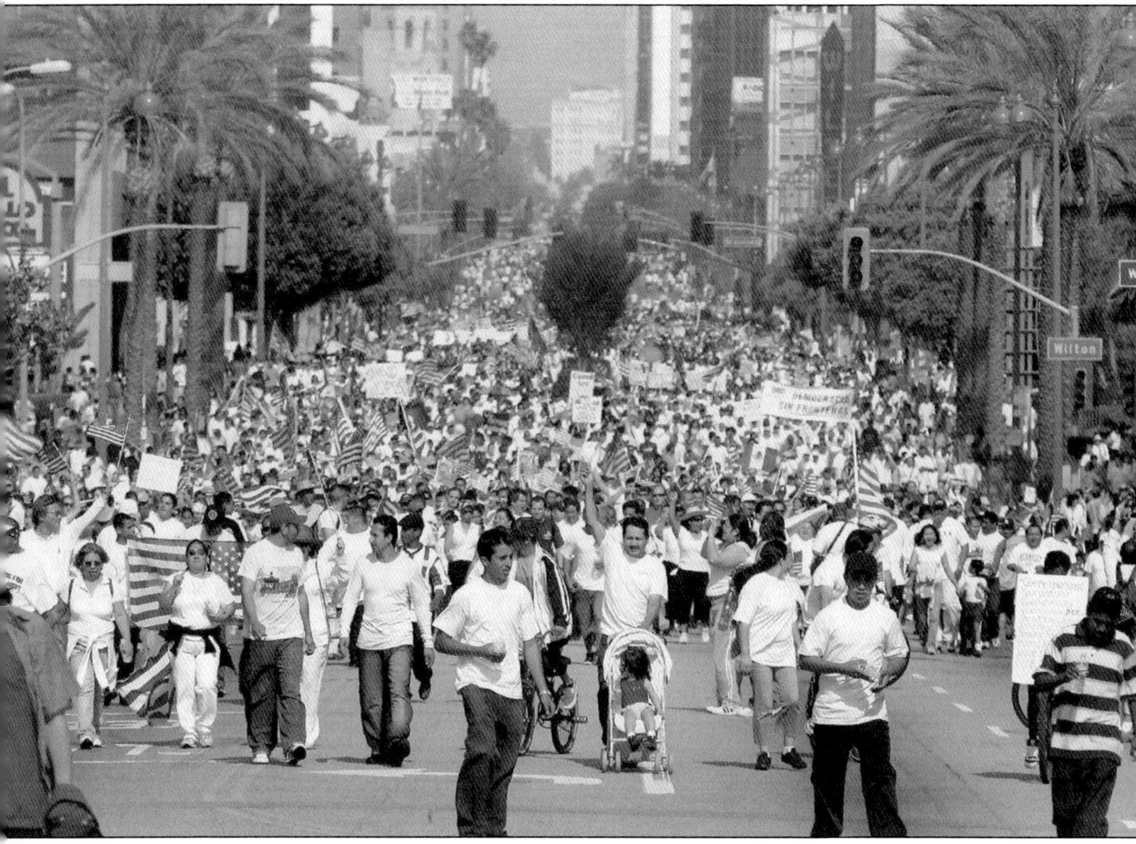

Some of the largest demonstrations to occur in MacArthur Park were related to the nationwide campaign for comprehensive immigration reform, organized by a coalition of hundreds of community organizations. Naturally, the park was the starting point for the hundreds of thousands of marchers as they proceeded due east towards city hall. The park continues to welcome pro-reform marchers every year. (Courtesy of Rick Loomis, 2006, *Los Angeles Times*.)

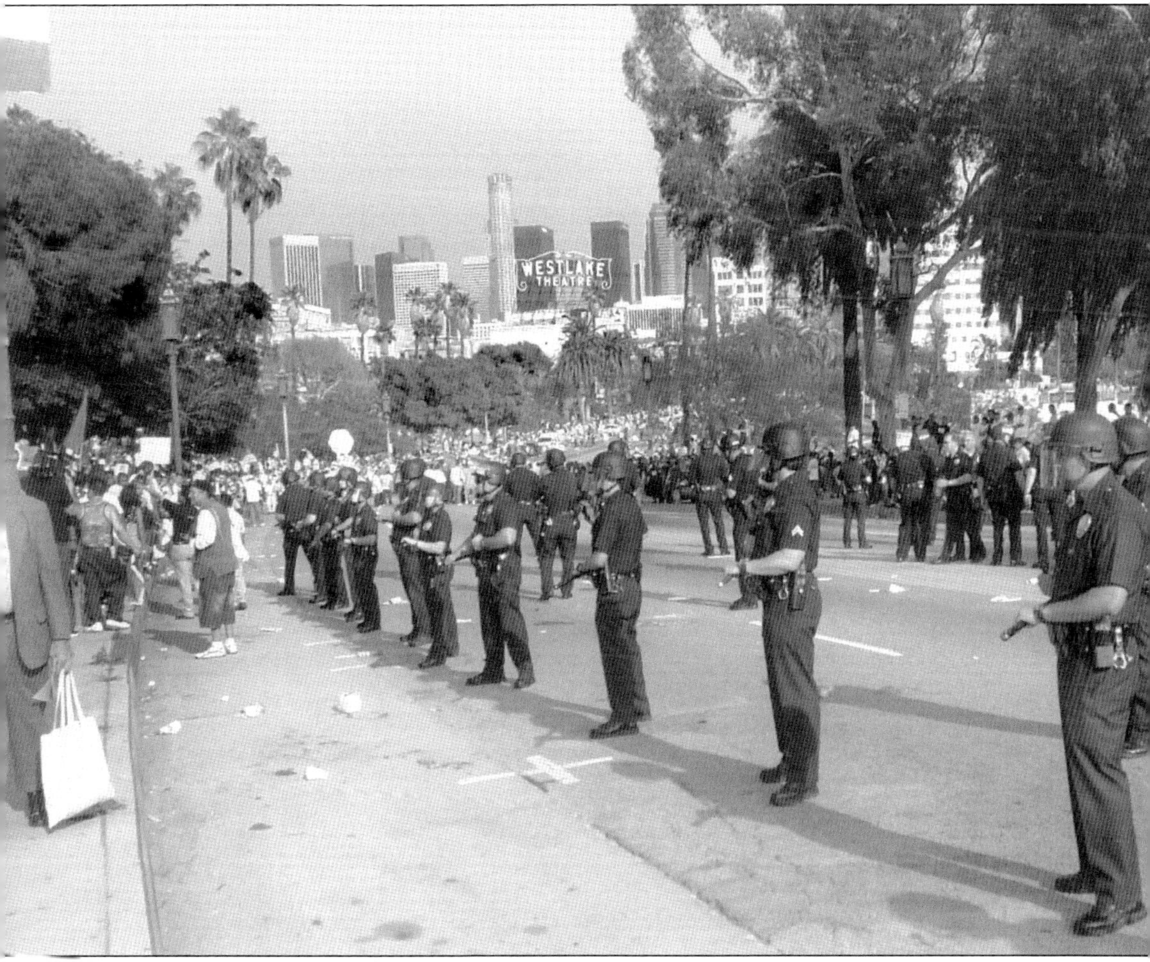

On May 1, 2007, the May Day rally at MacArthur Park became one of the most violent episodes in the history of political discourse within the park. Police reacted with heavy force in order to disperse the large crowd. According to police, some people began throwing bottles and rocks at officers. The LAPD attacked the crowd with batons and rubber bullets in a manner later found by the LAPD's own investigation to be excessive. After an extensive internal review, Chief William Bratton apologized; 17 officers faced penalties; and the city paid more than $13 million in damages. (Courtesy of Independent Media, Inc.)

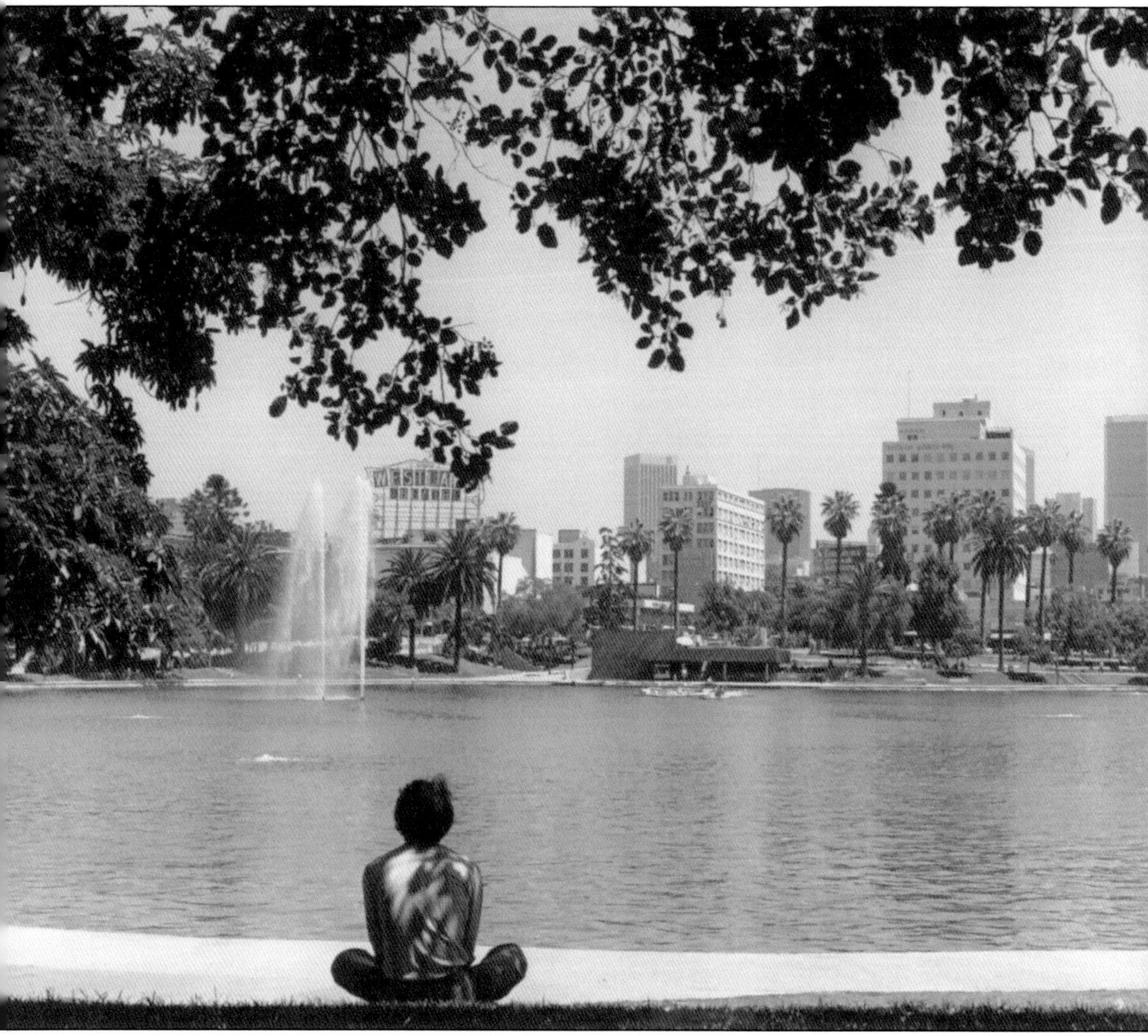

After more than a century of boating, floating miniature yachts, the pomp and circumstance of concerts, romantic carriage rides, chess playing, artistic creation, photograph taking, rallies, protests, and mock elections, sometimes the most democratic action that can occur in MacArthur Park is the simple act of contemplation. In the middle of a busy park that sits in the center of a crowded city, a young man possibly imagines the future. (Courtesy of the Los Angeles Public Library Photo Collection.)

Six

IMAGINATION OF THE PARK

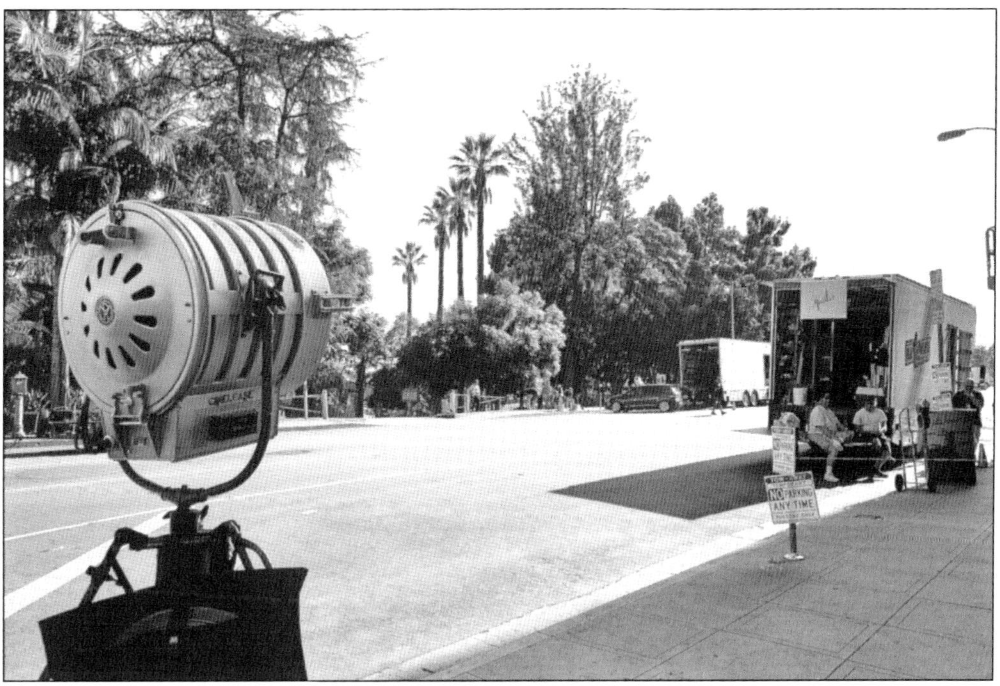

MacArthur Park fires up the imagination. It inspires writers, painters, filmmakers, architects, and, of course, children and adults alike. They find their muses within the landscape, amongst the nostalgic design of the park's architecture, or through the sights and sounds of people at play and prayer. The call for "Lights, Camera, Create" is part of the sound track of MacArthur Park. (Courtesy of Meeno.)

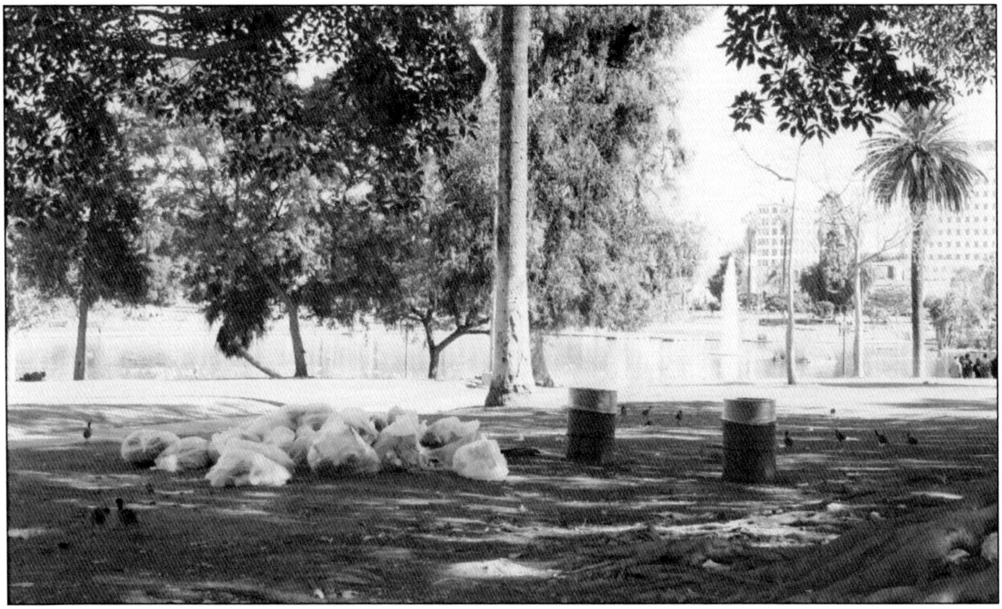

Westlake Park
"Twas twilight on the Sabbath Day,
The hour 'twixt dusk and dark:
Softly the evening shadows lay
O'er peaceful Westlake Park.
I saw tall trees in solemn rows
Their last obeisance make;
A picture of the divine repose
Was mirrored in the lake.
But through the shrubs and shady bowers
By lawns and grassy leas,
On winding walks and beds of flowers
And underneath the trees
Of stately gum and graceful ash
And all about the lake
Was such a hash of littered trash
As only man can make.
To show how human nature keeps
a pleasant holiday,
Were newspapers in shabby heaps
Left tumbled where they lay;
Torn, greasy bags and stubs and fags
And bottles dropped ker-flunk!
And peel and rind of every kind
And miscellaneous junk.
O prospect on so fair a plan
For higher joys designed;
Where beauty, since the world began,
Was ne'er more fltly shrined,
Look up, ye lower beasts, and mark
How only God-like man
Would turn a noble public park
Into a garbage can!

In June 1923, Harry Bowling posted in the *Los Angeles Times* a poem titled "Westlake Park." Note the "hash of littered trash" pictured here. (Above, author's collection.)

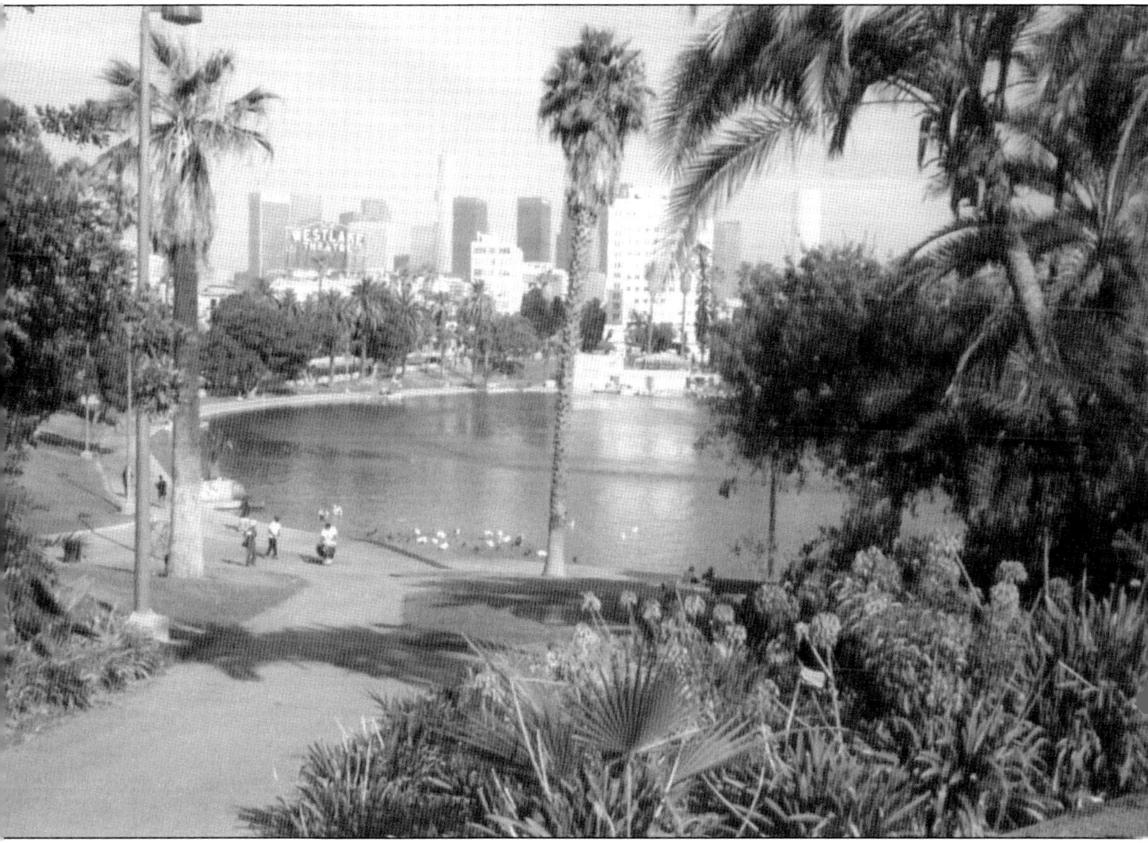

Here is a photograph reflective of the more pleasant lines in Harry Bowling's poem: "I saw tall trees in solemn rows / Their last obeisance make; / A picture of the divine repose / Was mirrored in the lake." (Author's collection.)

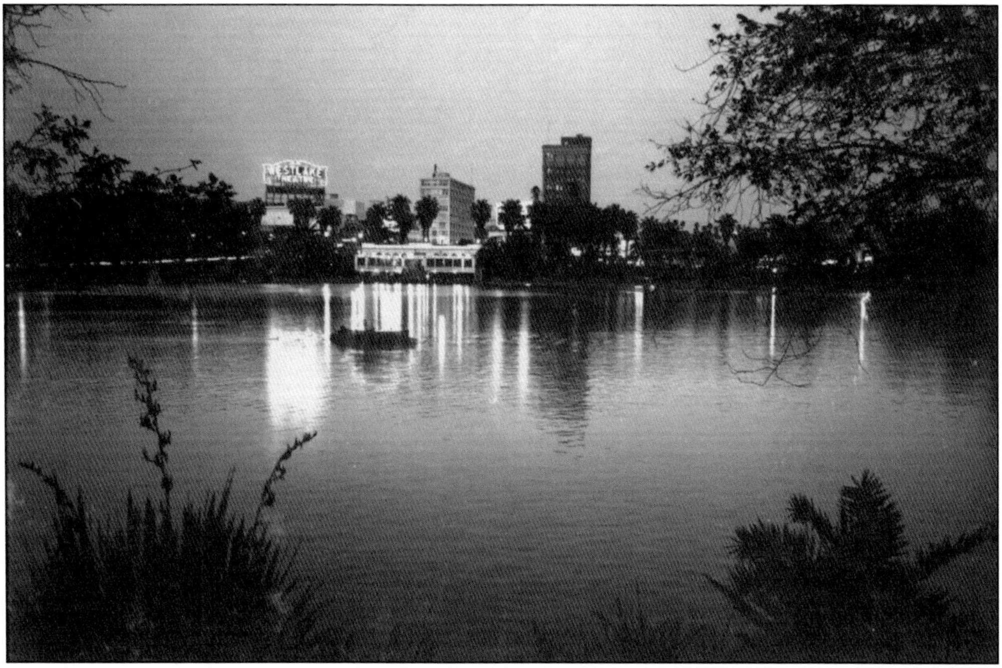

Westlake Park at Night
The lurid city-lights,
Reflected across the water,
Shimmer and dance,
Softened and lovely.
The harsh city noises
Are subdued to a murmur,
As they drift over the lake.
The pipe of a bird,
Sudden splash of a fish,
The croak of a frog,
Deny the city.
My city-thoughts steal away,
Greeds, lusts, and hatreds,
Dissolve under the spell of the lake.
Here, under the stars,
Like a faint perfume on the night breeze,
Is Peace,
And the old, forgotten thought of God.

"Westlake Park at Night" was penned by Laurence Faulkner Hawkins. This image accompanies the poem splendidly; note how the lights "shimmer and dance." (Both, courtesy of the Los Angeles Public Library Photo Collection.)

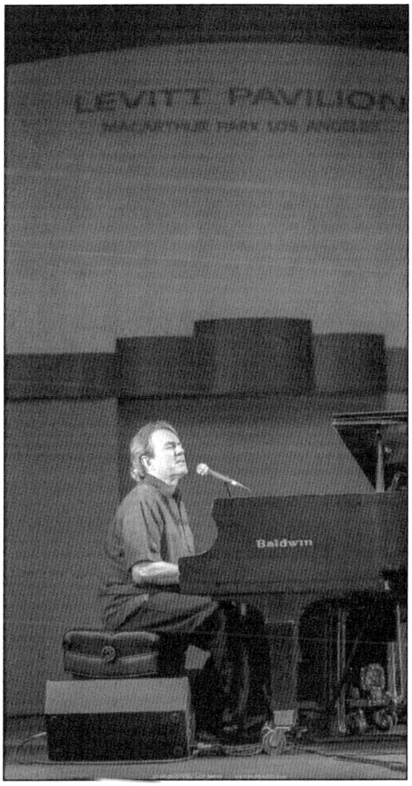

Jimmy Webb and Adrian Drover wrote in the late 1960s what are perhaps the most-recognized lyrics related to MacArthur Park. According to Webb, he drew inspiration for the song while visiting the park with his girlfriend during her lunch hour. (Above, courtesy of Levitt Pavilion MacArthur Park.)

MacArthur Park
Spring was never waiting for us, girl
It ran one step ahead
As we followed in the dance

Between the parted pages and were pressed
In love's hot, fevered iron
Like a striped pair of pants

MacArthur's Park is melting in the dark
All the sweet, green icing flowing down
Someone left the cake out in the rain
I don't think that I can take it
'Cause it took so long to bake it
And I'll never have that recipe again, oh noooooo

I recall the yellow cotton dress
Foaming like a wave
On the ground around your knees
Birds like tender babies in your hands
And the old men playing checkers, by the trees

MacArthur's Park is melting in the dark
All the sweet, green icing flowing down
Someone left the cake out in the rain
I don't think that I can take it
'Cause it took so long to bake it
And I'll never have that recipe again, oh noooooo

There would be another song for me
For I will sing it
There would be another dream for me
Someone will bring it

I will drink the wine while it is warm
And never let you catch me looking at the sun
And after all the loves of my life
After all the loves of my life, you'll still be the one

I will take my life into my hands and I will use it
I will win the worship in their eyes and I will lose it
I will have the things that I desire
And my passion flow like rivers through the sky

And after all the loves of my life
Oh, after all the loves of my life
I'll be thinking of you - and wondering why

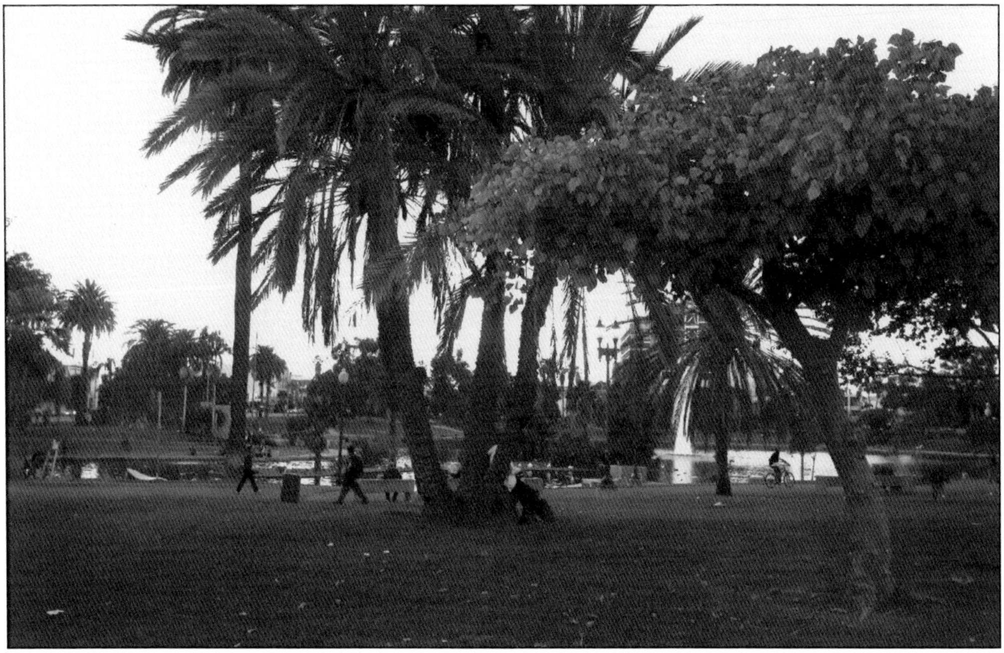

Author Hector Tobar writes in his novel *Tattooed Soldier* the following passage regarding the park: "After some gentle persuasion, Jose Juan agreed. They dusted themselves off and headed for MacArthur Park, where all the other Guatemaltecos and Salvadorenos and Mexicanos went, a little Parque Central almost like the ones back home." (Author's collection.)

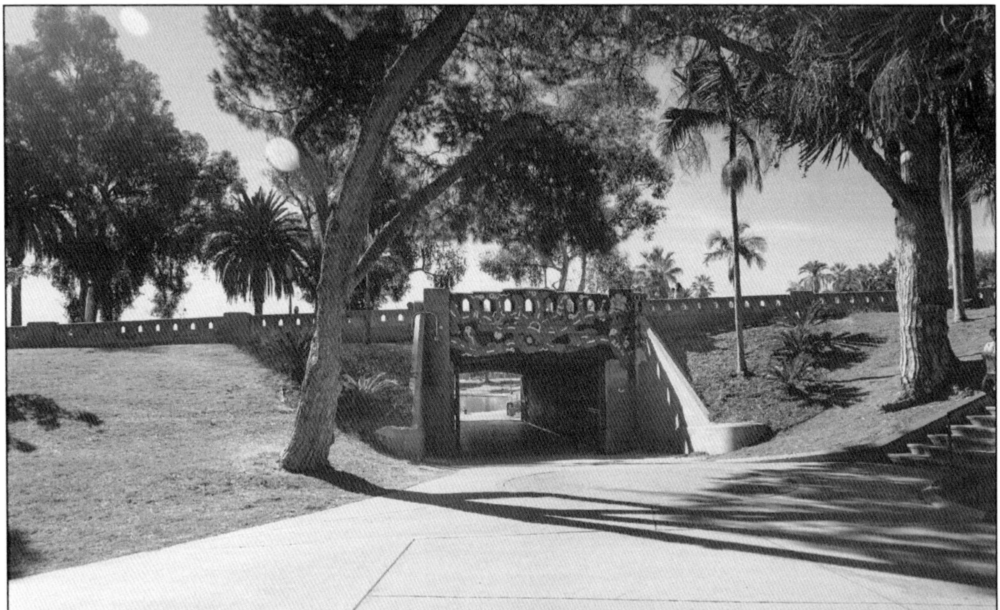

In his novel *This Wicked World*, author Richard Lange captures the dark underside of the park: "He sat up on the bench in MacArthur Park, and the pain that roared through him drove tears into his eyes. His arms, his legs–there was no part of his body that didn't hurt. He was full of liquid fire that burned him from the inside out." (Courtesy of Meeno.)

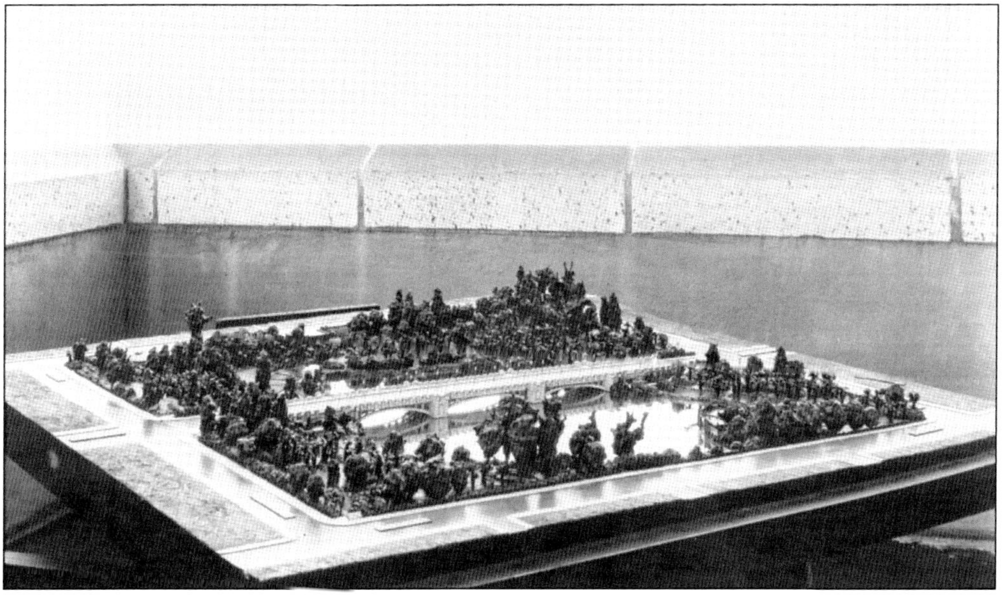

In anticipation of the public discussion about the proposed Wilshire Viaduct, city engineers commissioned the construction of a model that would depict a "roadway bridge" across Westlake Park. City officials estimated the cost of the bridge to be somewhere between $1.5 million to $2 million, four times more expensive then the proposed viaduct option. The bridge model was designed in the style of similarly envisioned bridges that were under consideration or were already under construction spanning the Los Angeles River. (Courtesy of the City of Los Angeles Archives.)

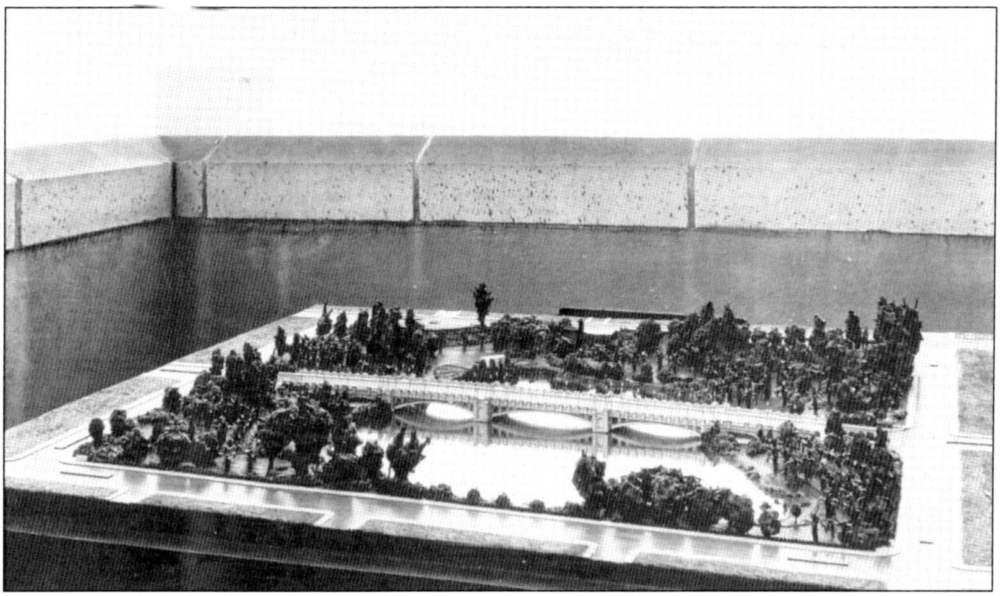

But the bridge option across the park had its critics. One local engineer opined that the bridge would essentially overwhelm the scale of the park and lake, arguing that the width of the park did not justify the construction of the bridge. The city's planning department was more succinct in its opinion of the bridge option: "This park is not of sufficient size to construct drives and still maintain its present character." The bridge option never received serious consideration, and the fate of the bridge model is unknown. (Courtesy of the City of Los Angeles Archives.)

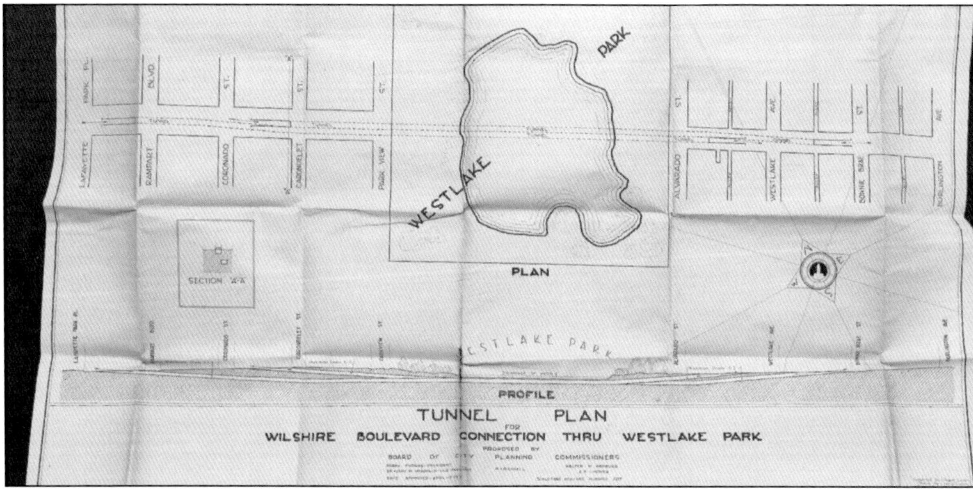

Of the four original options that were presented relative to completing the viaduct, the most expensive option was the Wilshire Tunnel alternative, at $2.5 million. This option was also the ideal choice of the city's planning department. In a multipage letter to the city council, the planning department staff wrote that "the tunnel method is the only one that would not be detrimental to the recreation of the public." This layout plan from 1931 even shows a profile of the depth of the tunnels. (Courtesy of the City of Los Angeles Archives.)

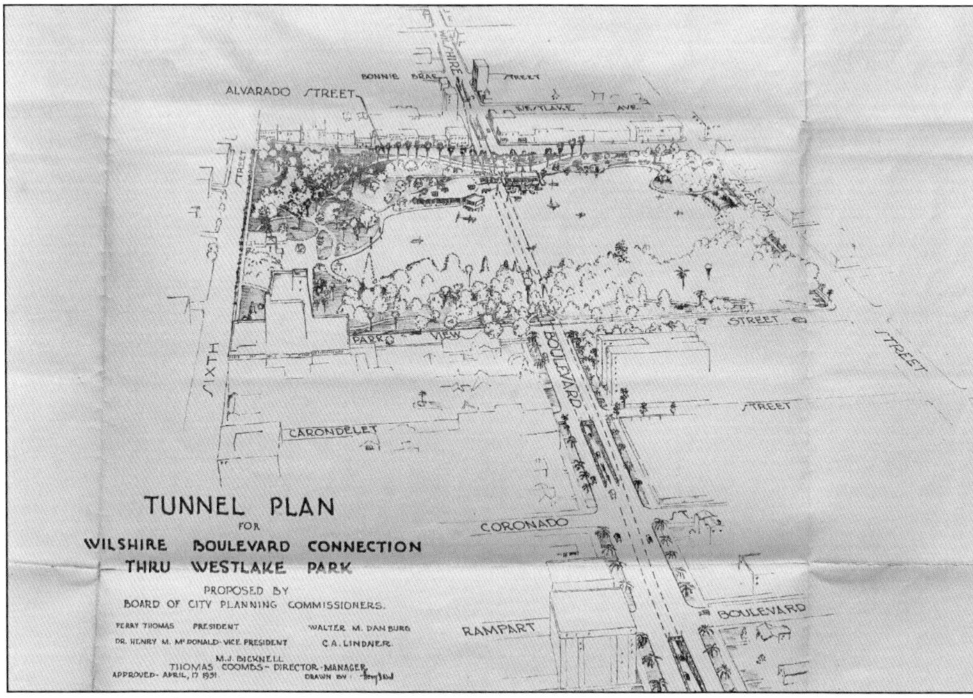

This rendering clearly shows the ingress and egress points for the tunnels that would have traversed under the park. Although the board of city planning commissioners "respectfully requested that the tunnel plan be given serious and definite consideration," the option was quickly dismissed as too expensive and would have required a longer time frame for construction. Thus, the roadway option at-grade emerged as the most viable, if least environmentally adequate, alternative for the Wilshire Viaduct. (Courtesy of the City of Los Angeles Archives.)

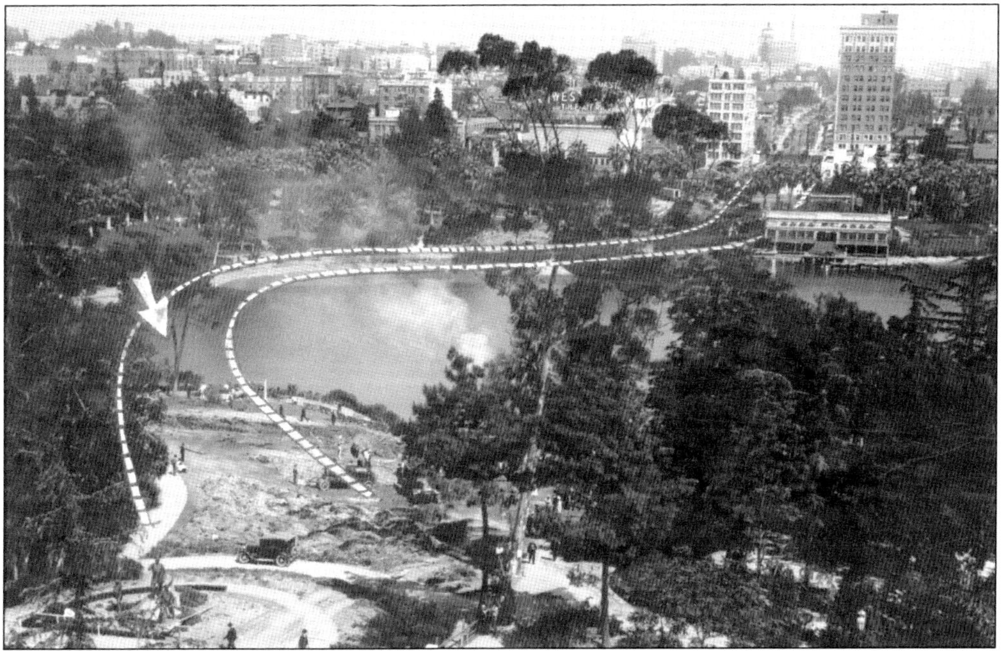

In this view looking eastward, city engineers prepared this somewhat exaggerated version of the already-approved roadway across the park. It is still unclear why the roadway designers chose to include the curvature for the street. One neighborhood old-timer communicated to the author that the roadway designers wanted to mimic a "European parkway" to mitigate the criticism of building a street across the park. (Courtesy of the Los Angeles Public Library Photo Collection.)

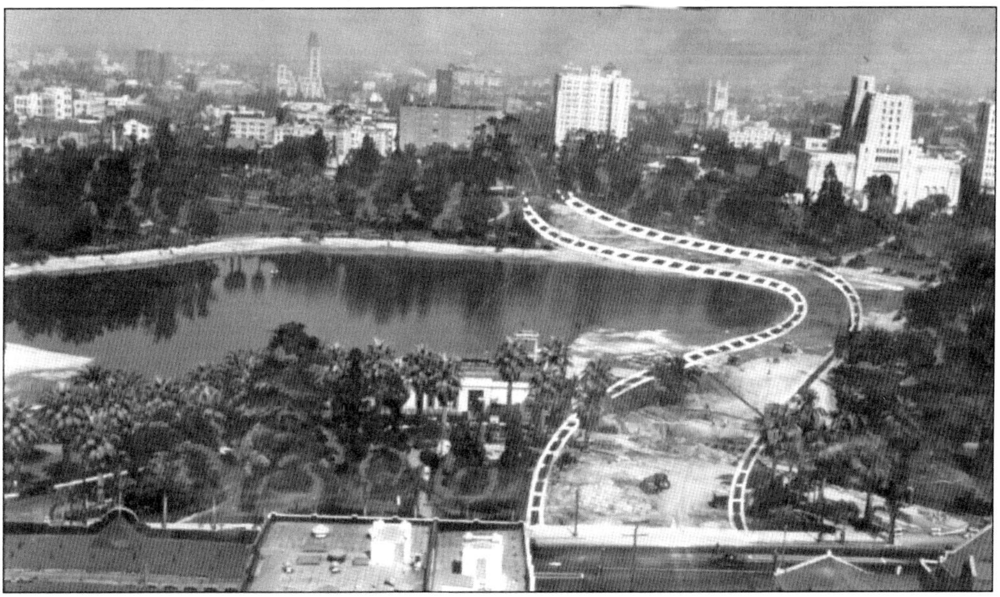

In this view looking westward, the same effect was created for the viaduct. In this photograph, the draining of the lake that was initiated as soon as the viaduct was approved is noticeable. Although much care was taken to ensure that the lagoon would remain, the miniature lake soon disappeared and was replaced with a grassy knoll that frequently needed maintenance due to the high water table. (Courtesy of the Los Angeles Public Library Photo Collection.)

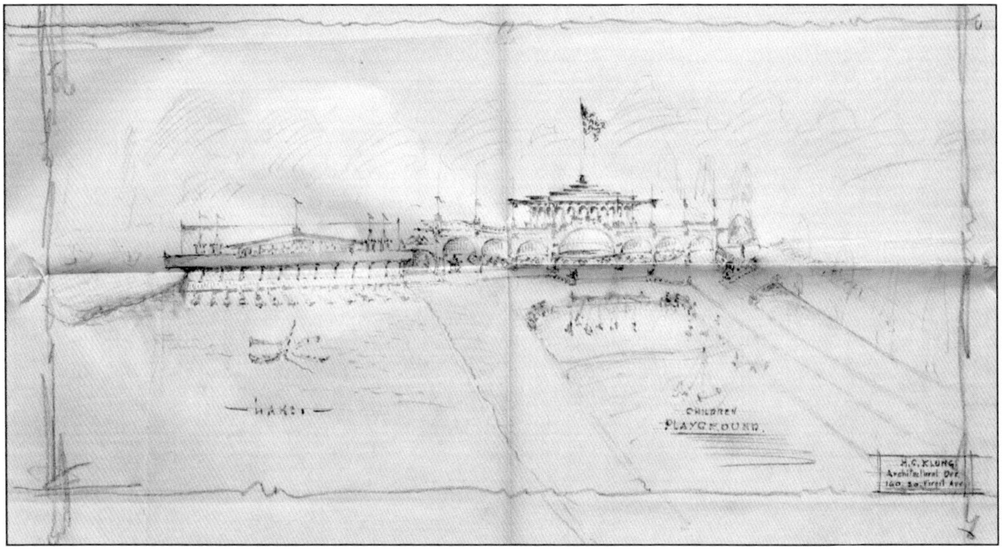

In the mid-1910s, local boosters proposed building this children's playground within a larger carousel complex inside Westlake Park. In a letter to the park commission, the applicants for the contract state, "There is no question but what clean amusements help to make a clean neighborhood." The proposal never went beyond this rough sketch of the project; the auxiliary playground was never built due to community opposition. (Courtesy of the City of Los Angeles Archives.)

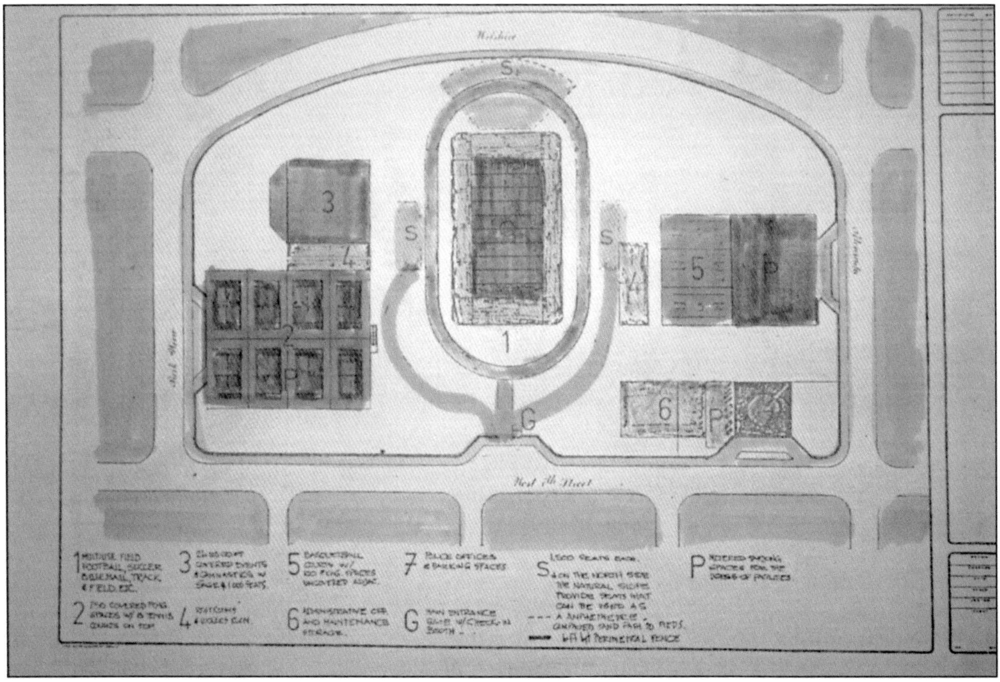

In the 1990s, a local property owner proposed a much more radical solution to the ongoing crime and delinquency problem plaguing the park at the time. He proposed filling in the lake and converting the entire southern side of the park into an active recreation area with soccer fields and basketball courts. Although never formally proposed, the plan would have surely entailed a long discussion with local park preservationists. (Courtesy of Daniel Berdakin.)

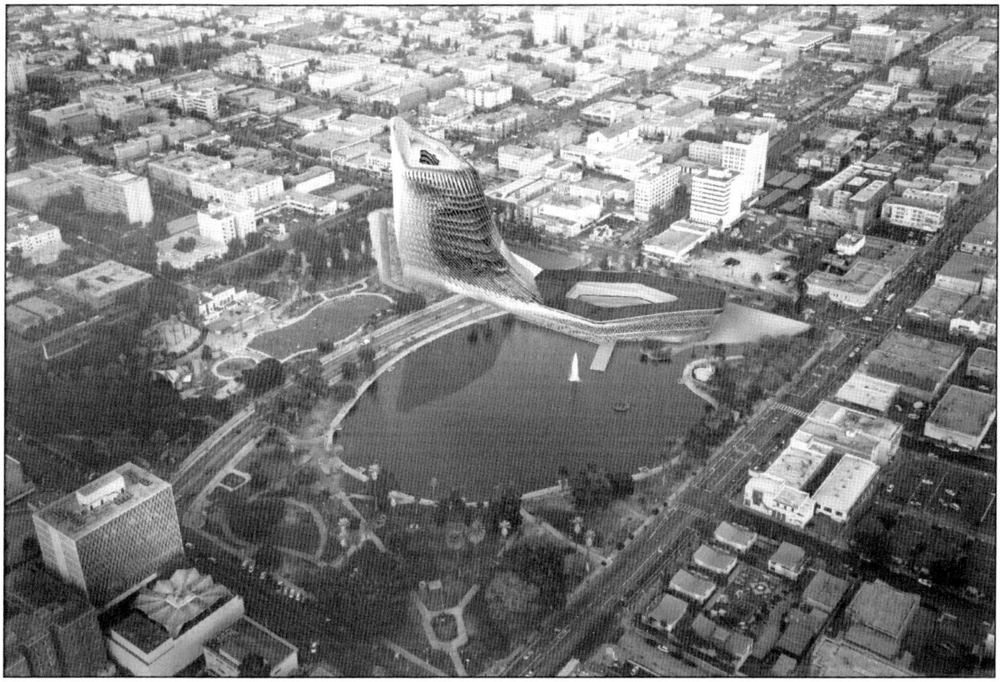

In the new century, as the park and the neighborhood were in clear ascent into some type of economic recovery, a local architect envisioned a "gastropolis" for one section of MacArthur Park. As one can see in this computer rendering (something unavailable to earlier dreamers of the park), the thoroughly modernistic mega-complex would have brought a science fiction vision to a 19th-century setting. (Courtesy of Allthatissolid and Noe Montes.)

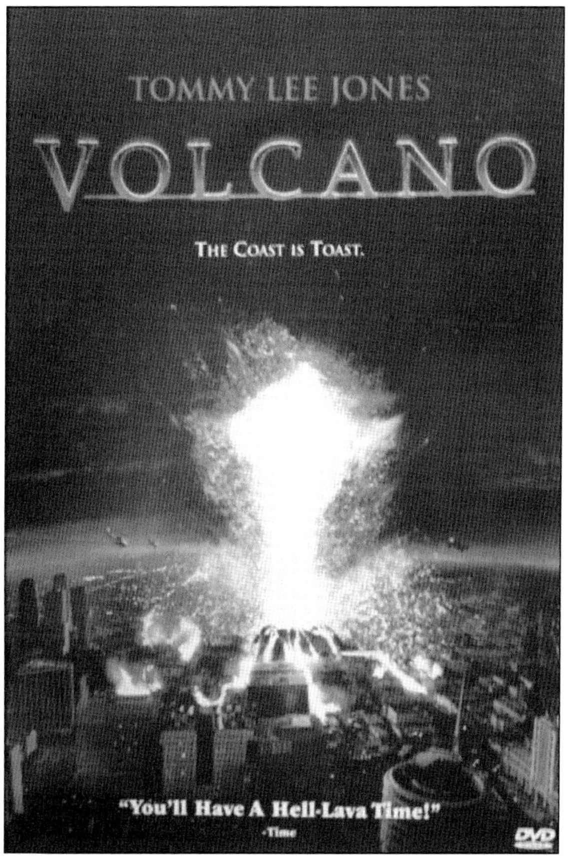

Hollywood with its movies and television output has played a key role in imagining and reimagining MacArthur Park into fictional and sometimes realistic settings. One of the more ironic depictions is from the 1997 movie *Volcano*. In the film, as lava pours down Wilshire Boulevard, MacArthur Park becomes a refugee camp for residents fleeing the impending disaster. Homeless camps were a very real issue in the park at this time. (Courtesy of 20th Century Fox.)

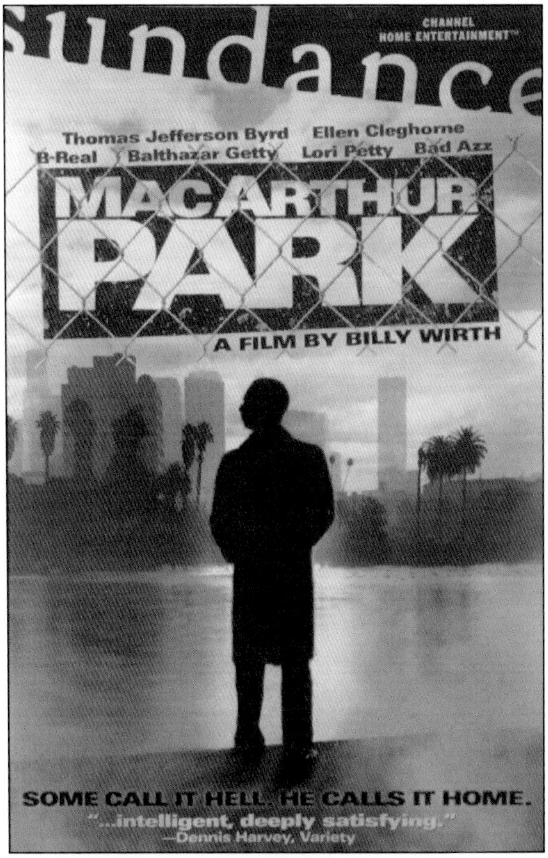

A more gritty depiction of the eponymous park appears in the 2001 movie *MacArthur Park*. The movie was not a critical success, but it gained notoriety for its realistic take on the surrounding environment. The park was still a hotbed of uncontrolled criminal activity around this time. (Courtesy of Sundance Studios.)

Perhaps the most important image-makers who have plied their wares inside the park have been the Polaroid photographers. Their story was beautifully documented by Esmeralda Bermudez in a *Los Angeles Times* article that artfully describes their nostalgic saga and slow departure from the park. Over the last five decades, they have visually captured via Polaroid shots countless scenes of children and families at play while visiting MacArthur Park. For many of these immigrant families, this is their first photograph in the new city and perhaps the first photograph that their families back home in the old country will see of their father, mother, son, or daughter. (Courtesy of Brian Vanderburg, 2010, *Los Angeles Times*.)

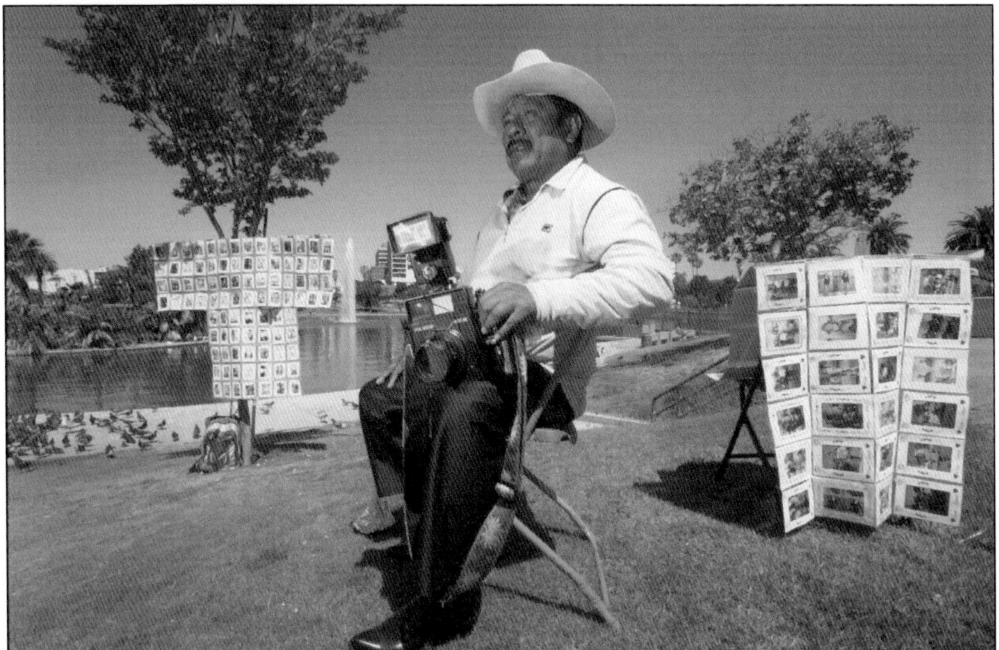

Seven

The Revitalization of the Park

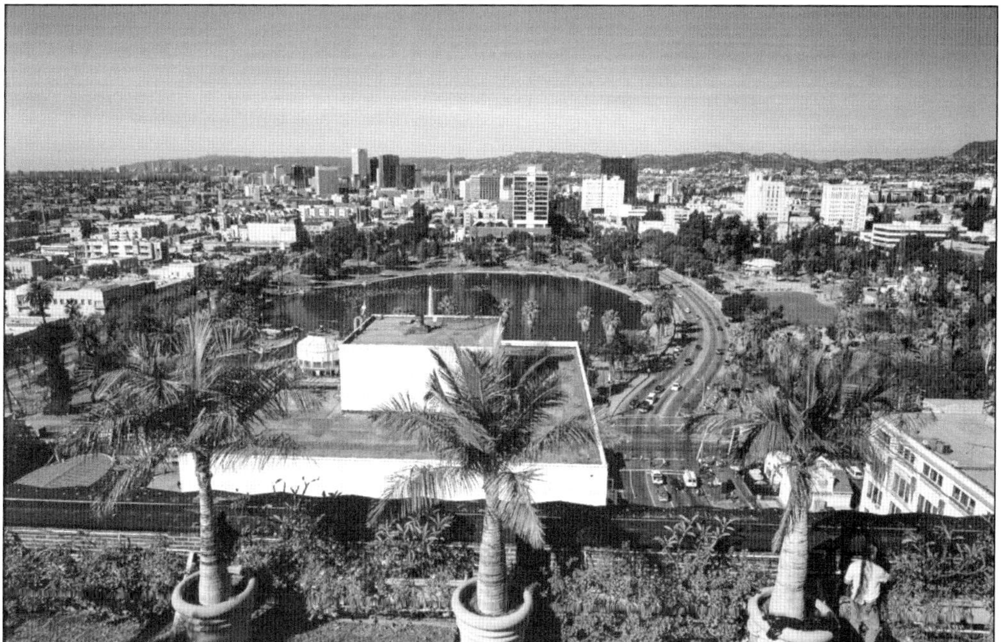

In a re-creation of an earlier photograph from the 1930s, MacArthur Park continues today as an urban oasis, flawed but still delivering the promises made by the founders—of providing respite in a crowded city. The revitalization of MacArthur Park cannot be described as a revolution in change, but rather a series of incremental reforms that have brought back public investment into the park's infrastructure. The first signals of reform occurred in the 1980s, when local property owners and artists, under the leadership of Adolfo Nodal from the Otis Arts Institute, initiated a series of public meetings to better understand the public's priorities for the park. (Courtesy of Meeno.)

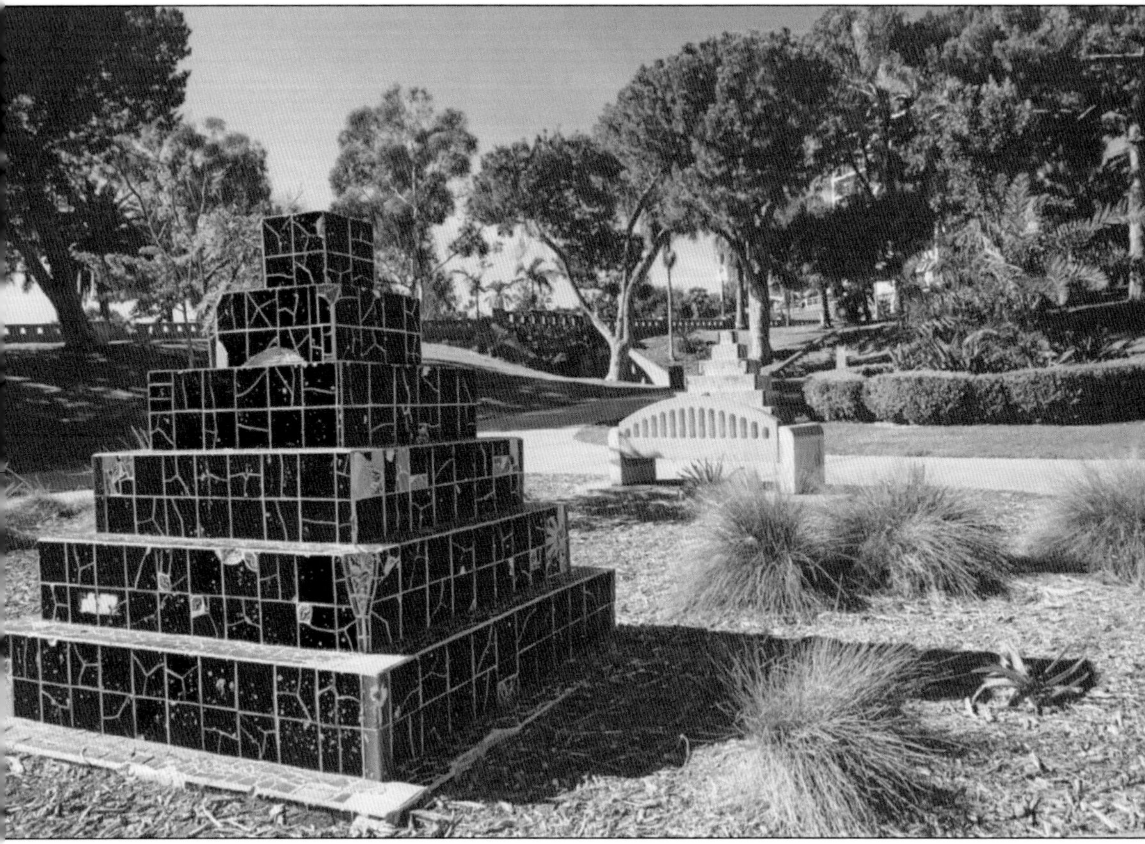

Named the MacArthur Park Public Art Program, the movement's main goal was to create "meaningful art and design, sensitive to both its multi-cultural community and its time." The initiative reflected the belief that "artists can be leaders in community revitalization." Situated adjacent to the band shell in the north side of the park, Judy Simonian's *Talking Pyramids* is representative of the program's objective. (Courtesy of Meeno.)

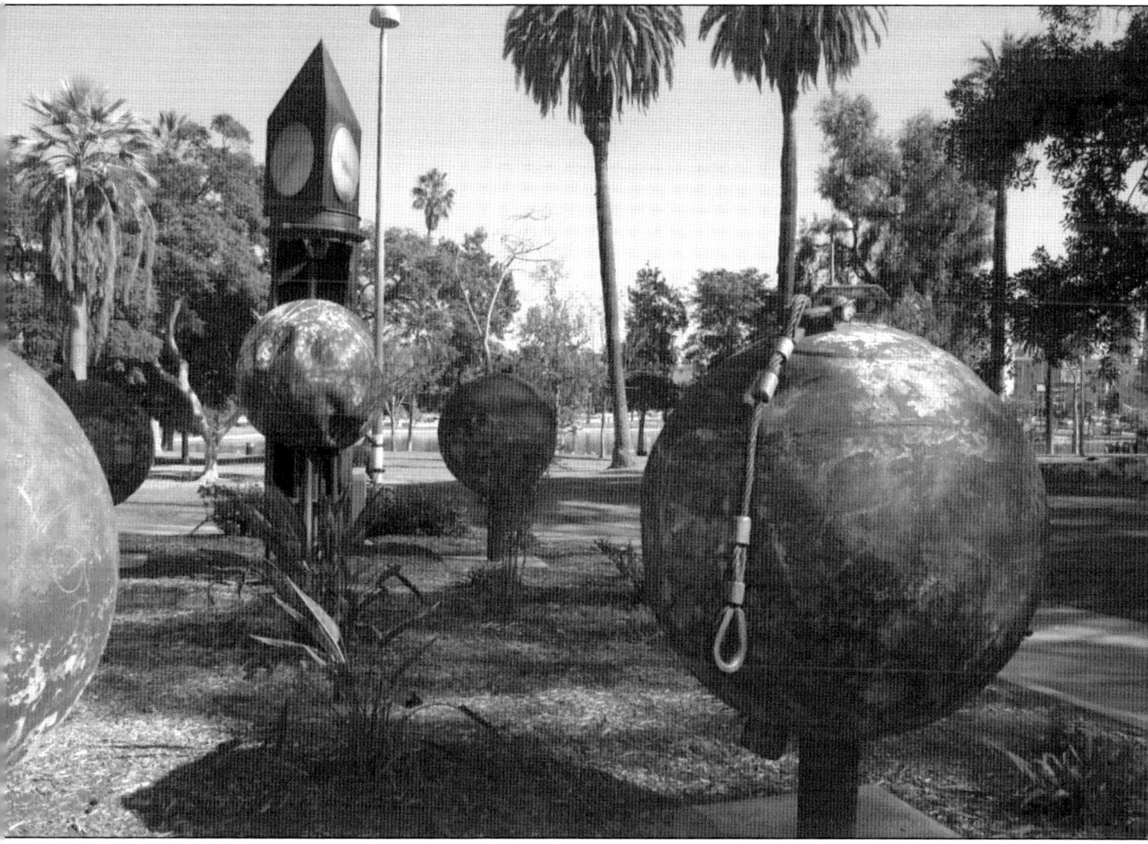

By all accounts, the introduction of the arts and culture in a structured fashion had a significant impact on the quality of experience for visitors to the park and local residents. Near the entrance to the park at Seventh and Park View Streets, George Herms created his art piece *Clocktower: A Monument to the Unknown*, which galvanized community participation in the creation of the sculpture. (Author's collection.)

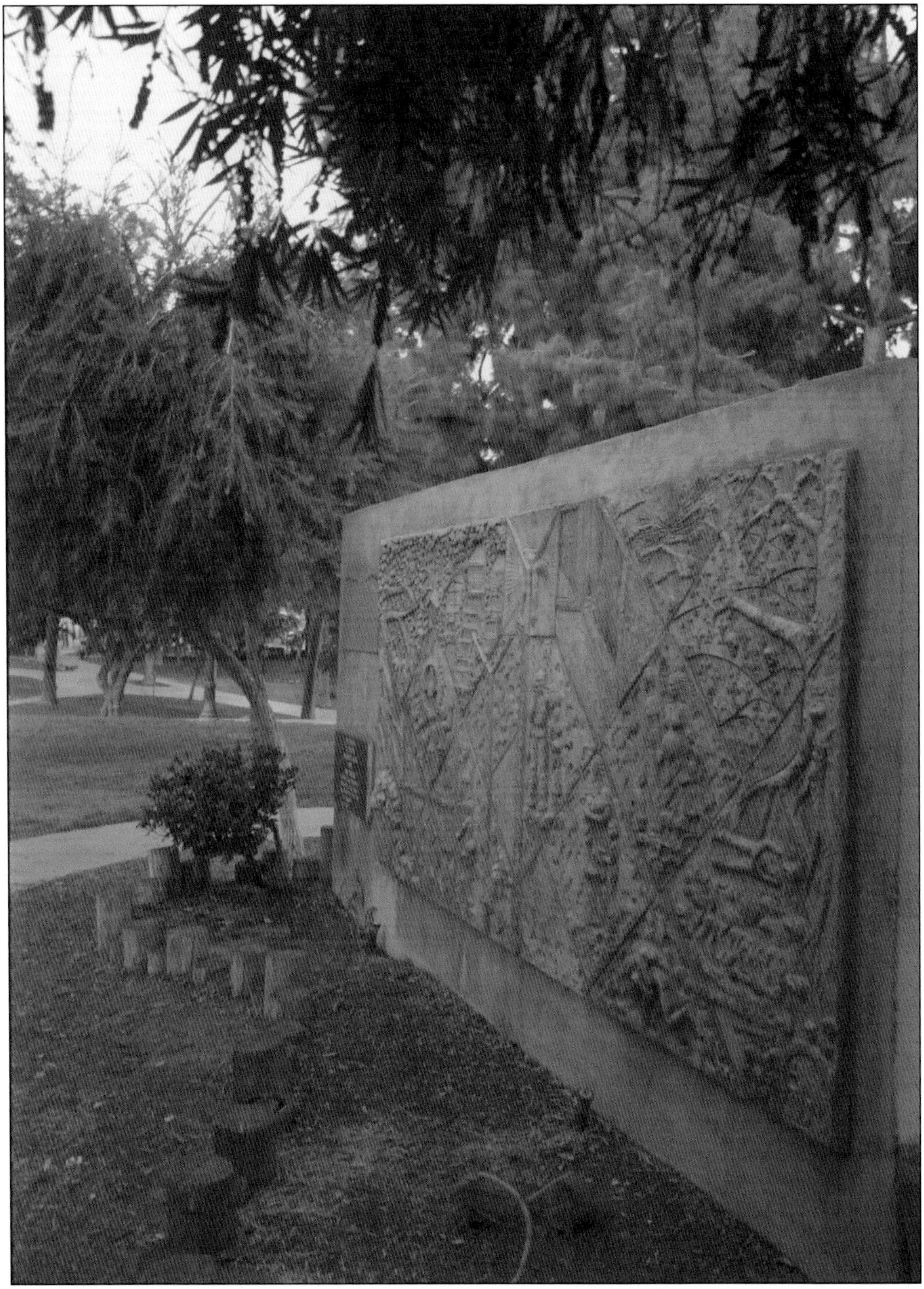

With the large presence of the Central American community in the Westlake neighborhood and the critical role that the park played as a site for political organizing, local immigrant rights activists organized the creation of the Memorial to the Immigrant located near the intersection of Wilshire Boulevard and Park View Street to commemorate the "struggles of the immigrant" in Los Angeles. (Author's collection.)

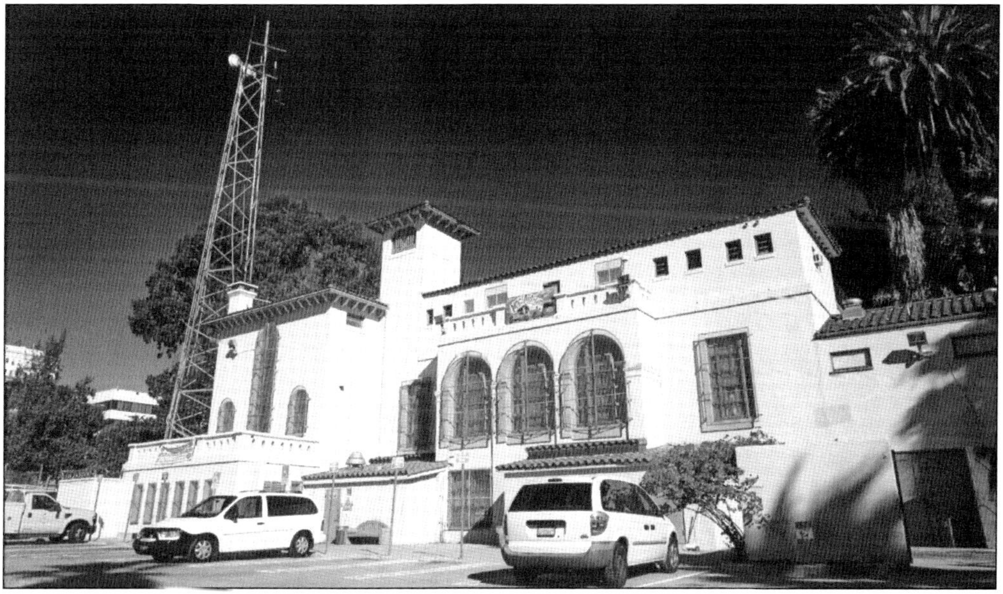

By the 1990s, the city's department of recreation and parks had taken over the operation of the Signal Building from the fire department. Soon after, work began to restore two of the three floors to bring back youth and senior programming to the park. Today, the building's exterior awaits restoration to reconnect with the park and its users. (Courtesy of Meeno.)

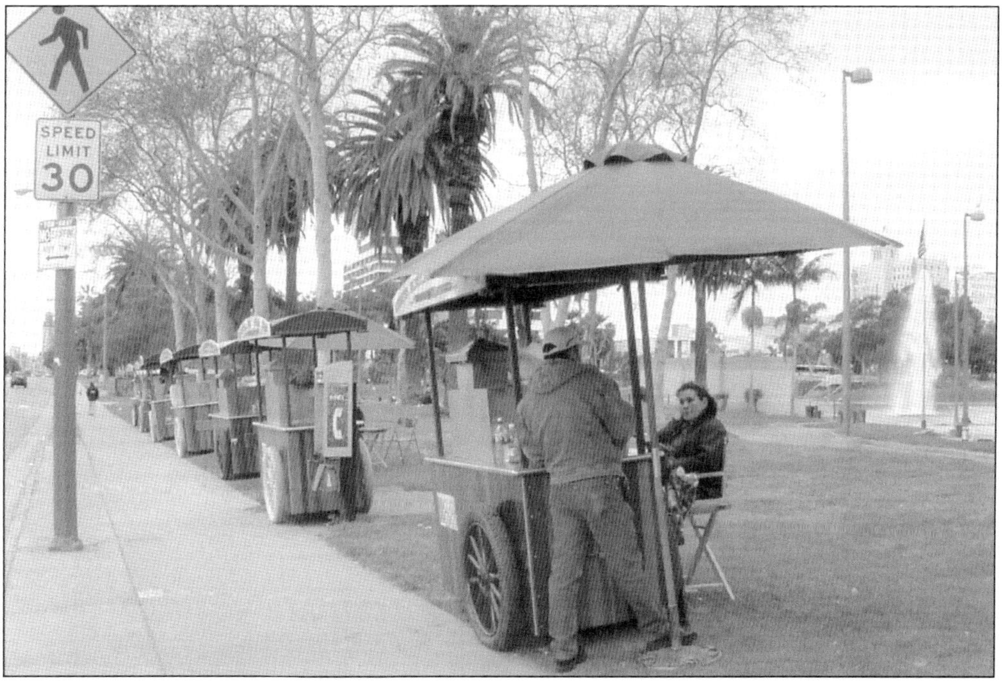

During the same decade, local leaders, recognizing that the neighborhood needed revitalization as well in order for the park to succeed, initiated an effort to legalize street vending in and around MacArthur Park. By 1999, community leaders celebrated the first street-vending district in the entire city. Through the district, 48 street vendors were permitted to sell along the Alvarado Street and Seventh Street perimeters of the park. (Courtesy of LA Commons.)

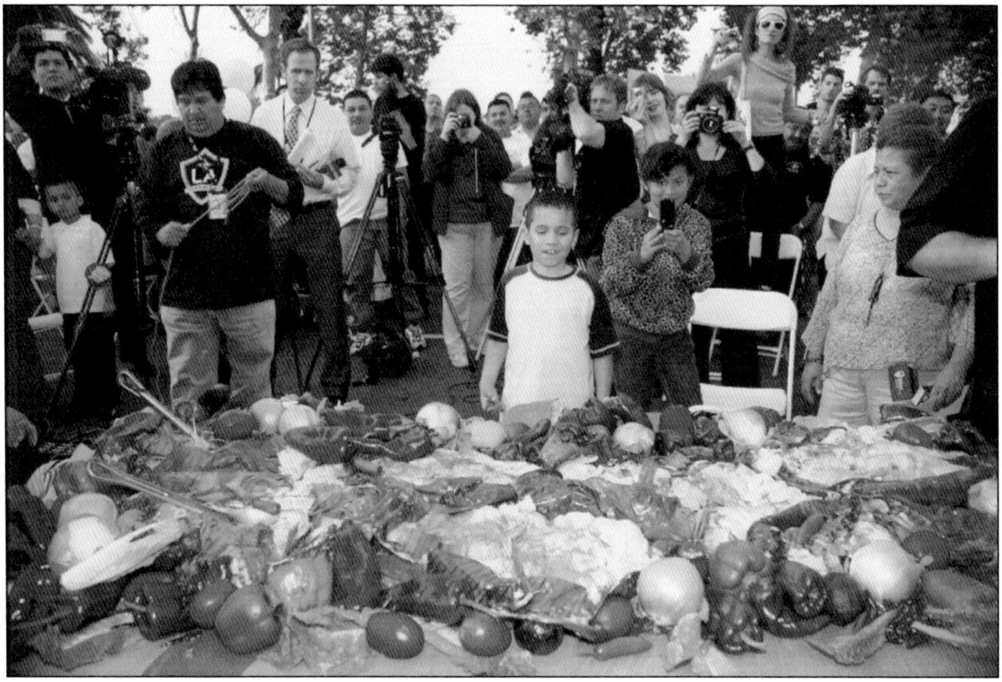

As an offshoot of the street-vending district, program coordinators created Mama's Hot Tamales on Seventh Street, a sit-down restaurant that showcased dozens of types of tamales. This restaurant quickly became a landmark, hosting special events and other culinary activities. One of the special events was the annual Tamal de la Paz (Tamale of Peace). (Courtesy of Mama's Hot Tamales.)

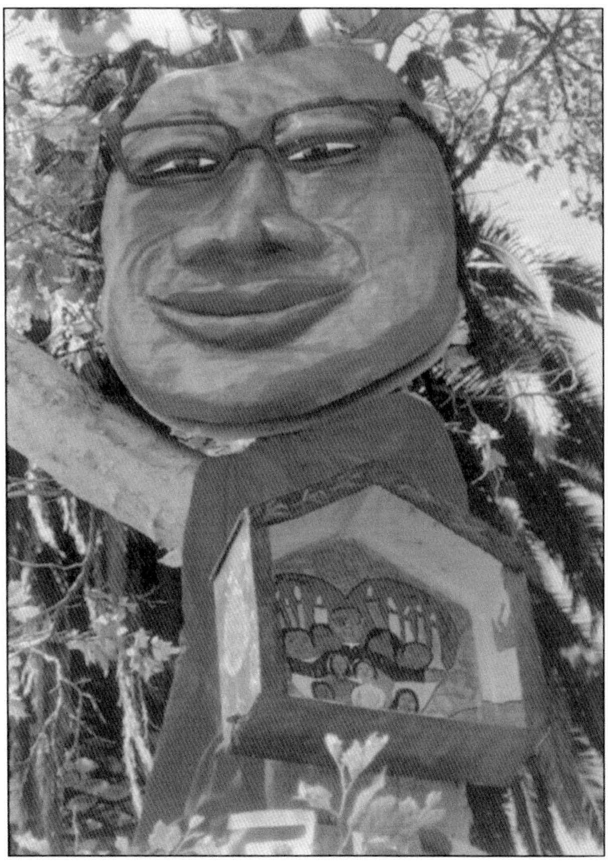

As a continuation to the arts and culture theme that started in the 1980s, the community-based LA Commons sponsored a series of artworks inside MacArthur Park to encourage place-making activities for local residents. Working with local youth, program organizers created outsized masks that were hung from trees throughout the park. Other activities included educational workshops and informational tours. (Courtesy of LA Commons.)

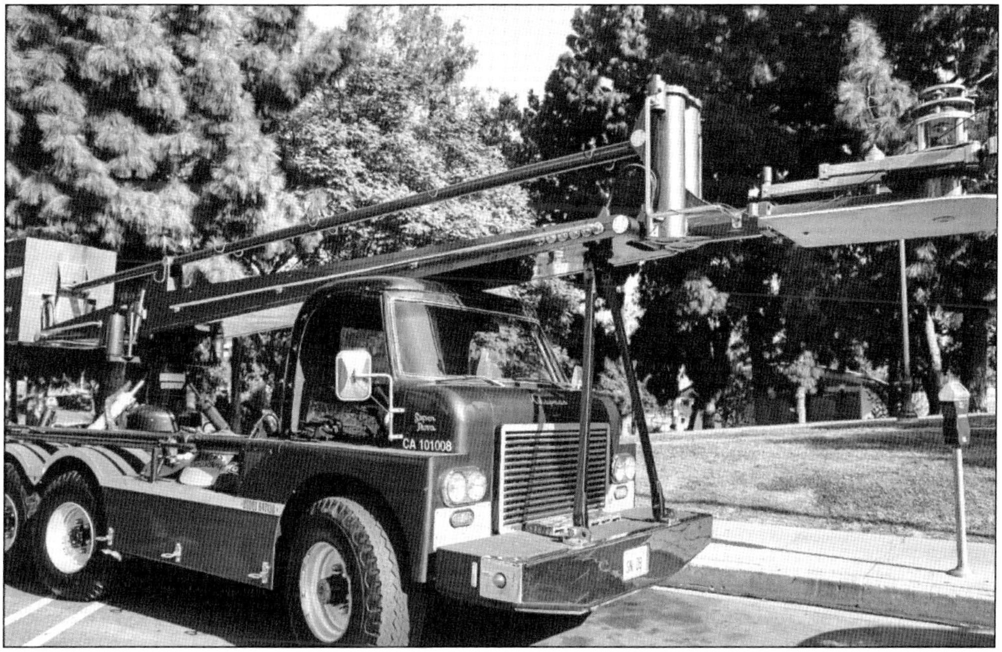

As described earlier, Hollywood and its moviemaking machine have been inspired by the daily realities of MacArthur Park. But it is also important to recognize that this creative activity has contributed to the revitalization of the park and local landmarks like the Park Plaza and the Bryson Apartment House. Park Plaza is so popular as a movie set that Park View Street is frequently closed to accommodate movie production equipment. (Courtesy of Meeno.)

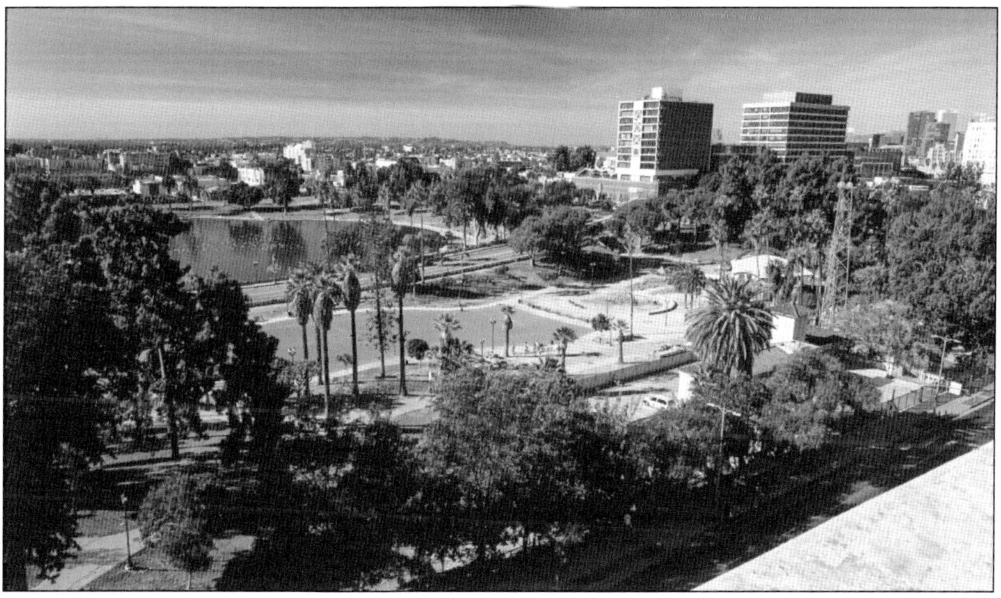

By far, it was the north end of MacArthur Park, seen here in the lower portion of the photograph, that received the lion's share of public investment during the last 10 years. The improvements included a new synthetic turf meadow, period lighting, a restored band shell, and a new children's play area. Although the park maintained its passive designation, it was clear that active recreation had returned to the natural area. (Author's collection.)

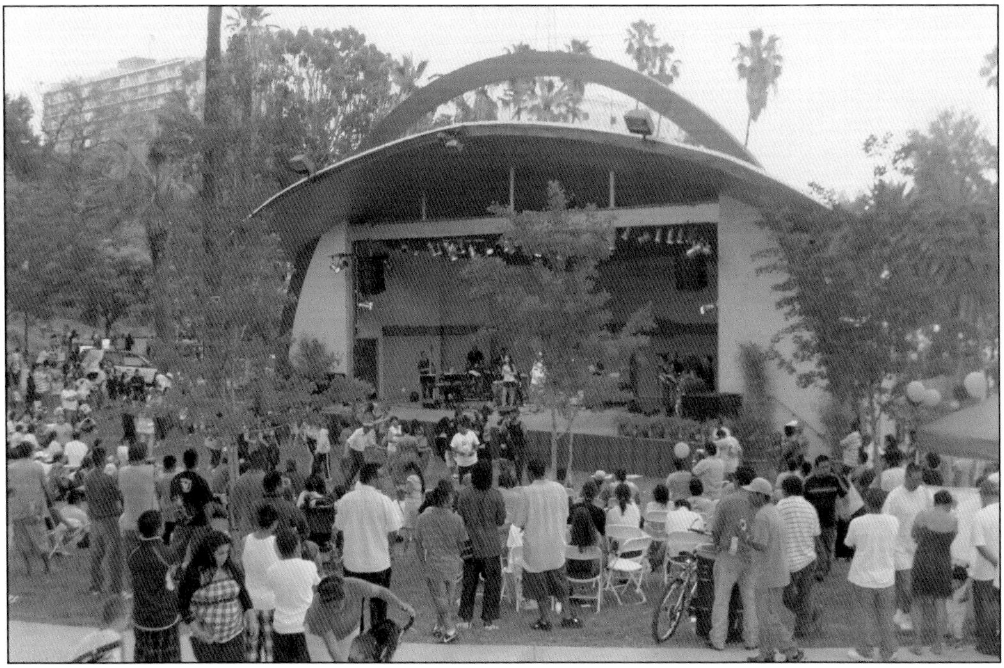

In 2005, the Mortimer Levitt Foundation, led by Elizabeth Hirsch and the City of Los Angeles, provided funding for the full restoration of the band shell as well as supporting a summer concert series organized by the foundation. The concert series has been an overwhelming success in bringing to the park top-quality, multicultural, and multi-genre musical performers. Thousands have attended the concerts over the years. (Courtesy of Tony Perez.)

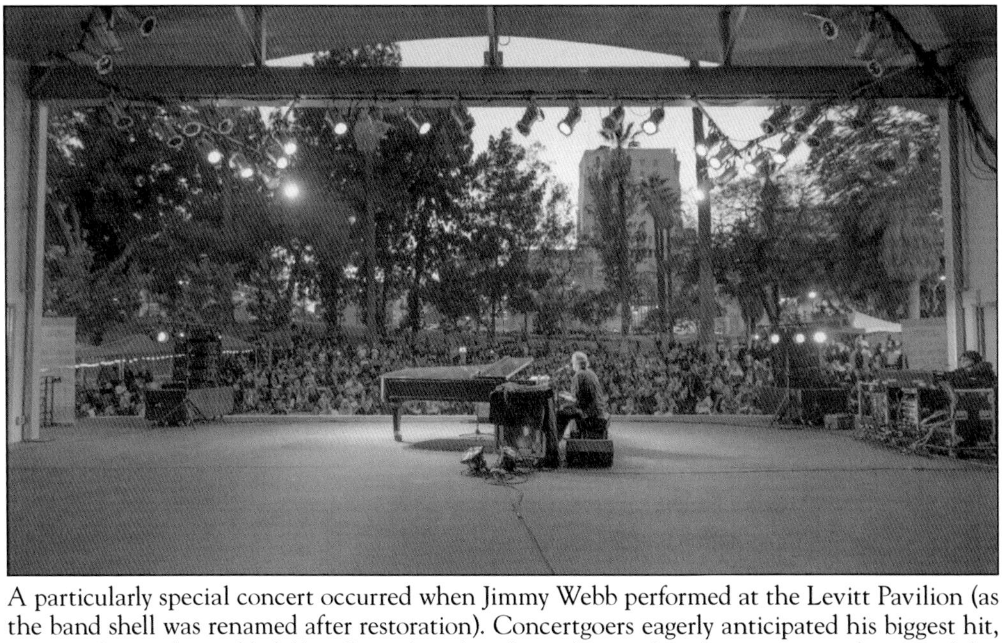

A particularly special concert occurred when Jimmy Webb performed at the Levitt Pavilion (as the band shell was renamed after restoration). Concertgoers eagerly anticipated his biggest hit, "MacArthur Park." Webb did briefly explain that the park was a favorite spot to spend time with his girlfriend during her lunch hour, but he never expounded on the meaning of the song's lyrics. The "sweet, green icing flowing down" will continue to intrigue his fans. (Courtesy of Tony Perez.)

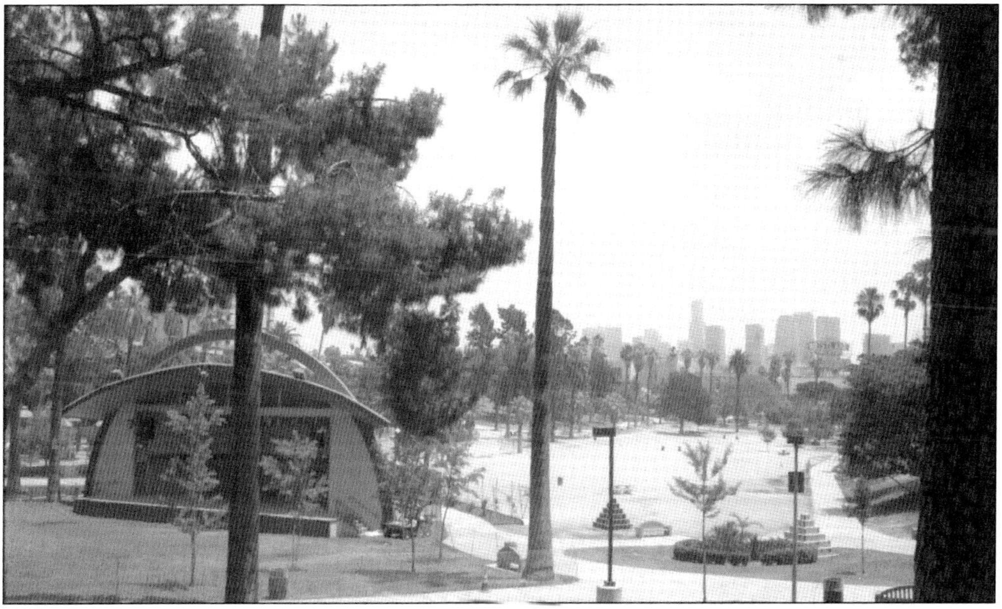

After the bisection of the park by the Wilshire Viaduct, the north side of MacArthur Park presented the city with challenges and opportunities. The deepest challenge was the high water table found in this section of the park. More recently, the open meadow layout of the space behind the band shell encouraged local youth to play soccer and other games. The result was an area that was usually without grass and dusty, a historical issue awaiting a modern resolution. (Courtesy of Tony Perez.)

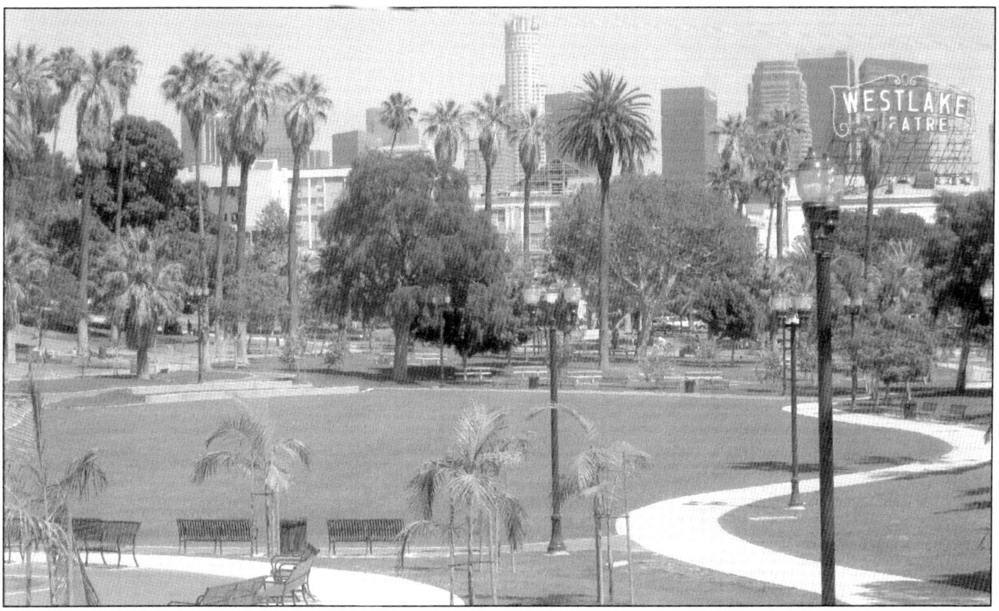

The modern resolution came in the form of a synthetic turf to replicate a grassy meadow. After much discussion as to its appropriateness within a historic park, the City of Los Angeles Bureau of Engineering project managed the installation of the carpet. The natural slope of the former lake bottom was not disturbed (balls roll west even without being kicked). A water pump was installed to address the high water table. (Courtesy of Tony Perez.)

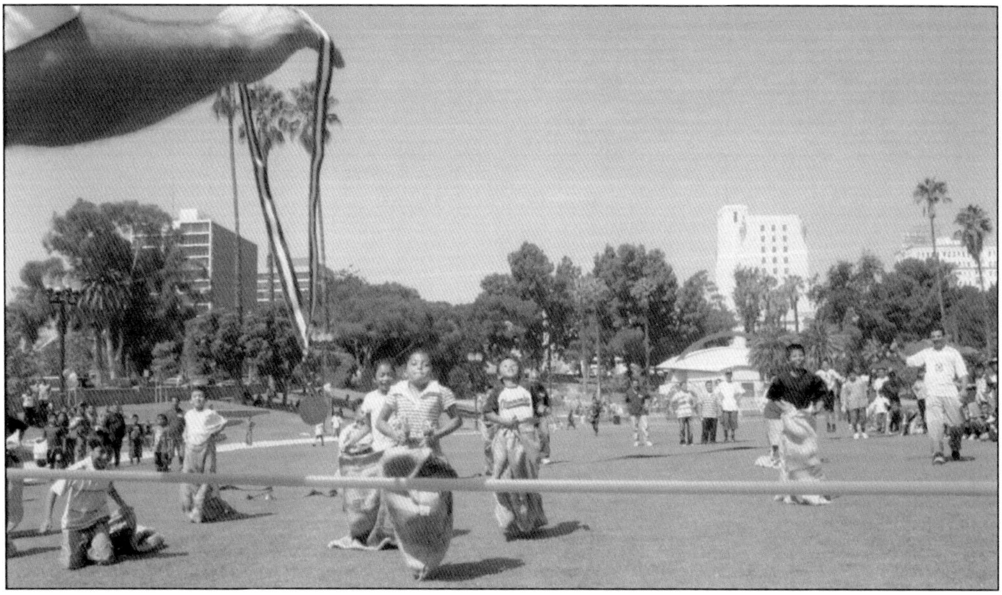

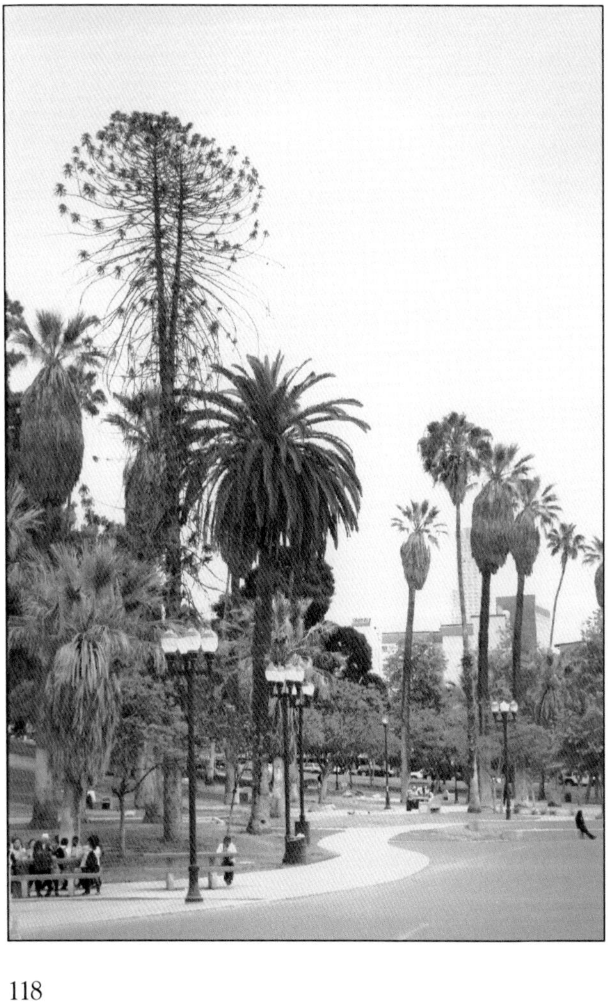

Today, young people are playing in MacArthur Park again. On any given weekend, hundreds of soccer players and their parents enjoy the sun, the field, and the park. Not coincidently, the incidence of vandalism and other criminal activity has dramatically dropped within the park. The space is once again for the "enjoyment of all people." (Courtesy of Tony Perez.)

Another important infrastructure improvement inside the north side of the park was the installation of period lighting around the new meadow and along the walkways. Local residents had long advocated for more lighting to discourage delinquent behavior. After the lights were installed, the LAPD coordinated the installation of security cameras throughout the park. (Author's collection.)

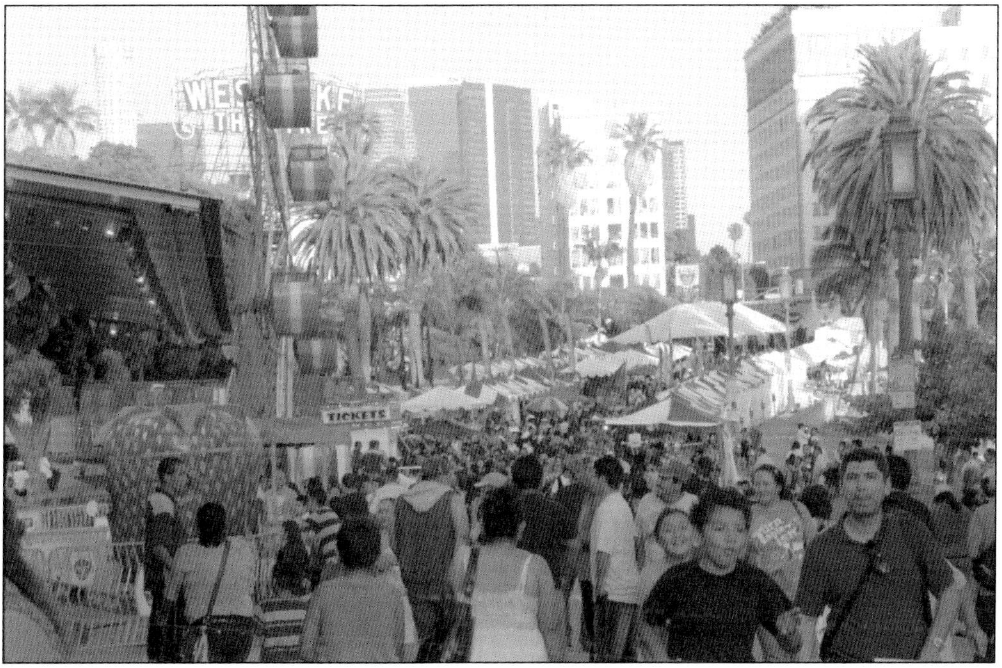

One of the more popular community festivals in MacArthur Park is the annual Feria Agostina, sponsored by a coalition of local Central American nonprofits. The August festival mimics the traditional town festivals held throughout Central America. The local festival hosts music, food, and an information fair that provides services on matters ranging from health care to financial services. (Courtesy of Salvador Sanabria.)

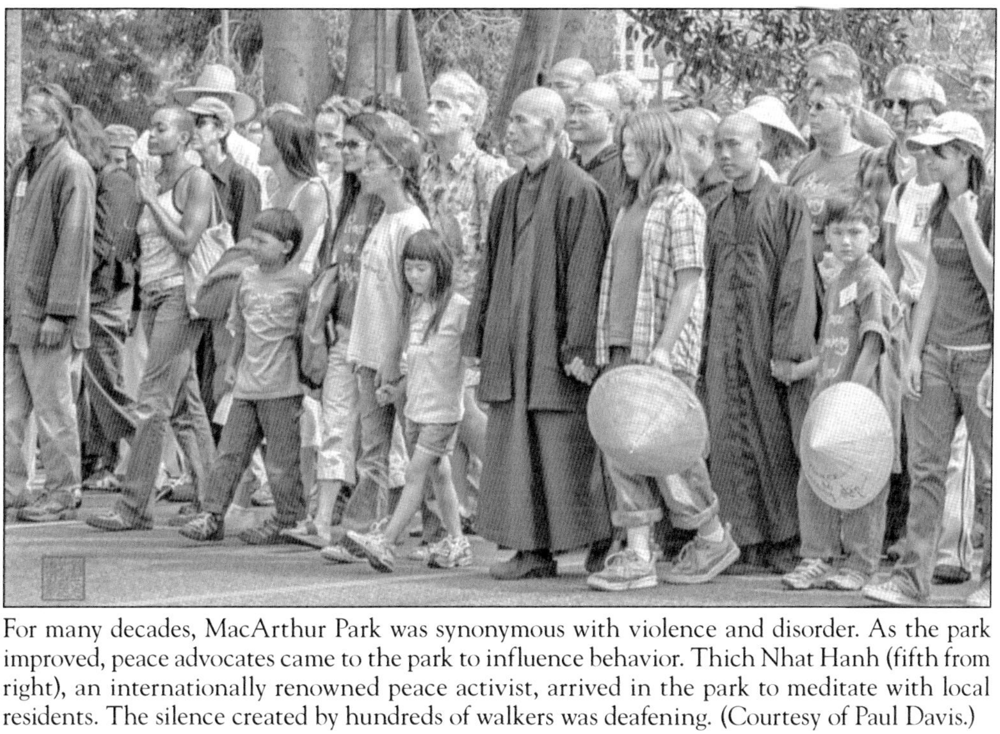

For many decades, MacArthur Park was synonymous with violence and disorder. As the park improved, peace advocates came to the park to influence behavior. Thich Nhat Hanh (fifth from right), an internationally renowned peace activist, arrived in the park to meditate with local residents. The silence created by hundreds of walkers was deafening. (Courtesy of Paul Davis.)

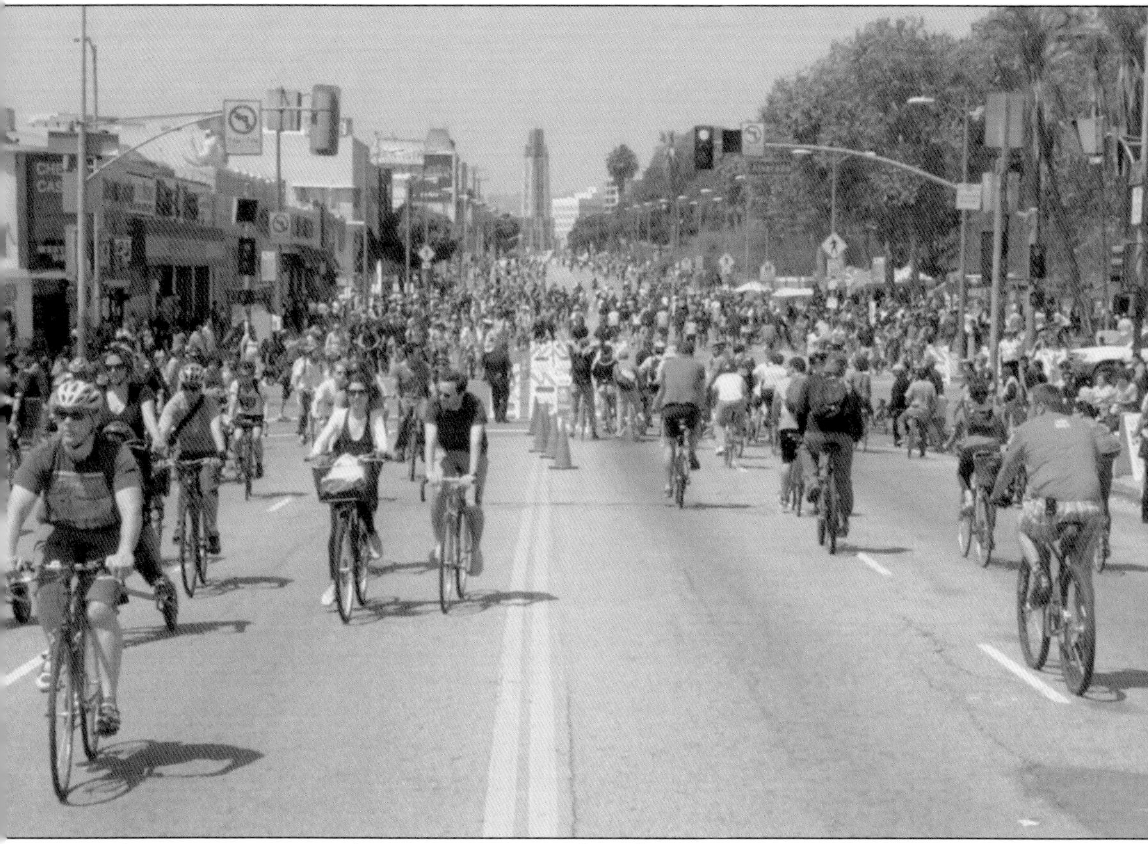

Like many cities across the country, Los Angeles is beginning to celebrate alternative modes of transportation. The bicycle is gaining prominence in the capital of cars and freeways. Leading the way in this transformation is the CicLAvia festival, where streets are closed to cars and thousands can then enjoy the city on bicycles, skates, and on foot. Many participants have enjoyed MacArthur Park during several CicLAvias held over the last few years. (Courtesy of CicLAvia.)

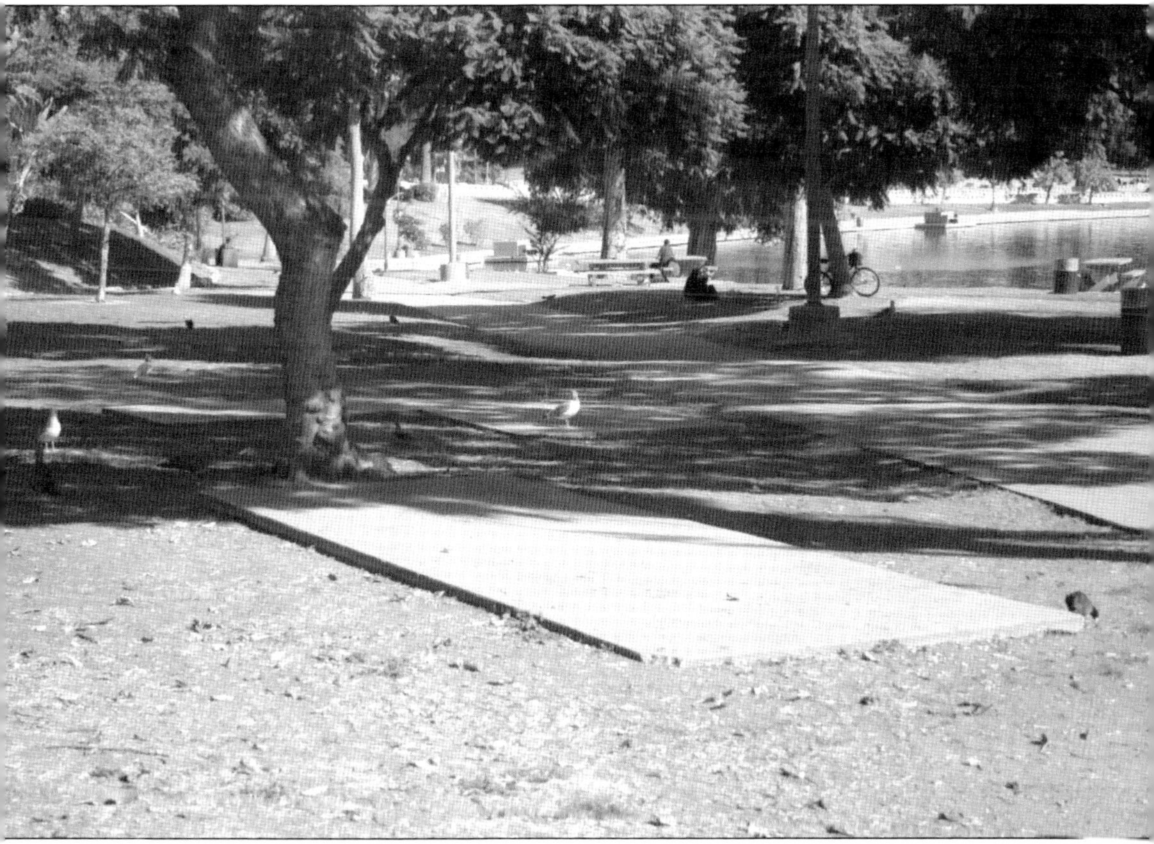

As stated earlier, the chess tables were removed from the southwest corner of the park for security reasons. The concrete platforms for the tables sit empty, awaiting the return of one of the most traditional activities within MacArthur Park. Local stakeholders are beginning an effort to restore the chess tables to their original location. (Author's collection.)

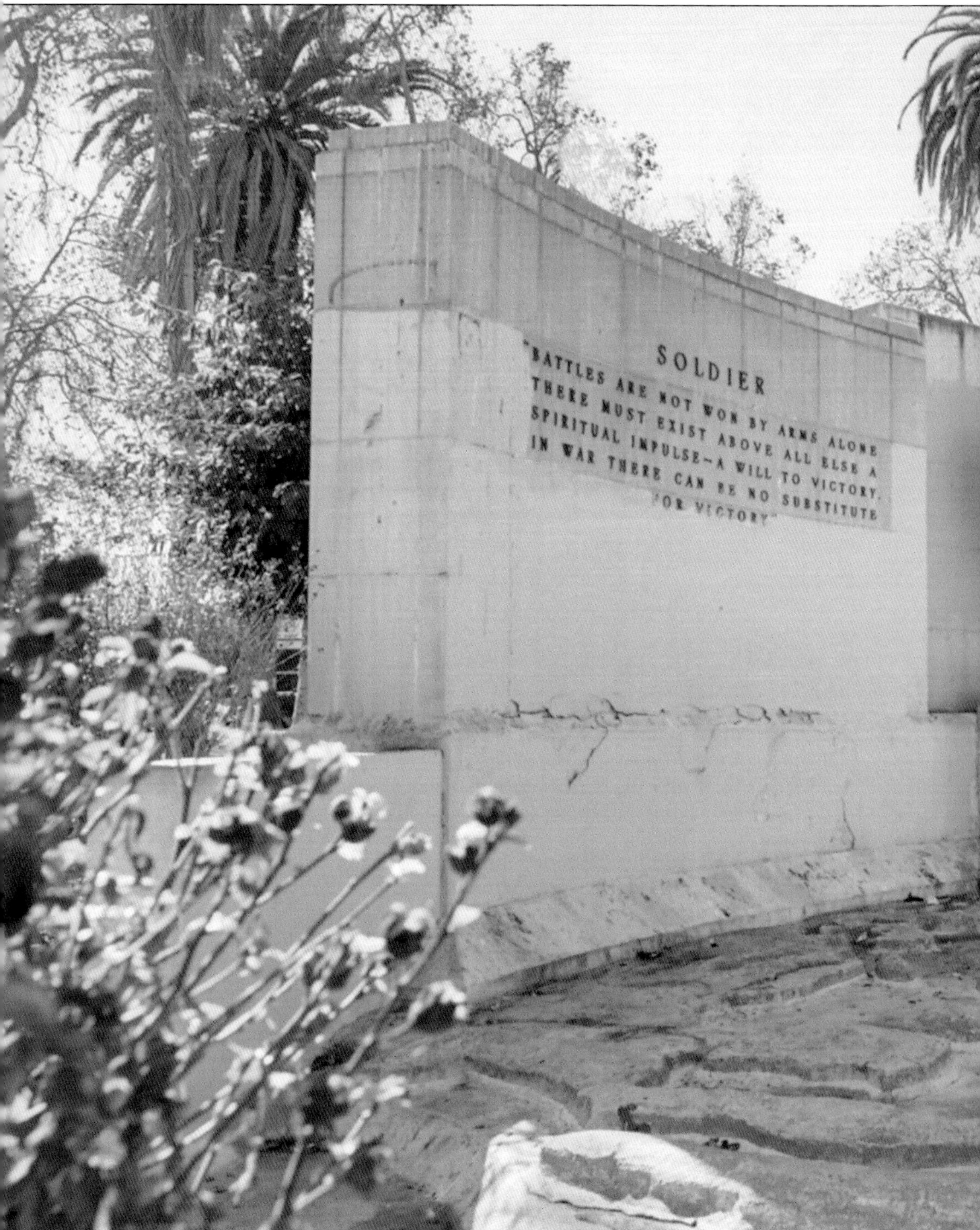

While much has improved in MacArthur Park over the last decade, several issues remain. Perhaps the biggest irony is the current condition of the General MacArthur statue inside the park named after him. The memorial is in dire need of restoration. Vandalism and biological damage wrought

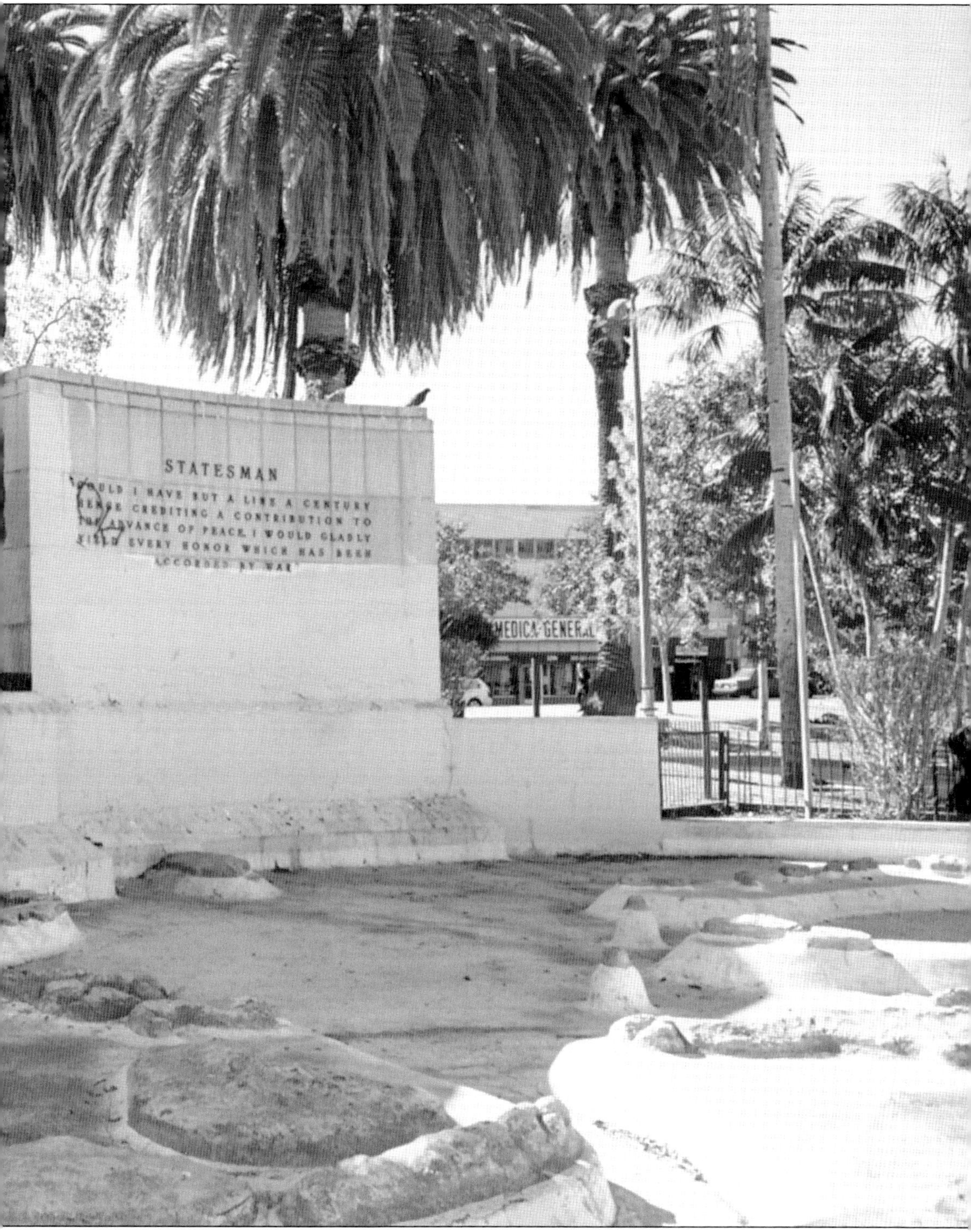

by ducks and seagulls have taken their toll on the general. (Courtesy of the Los Angeles Public Library Photo Collection.)

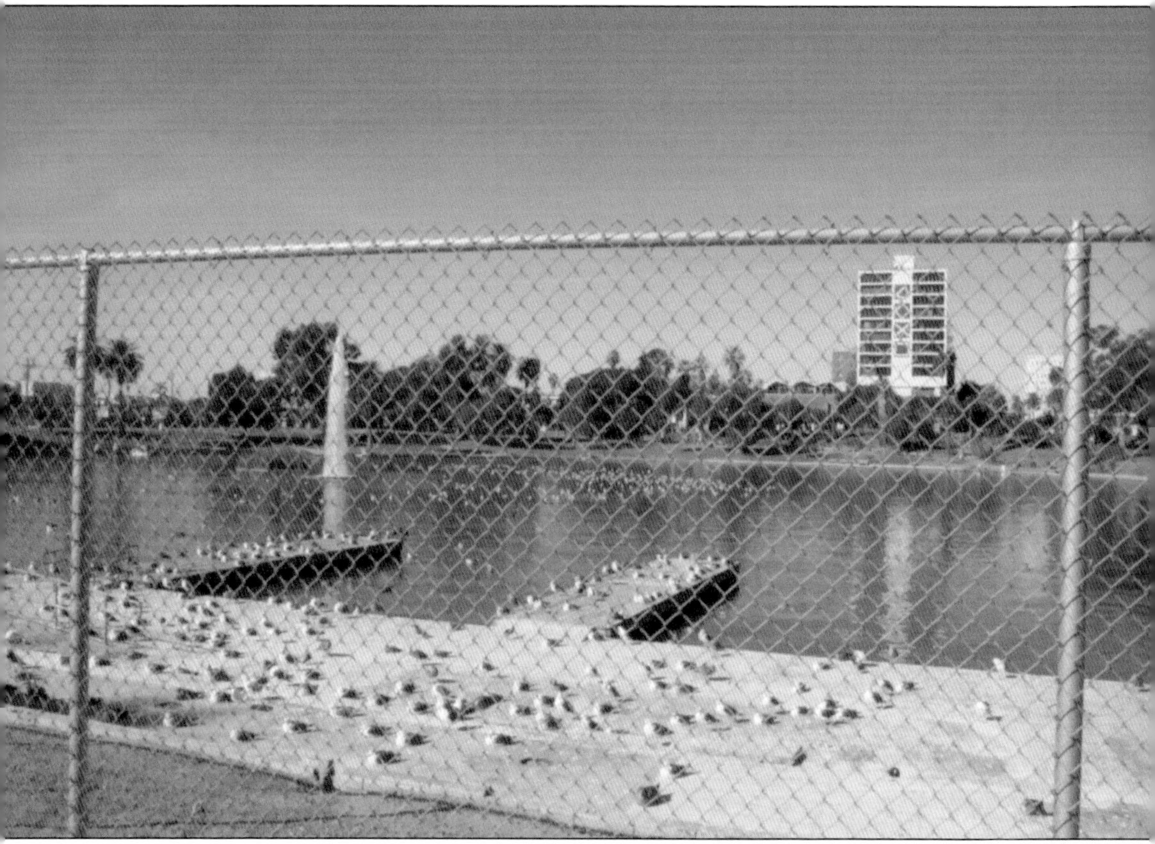

Boating has been the oldest water-related community activity at Westlake/MacArthur Park since the first rowboat permit was issued in 1895. In order to have boating, the park must have a boathouse again. In order for this to happen, the city must make it a priority to rebuild a boathouse at the lake's edge, preferably one that reflects the legacy of its architecture. (Author's collection.)

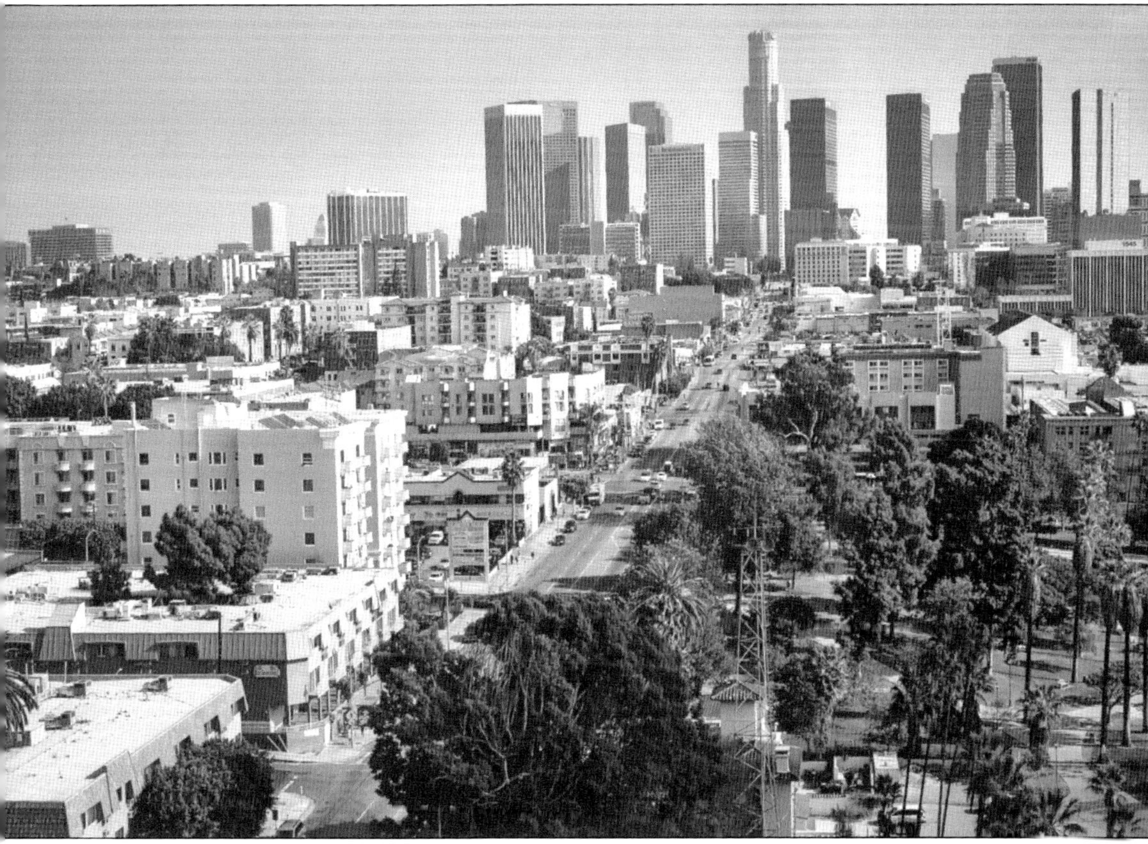

The elegant apartment houses along Sixth Street are long gone, and only the Bryson and Ansonia buildings remain on the street. As the main residential edge along the northern perimeter of the park, the Sixth Street park frontage today is dark and starkly inaccessible to pedestrians. Indeed, crossing Sixth Street on foot is considered dangerous. What will the coming century bring to Sixth Street? Will it be another car-dominated invisible commercial throughway to get to downtown or the westside, or will the city facilitate a vision that will reignite the architectural passion that brought Los Angeles one of its most vibrant neighborhoods? (Courtesy of Meeno.)

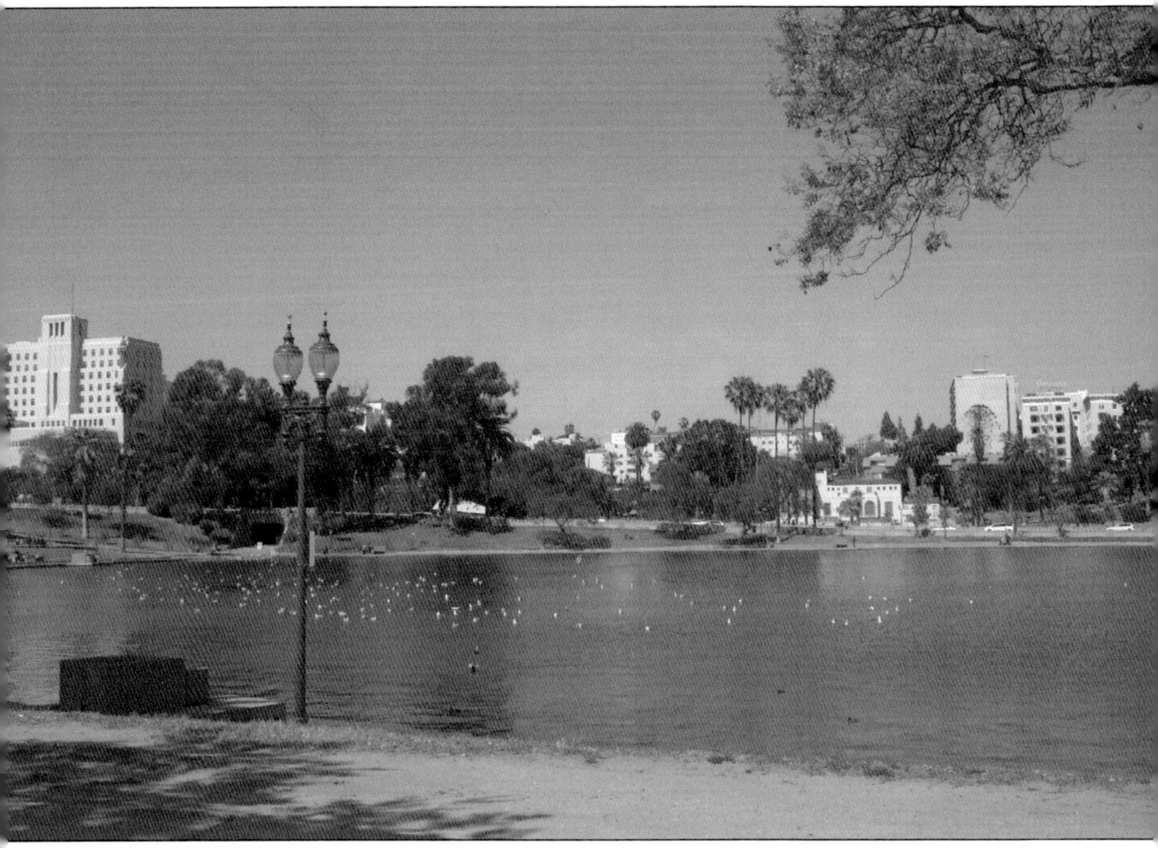

MacArthur Park is a beautiful space in a beautiful city. Like its city, the park has welcomed everyone—children and parents, dreamers and the close-minded, lovers and haters, the fortunate and homeless, the sane and insane, the builders and destroyers, and nativists and immigrants. The park has withstood crime, official neglect, roadway construction, and a subway trench. But it has never lost its original intent of providing a green oasis in the middle of the city. (Courtesy of Meeno.)

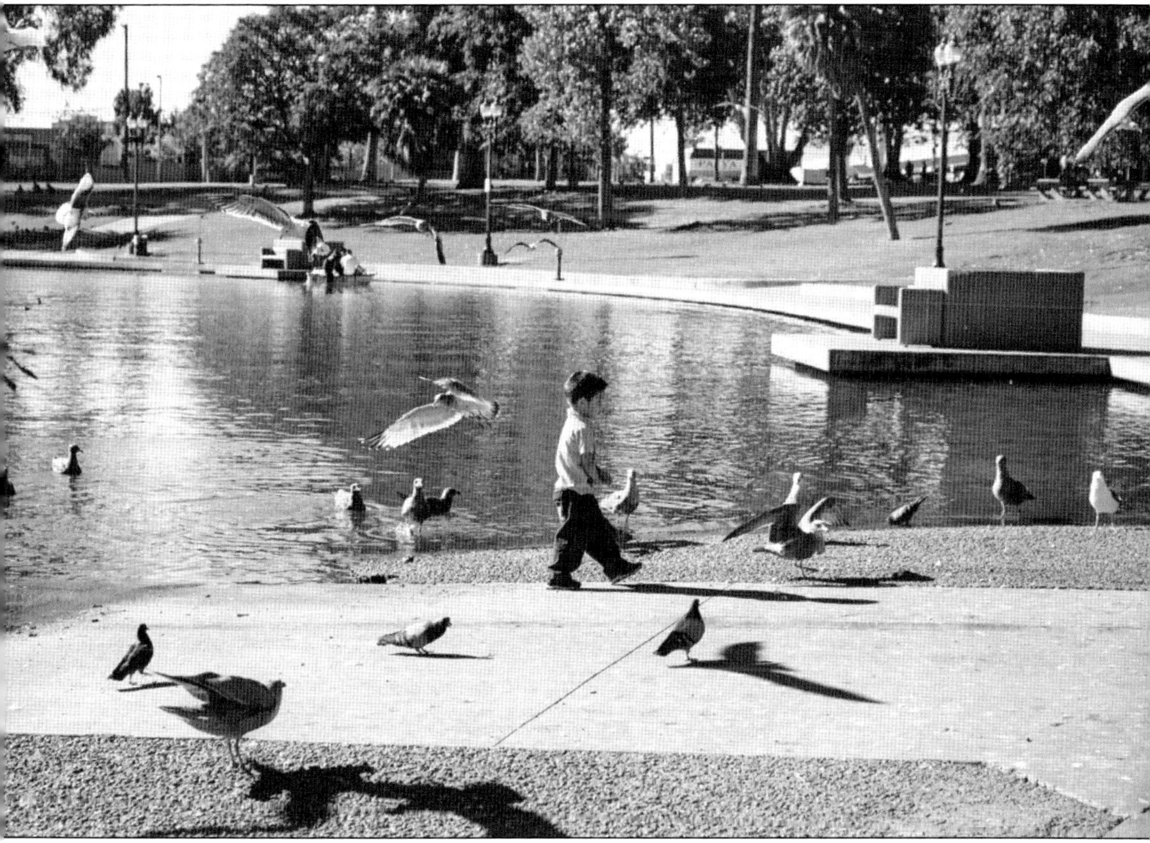

If MacArthur Park, like Los Angeles, is an unfinished story, what story might this little boy tell about the park in the future? (Courtesy of Meeno.)